Reimagining God

Johanna W. H. van Wijk-Bos

Reimagining GOD

The Case for Scriptural Diversity

Westminster John Knox Press
Louisville, Kentucky

Grateful acknowledgment is made for permission to quote from the following sources:

TANAKH: The New JPS Translation According to the Traditional Hebrew Text, © 1985 by the Jewish Publication Society, Philadelphia; "Blessing Song" from *WomanPrayer, WomanSong—Resources for Ritual,* words by Miriam Therese Winter, © 1987 by Medical Mission Sisters; *WomanWisdom* by Miriam Therese Winter, © 1991 by Medical Mission Sisters, reprinted by permission of The CROSSROAD Publishing Company, New York; Claudia V. Camp, *Wisdom and the Feminine in the Book of Proverbs,* Bible and Literature, vol. 11, © 1985, Sheffield: Almond [JSOT].

Scripture quotations marked NRSV are from the New Revised Standard Version of the Bible, copyright © 1989 by the Division of Christian Education of the National Council of the Churches of Christ in the U.S.A., and are used by permission. All other Scripture quotations are the author's own translations.

Book and cover design by Drew Stevens

First edition

Published by Westminster John Knox Press
Louisville, Kentucky

This book is printed on acid-free paper that meets the American National Standards Institute Z39.48 standard.⊗

PRINTED IN THE UNITED STATES OF AMERICA

95 96 97 98 99 00 01 02 03 04 — 10 9 8 7 6 5 4 3 2 1

Library of Congress Cataloging-in-Publication Data

van Wijk-Bos, Johanna W. H., 1940–
    Reimagining God : the case for scriptural diversity / Johanna W. H. van Wijk-Bos. — 1st ed.
        p.   cm.
    Includes bibliographical references and index.
    ISBN 0-664-25569-8 (alk. paper)
    1. Femininity of God.   2. God—Motherhood.   3. Bible.   O.T.—Criticism, interpretation, etc.   I. Title.
BT153.M6V36   1995
231'.4—dc20   94-36909

לְדָוִד

Contents

Introduction   ix

1. Naming the Holy One   1
   Two Images
   Issues and Questions
   Naming the Holy One and Holy Scripture

2. "To Whom Then Will You Compare Me?"   11
   Exile and Crisis
   Speaking of God
   "Your Ways Are Not My Ways"

3. Names and the Gender of God   23
   Elohim
   El Shaddai
   The Unpronounceable Name
   The Holy One of Israel

4. To Whom Does Scripture Compare God?   35
   Speaking of People—Speaking of God
   Is God a Man of War?
   God as Male Authority: King and Lord
   God as Teacher
   God as Kinsman: Father
   God as Rock
   God as Maker and Mender
   In Summary

5. God—Maker and Mother   50

A Woman in Childbirth
A Child's Protest
A Mother's Responsibility
Can a Child Forget?
A Mother's Protest
A Mother Comforts
In Summary

6. God—Eagle and Spirit   66

As an Eagle . . . as a Hen
The Presence of God in the Spirit
She Who Gives Life
She Who Empowers
She Who Educates
In Summary

7. The Paths of Wisdom   78

Who Is Sophia?
What Is Wisdom?
Who Is Woman Wisdom?
Is Woman Wisdom God?
Woman Wisdom and Women
In Summary

8. "I Will Be Who I Will Be"   89

A Conversation in the Desert
The Impossible Name
Promise of Presence
The God of the Future

Conclusion   99

Glossary   102

Notes   105

Selected Bibliography   114

Scripture Index   117

Introduction

How do believers talk about God and to God in a way that is not exclusively male and that is biblically responsible? That is the question explored in this book. This volume is written as a study book for folk who are willing to entertain the idea that God is not male. Much that I say in these chapters has already been stated by others but perhaps not in ways that are accessible to those who lack expertise in the technical language of theology or biblical scholarship. It is not so much my intention here to break new ground as it is to offer a bridge between one world and another, to "translate" for a general readership what has been available to a smaller group. Although I am a Presbyterian, I have not written for Presbyterians alone nor only for Christians. It is my hope that many who engage themselves with these questions from different perspectives will find something here to interest them.

A brief explanation about the scope and limitations of this book may be helpful here. This is not a book that discusses at length feminist theology or biblical authority. Those are important issues that have been addressed widely and that I have dealt with in a previous book. I am concerned here with exploring biblical images for God—in names, titles, and designations—that offer alternatives to exclusively male imagery. In this effort, I hope to help reimagine God in a way that contributes to the transformation of present structures and concepts and that is at the same time continuous with the biblical tradition.

Unless noted otherwise, the translations of biblical material in this volume are my own. In translating, I have kept to the practice of rendering Hebrew verb forms in reference to God with a masculine pronoun and an English verb, where this is unavoidable. There are a number of reasons for being so literal in translation:

the most important one may be that translators should not attempt to "cover up" the patriarchal setting of the Bible. It goes without saying that in this practice I am in no way stating opposition to more inclusive readings of the biblical text, especially in a context of worship. Translating is a precarious enterprise. I offer my translations in the spirit of the principles of Bible translation held by the renowned Jewish scholar Martin Buber. First, I have translated every Hebrew word with the same English word where at all possible. Second, in transposing Hebrew into English, I have attempted to keep the rhythm and word order of Hebrew. The result may strike the reader at times as awkward, but fresh insights may arise from unfamiliar readings and may thus turn the somewhat alien character of the biblical text to an advantage.

After setting the stage, I focus the discussion on the Bible. My emphasis is on the Old Testament, or Hebrew Bible (see the glossary), as a rich source for images of God. My overall approach is to consider first the incomparable nature of God as it is expressed in the biblical text, and whether on biblical grounds it is necessary and unavoidable to speak of God in male terms only. Then I invite consideration of the most frequent male images for God, pondering alternatives and expanding the imagery in a more inclusive direction. Key passages in the Bible that speak about God as a female presence are next examined in detail. Finally, I take up the promise of God's self-revelation in Ex. 3:14 as pointing to the necessity of continuing with our reimagining of God.

More specifically, in chapter 1 I review language for God as an essential component of women's quest for human dignity. In the articulation of this concern, a new stage is distinguished by the move beyond a critique of male language for God to a construction of alternative images. Through the work of Elizabeth Johnson and the 1993 Re-Imagining Conference, a powerful witness arose for the use of female imagery for God. I intend this book to be consistent with this effort.

When Christians ask about the right way to speak about God and to God, they look to the Bible as source and inspiration. Briefly, I outline from a Christian standpoint the significance of a biblical orientation in view of the fact that a large part of the Bible was not composed by and for the Christian church. In the chapters that follow, then, I explore the biblical terrain for possibilities and openings toward a reimagining of God.

Chapter 2 proceeds from the starting point that God transcends human categories, is incomparable, and cannot be grasped in human language. I discuss Isaiah 40–55, especially portions of chapters 40 and 55, with a detailed review of the context of these chapters, insofar as it precipitated particular questions about the identity of the ancient covenant community in its relation to God and about the nature of God. I invite readers to seek connections between questions and responses from the biblical time that arose from the conditions of exile, and those from our time that arise from the conditions of patriarchy. Isaiah 40 and 55 speak to God's incomparable nature, specifically as this nature is cast in terms of God's love for the human community.

Chapter 3 reviews names of God in the Bible, highlighting God, El Shaddai, and Adonai. I examine Gen. 1:26–27 in view of the implications of this text for the image of God. "El Shaddai" points almost certainly to an original female image; and "YHWH," or "Adonai," guides us back to God's mysterious nature. Somewhere between a name and a title, "the Holy One of Israel" emphasizes the "otherness" of God while making a claim on the faith community to act in ways that mirror God's inclusive nature.

Chapter 4 examines the connection between experience and our naming of God. Because of the challenge to patriarchal language of the past decades, male language for God today is experienced by many as exclusive. This chapter surveys a number of male images of God in the Bible: "man of war," "king," "lord," and "father." In seeking out alternatives, I attempt to stay close to the intent of Scripture and at the same time look for resonance with contemporary human experience.

Chapter 5 explores images of God in the Bible that reveal God as mother. Texts from Isaiah, Exodus, Numbers, and Hosea provide a rich tapestry demonstrating God's maternal nature. Although birth-giving and nurture are essential to these evocations, maternal language for God is not limited to such traditional motherly qualities. The maternal references stress also God's creative power, God's responsibility, the pain God bears on behalf of the human community, and the comfort of God's presence.

In chapter 6, I connect the images of God's presence as eagle and as spirit by means of wing imagery. God's parental presence as eagle is protecting and educational, as expressed in two texts in particular, Ex. 19:3–6 and Deut. 32:10–13. The word for spirit has feminine gender in Hebrew. God's Spirit bears the characteristics of life-giving, empowering, and educational presence.

In chapter 7, I examine the significance of the female personification of wisdom. The description of Woman Wisdom's activities makes use of terms employed elsewhere in the Bible for God's activities: Woman Wisdom calls, reproaches, gives life, and guards justice. As Woman Wisdom theology developed, she became a personification of God's being, as evidenced by the Wisdom of Solomon, one of the deuterocanonical books (see the glossary). This development had its repercussions also for early concepts of Christ. Jesus was considered to be the personification of wisdom, *sophia* in Greek, according to the earliest witness of the New Testament. Yet Sophia disappeared from the awareness of believers. How can we reclaim Woman Wisdom as an empowering symbol for women today?

Chapter 8 analyzes portions of Ex. 3:1–4:17, especially 3:14: "I will be who I will be." This rendering of God's self-revelation includes a reference to God's mysterious nature and to the human inability to grasp God in name or title. This phrase also contains a promise of presence, according to the manner in which God wills it. Last, the phrase emphasizes God's freedom to exist dynamically, opening up to new and different ways of God's manifestation in the creation, thus giving room for imagining God in female images.

In a brief conclusion, I summarize the insights gained from Scripture and their significance for our existence as a community with one another and with God.

Much of the textual work presented here is the product of years of teaching and preaching. To my students and co-learners go my thanks for their encouragement in this endeavor. This book could not have been written without three motivating events. My gratitude goes to Elizabeth Johnson for her inspiring work and her presentation of it at Louisville Presbyterian Theological Seminary in the fall of 1993. The enthusiasm and hope created by the Re-Imagining Conference in Minneapolis in November 1993 provided the second impetus; my deep and abiding thanks go to the organizers of that event, especially to Mary Ann Lundy, formerly with the national offices of the Presbyterian Church (U.S.A.), and to the presenters at the conference, and to all my sisters and brothers who sang and danced with me there. Last, I am grateful for the opportunity afforded by the request for this work from publisher Davis Perkins and managing editor Stephanie Egnotovich at Westminster John Knox Press.

I thank also Brian Wren for his encouragement and critique of the work while it was in progress and for the generous provision of his poetry. My husband David was a staunch supporter and offered valuable insight and critiques throughout the process of writing. Without his commitment to feminist theology and its vision, I would not have the hope I have for the future.

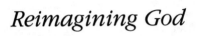

Reimagining God

Bring Many Names

Bring many names, beautiful and good;
celebrate, in parable and story,
    holiness in glory,
    living, loving God.
Hail and Hosanna!
bring many names!

Strong mother God, working night and day,
planning all the wonders of creation,
    setting each equation,
    genius at play:
Hail and Hosanna,
strong mother God!

Warm father God, hugging every child,
feeling all the strains of human living,
    caring and forgiving,
    till we're reconciled:
Hail and Hosanna,
warm father God!

Old, aching God, grey with endless care,
calmly piercing evil's new disguises,
    glad of good surprises
    wiser than despair:
Hail and Hosanna,
old, aching God!

Young, growing God, eager, on the move,
saying no to falsehood and unkindness,
    crying out for justice,
    giving all you have:
Hail and Hosanna,
young, growing God!

Great, living God, never fully known,
joyful darkness far beyond our seeing,
    closer yet than breathing,
    everlasting home:
Hail and Hosanna,
great, living God!

Brian Wren, 1988, revised 1993. © 1989 Hope Publishing Company,
Carol Stream, IL 60188. All rights reserved. Used by permission.

1

Naming the Holy One

I will tell of your name to my brothers and
sisters; in the midst of the congregation I will
praise you.

Psalm 22:22, NRSV

In his hymn "Bring Many Names," Brian Wren speaks about the
"living, loving God" as both mother and father. As he does so,
he uses unexpected adjectives, moving the language away from
stereotypes. The hymn testifies to a widespread concern in many
branches of the Christian faith for transformation from patriarchal
structures and language that promotes such structures to a community that exemplifies the oneness in Christ of male and female.
We have reached a new stage in the search for God-language
that reflects this concern in the different denominations, a stage
marked by significant events and controversies freshly stirred in
the Church.

Feminist theology has been on the scene for a good number
of years. From its beginning, its proponents analyzed the importance of language in reference to humanity and advocated
change from exclusive to inclusive language for people. Although
this focus was not peculiar to feminist theology and was raised
by many branches of feminism, feminist theologians faced a
unique task. Language for people and language for God are not
separate issues. Thus, early on, the concern arose to find ways
of speaking about God that offer alternatives to exclusively male
references. Much excellent work in reimagining God has been
done over the last twenty-five years by religious scholars from
different perspectives. Not only scholars but pastors and members of congregations have engaged themselves with this effort.
Yet for many participants in religious structures, this challenge to
traditional language and images for God has remained a difficult
issue toward which they feel hostility. Above all, it seems unbibli-
cal to speak of God in other than male terms. It is important, then,
to revisit the Bible on this issue.

Many events have taken place in the past twenty-five years that

1

have pressed the issue of exploring alternative language for God. Women-Church, for example, held regular national conferences.[1] Workshops and study groups took place in congregations and regions across the nation. Two events that occurred toward the end of 1993 clearly heralded a new stage in the course of the inquiry.

Two Images

On the evening of October 27, 1993, my husband and I arrive at my place of work to attend a lecture. The presentation will begin at 7:30. We have hurried to be on time, for earlier in the day rumors had it that this event will be well attended, and, to accommodate a potential crowd, the location has been moved from a lecture hall to the chapel. I am confident that at ten minutes past seven o'clock we are in time to find good seats; after all, the chapel can hold at least four hundred people. I am caught by surprise as we enter the seminary grounds together with a steady stream of cars, obviously all headed for the same destination. As we walk into the chapel, it is clear that not only are the good seats gone, there are no seats to be had at all. Already, groups of people are milling around in the vestibule, heading upstairs to the organ loft or downstairs to the basement where monitors are set up. We go inside and find an empty windowsill. These places and the aisles are beginning to fill up also. A friend sees me and offers a few inches of chapel bench next to her and her mother. I manage to squeeze in beside them while my husband remains perched on his windowsill. By 7:30, not a square inch of floor space is left unoccupied. The aisles and the entire chancel are filled with people sitting on the floor. Windowsills have become a precious commodity. There is a kind of breathless hilarity in the air. Never have I seen this building so thronged, not even when the famous Roman Catholic theologian Hans Küng came to speak, and it was filled then. Later we learn that more than two hundred people had to be turned away.

The occasion that has drawn such a multitude is a lecture by Elizabeth Johnson, who will speak on her book *She Who Is,* a work for which she has won the 1993 Louisville Grawemeyer award in religion.[2] People of all ages are listening as Professor Johnson presents to her audience in one hour the main arguments of her book. There are many women, but also men; a great number of students have come, a notoriously difficult group to attract to lectures outside of their curricula. A number of young women are accompanied by an older companion, a mother or a grandmother. To attend any kind of meeting after a day's work is, for me, usually a mixed blessing; evening lectures may find me dozing off. But not this evening; not this lecture. We all listen intently as Elizabeth Johnson pursues her discourse of the "right way to speak about God." When she is done, the crowd rises to its feet and honors her with a standing ovation.

The second image is of an event a few weeks later, in Minneapolis, Minnesota. On a Sunday morning, in a hotel ballroom, a large crowd of women and a handful of men celebrate the last moments of a conference that began three days earlier. We have made speeches and listened to them, we have eaten and sung together, we have applauded, we have talked and laughed, we have frowned sometimes. Now it is time to dance. We dance a long snake dance around tables and chairs and sing one of the most beautiful freedom songs ever written: "We Are Marching in the Light of God." I have known this song for a long time. I have sung it, I have spoken about it, but I have never *done* it. Now here we are, approximately two thousand of us, singing at the top of our lungs and dancing, marching and dancing in the light of God. It goes on for a good long while, and when it is over, it is still too soon for me.

The conference that had just come to an end was called Re-Imagining. It had been two years in the planning and was held under the auspices of the World Council of Churches Decade in Solidarity with Women. Women came from all over the world, from many cultures, and from many regions of the United States to probe together the right way to speak and think and dream about God. I had looked forward to participating in this event and felt it had turned out to be all that I had hoped for. Afterward, people back home asked how it had been, and I said, "I am so glad to have lived to be a part of it." In view of the vigor and enthusiasm, the courage and hope that were present at the conference, the subsequent reactions should perhaps not have been surprising. Denunciations of the conference and the participants were issued by various conservative publications, originating with self-appointed guardians of orthodoxy and of the right way to speak about God in different denominations.

Issues and Questions

What was going on to cause the intense and numerous participation in these events? What caused the reaction to the Minneapolis conference? When Elizabeth Johnson asks in her book about the right way to speak about God, she sets this question in a particular context. She asks, "What is the right way to speak about God in the face of women's newly cherished human dignity and equality?"[3] The issue from which the questions arise is precisely this newly cherished human dignity and equality of women. Patriarchy creates an organization of structures with men in charge of all arrangements and in which only men have the right to public power. In a patriarchal society, women exercise power legitimately only in the private sphere. Within this construct exist no equality and no equal human dignity for women. Feminist theologians view patriarchy and its attendant attitudes as a sin, in agreement with Elizabeth Johnson's statement that "sexism is a sin, because it is contrary to God's intent and breaks the basic commandment 'You shall love your neighbor as yourself.'"[4]

How destructive the present structures are for women was recently made clear once again. On February 4, 1994, the *New York Times* reported on the abuse of women across the world in an article on recent findings by the U.S. State Department. Timothy Wirth, the State Department's counselor, is there quoted as observing, "There is a problem of rampant discrimination against women, and physical abuse is just the most obvious example." The findings review many situations of abuse in different countries and estimate that in the United States alone more than one million women were attacked by their husbands or companions in 1993.[5] Shortly before this report, the U.S. Justice Department released a study that found "two and a half million of the nation's 107 million women 12 and older were raped, robbed, or assaulted, or suffered a threat or an attempt of such crimes." The same study reports that "injuries were nearly twice as likely to occur if the offender was a husband or boyfriend than if the attacker was a stranger."[6]

What is at stake is life. Women's and children's lives, all poor people's lives, the life of the planet—all are endangered today by the interlocking patterns of patriarchy.[7] Many women and men are more ready than ever to challenge patriarchy and the injustices it creates; they are more willing than ever to call into question the ideas and principles that support patriarchy. Is the church willing to sound a voice of protest against these dehumanizing and destructive arrangements? Even more important, is the Church prepared to face its own destructive patterns of patriarchy, and is it willing to repent and to turn to a transformed existence?[8]

Changing patriarchy does not mean allowing women entrance into the structures as they are, giving them access to power within the patriarchal setup while leaving this setup unchanged. To believe that a more equitable sharing of power between women and men within the existing structures will create change is a misunderstanding. We need to change our entire way of thinking, being, and acting with each other. Patriarchy is an ethical system that needs change from the ground up. The positive reaction to Elizabeth Johnson's presentation in Louisville, together with the enthusiasm that the Re-Imagining Conference created and the negative reaction to it, witness to the fact that both events raised issues and questions that struck at the very roots of the patriarchal system. They also give testimony to the eagerness with which many look forward to changed relations in the faith community and to the fear and condemnation with which others view these anticipated changes.

"What is the right way to speak about God?" Johnson calls this a "crucial question." It is crucial because it matters greatly how the faith community speaks about the One it considers most holy. It matters for this community's understanding of God and of itself. How we speak about what we value most speaks to who we are and how we live. The concern with language about God in this context is not new. For example, both The United Presbyterian Church in the U.S.A. (UPCUSA) and the Presbyterian Church in the United States (PCUS) produced study papers on this subject in the late 1970s and early 1980s. Both denominations agreed that current Church usage reflected names and pronouns for God that were more limited and limiting than is warranted by Scripture. As the report "Language about God" from the PCUS puts it, "Those of us who habitually speak of God only in male terms need to reassess the intention of Scripture's metaphors and to employ the richer variety and greater inclusiveness offered by Scripture." This report also urges "strenuous efforts" and "ongoing reflection and discussion."[9]

In line with the same concern, the National Council of Churches of Christ (NCC) launched a project in 1980 that issued in an inclusive translation of Bible passages regularly used in Sunday worship. Called *An Inclusive-Language Lectionary,* the first volume appeared in 1984, and the furor it created is well remembered by many.[10] In addition to denominational engagement, the same questions and concerns were raised in numerous books and articles in the late 1970s and early 1980s.[11]

Language not only represents or reflects experience but also shapes it.[12] What is true for all language is also true for religious language. Language for God that is exclusively male, in Elizabeth Johnson's words, "serves . . . to support a world that excludes or subordinates women. Wittingly or not, it undermines women's dignity as equally created in the image of God."[13] Speaking about God in terms other than male becomes, then, an essential part of the challenge to patriarchy and of the effort to turn toward transformed existence as women and men in the community.

The two events I have described at the start of this chapter are evidence of the continuing efforts in the faith community to deal with the challenges that feminist theology poses to the way we speak and think about God. Both Elizabeth Johnson's work and the Minneapolis conference moved the issue to new ground, going beyond a critique of male language for God to using female alternatives. It is one thing to discuss female symbols and pronouns for God as a possibility. It is yet another step to use such symbols and pronouns, as Johnson does throughout her book. She points out that she endorses *equivalence* of female and male terms for God, but because female symbols for God are unfamiliar to mainstream Christian language and practice, Johnson uses only female terms for God in her book. Thereby she explores a suppressed world in order to find "the design of a new whole."[14] The Re-Imagining Conference, operating with a similar agenda, used both male and female images and names.

What happened in Louisville and in Minneapolis were two different events. They were not planned by the same people, and it was not by design that they took place at approximately the same time and revolved around the same concerns. Yet this simultaneous occurrence was not entirely random or accidental. While the question of how to speak about God within a context of women's dignity and full humanity is not new, concern over this issue has taken on greater urgency and momentum. If it is clear, as I have said, that the very lives of women are at stake, it may also be more clear today than ever that the very vitality of the Christian faith is at stake.

Protests about the inappropriateness of thinking and speaking about God in female as well as male terms generally arise from two very different and opposing groups. For one group, traditionalists, it is inappropriate, perhaps even idolatrous, to "change" language that is mandated by the Bible and by the traditions of the Christian faith. This group will not entertain the notion of "equivalent" language for God and insists on traditional formulations. Another group, radical feminists, also rejects the possibility of change but ends up in an entirely different position from that of the traditionalists. According to these latter critics, the Christian faith is, both in its biblical roots and in its traditional expression, so patriarchal in its core that to change these expressions would be to change the faith itself. This change would be so radical and thorough that, in the end, it would no longer be the Christian faith. According to both extremes, then, Christianity and feminism are, at heart, incompatible. For radical feminists, this conviction usually results in a separation from Christianity.[15] In between these two groups are those of us who find in the Bible and in traditional theologies hope that our faith and its formulations are open to new directions. We still have hope for the Church and for the Christian faith. We hope that there is a place for women's human dignity and equality within the Christian faith. For us, our faith and the God of our faith are neither so rigid nor so tied to one type of language that they cannot stand adaptation and change. So we continue to explore scriptural and traditional roots for possibilities to open up new vistas and directions in our search to speak about God in a way that supports transformation and change of the community in the direction of greater inclusivity.

In one aspect, at least, the protesters and critics are correct: The issue is a crucial one. It is essential for the community of women and men in the Church and for the Christian faith to ask how we should speak about God in the face of our hope. We should be clear from the outset about the vital nature of the question and about the radical changes required to move toward a more human way of existing together now being envisioned by a Church that was patriarchal from the start. Nor are we entering into this stage with previous knowledge and experience. Never before has there been a challenge so sustained, so far-reaching, across so wide a diversity of people. We are in uncharted territory. The question is: Can the Church entertain the question?

Naming the Holy One
and Holy Scripture

When Christians ask about the right way to speak about God, they look to the Bible as source and inspiration. Before we begin our examination of scripture, we should consider briefly the names and the nature of the Christian Bible.

For Christianity, the Bible comes in two collections of writings called the Old and the New Testaments. The two testaments together form one Scripture. Scriptural authority rests in both testaments, not in one more than in the other. The word "old" in Old Testament indicates "first," "what came before," that in which the New Testament is rooted. "Testament" derives from the Latin word *testamentum,* which translates a Greek term meaning "covenant." The new covenant made with Gentiles in Jesus Christ

arose out of the old covenant made with Israel. This new covenant cannot be understood properly without the first or "old" covenant and does not exist separately from it. The two covenants
are interwoven and connected. Both the neutral meaning of "old"
and the sense in which it means that which is to be especially
respected and held in honor do not reflect current usage. In contemporary English, "old" indicates easily that which is useless, has
become superfluous, and may be thrown out. Consider to what
lengths we go to avoid the word "old" when it comes to human
beings. We prefer to use words such as "old*er*," "senior," or "re-
tired" when referring to people.

The word "old" may not be the best one for naming the first
part of the Bible in light of the problems it raises. There is also
another reason to choose an alternative term: Christians often ignore the fact that the Old Testament is the entire Scripture for
Judaism. Throughout its history, Christianity's attitude and behavior toward Judaism and toward the Jewish people have been
painful and shameful, marked by ignoring and ignorance, blame
and persecution. Christianity has often ignored the fact that the
first covenant was not canceled by God but found a continuation
in Judaism. In the terminology of John Calvin, the sixteenth-
century Protestant reformer, Christians are the adopted children
of God's covenant, whereas the Jews are direct descendants of
the first covenant community. To recognize the authenticity of
the Old Testament as the entire sacred Scripture for the faith community of Judaism, it has become customary in some Christian
circles to refer to this part of Christian Scripture as the Hebrew
Bible: Hebrew, because the text of the Old Testament was written
almost entirely in Hebrew. (A small part is written in Aramaic, a
close relative of the Hebrew language.)

There are clear advantages to what is, for many, a new term.
When Christians use the name Hebrew Bible, we stand in humble
recognition of and gratitude for our share in the gifts originally
intended for those "born in Zion." We also recognize that this
collection is still the whole of sacred Scripture for Judaism. In
naming the Old Testament "Hebrew Bible," the Christian community repents of a past in which it denied this authenticity to the
Book and to the people of the Book, the Jewish people. It repents
of past treatment that dehumanized these same people. It is a
beginning point that is relevant to our inquiry. Repentance and
a desire for renewed and healed relations between Jewish and
Christian faith communities are entirely within the realm of a concern for inclusivity and human dignity. The term *Hebrew Bible*
may also have the advantage of helping us to understand the distance between ourselves and the biblical text. Distance may not

sound like an advantage until we consider the implications. The text of the Hebrew Bible was composed by and for the faith community of Ancient Israel. When Christians direct their attention to this part of the Bible, they are tapping into sources that were not directly created by and for the Church.

When we look to the Hebrew Bible with our questions of the right way to speak about God, we need to be aware, first of all, that there is distance between ourselves and Scripture. To understand the text and to arrive at a productive engagement with it in light of our questions, we need to know what was going on with the first covenant community, Ancient Israel, by whom and for whom the Book was formed. We need to know about the life of the community, about its concerns, what was happening at the time. Because the languages in which the Bible was composed differ from our own, we ask also about words and their meanings in the original languages. Sometimes we are uncertain as to our answers, but we must ask the questions, always. If we begin by allowing distance between ourselves and the Bible, we are at least at a good starting point for our exploration.

There is distance and discontinuity between ourselves and Scripture. Yet we may also assume closeness and continuity. As we ask how the community of the past spoke about God and how it thus saw its own identity and understood the directives of God for its life, we ask also about our own naming of the Most Holy One, about our own identity, and about God's direction for our lives. In Jesus, those outside Israel are embraced in the love of the God of Israel. Out of Christian engagement with Scripture, out of our urgent and honest questions put to the text, new understandings of God and ourselves may indeed emerge.

What I have said about distance and the biblical text goes for the New Testament also. I have emphasized the relation of the Christian community to the Old Testament because that is where I am focusing my attention in this book. I look to the Hebrew Bible as the authoritative source and inspiration for our speaking of God. If, in Protestant Christianity, one testament is not superior to the other, yet the testaments may be understood as offering different gifts. One of the gifts of the Hebrew Bible is that it reflects the birth and the life of the prior covenant community, with all its ups and downs, and offers a great diversity of perspective on the presence of God in the daily life of the community. This birth of the community took place and its life developed with a belief in and a sense of the presence of God for this particular community and through it for the whole creation. The goal of God's involvement with the creation is understood in the Bible to be the *shalom,* the wholeness or health, of the covenant community and of all created existence. In patriarchy, human relations are unequal, broken in principle, and wholeness, shalom, is an impossibility.

The text of the Bible reflects and promotes the overarching concern of God for the creation, focused in the faith community called Ancient Israel. Was this community, then, not patriarchal, and does the Bible not also reflect and promote this patriarchy? This question requires a complex answer.

First, Ancient Israel was indeed a patriarchal society, just as the Church later became a patriarchal organization. This patriarchy and its attendant attitudes are reflected everywhere in the biblical text. We must nevertheless take care not to read our own patriarchal concepts and subliminal convictions into the text. The patriarchal structures of Ancient Israel were not identical to our own and were perhaps not as rigid as our own. In particular, times of great crisis and travail may have created openings for a different way of thinking, a different way of being. We look for these different perspectives in the biblical text. Second, the Bible as source and inspiration is also more than a text that reflects human experience; it is more than the sum of its parts. We hope to find there God's word for our time, which is no less a time of crisis and travail than was the time of the birth and rebirth of the ancient covenant community. For that word we search in story and song, in prophecy and proverb. We look with interest, eagerness, and hope, for we believe with songwriter Brian Wren that God is, above all, a "living, loving God."

For Reflection and Response

1. What does the word "patriarchy" mean to you? How do you see patriarchy at work in the world? Can you give examples from larger and smaller contexts, for example, from the workplace and the family? How does it work in the church?
2. What does feminism mean to you? What is "feminist theology"? Do you think of yourself as a feminist? Is feminism only for women?
3. How is the Bible patriarchal? Think of specific examples. Do you believe that the Old Testament is more sexist than the New? How is Scripture used today to justify patriarchy? How is Scripture used to promote inclusivity?
4. Is there an advantage in using the term *Hebrew Bible* instead of *Old Testament?* In which context might it be a disadvantage?
5. Are there common elements between sexism and anti-Judaism?

2

"To Whom Then Will You Compare Me?"

> Great, living God, never fully known,
> joyful darkness far beyond our seeing,
>   closer yet than breathing,
>   everlasting home:
> Hail and hosanna,
>   great, living God![1]

In this last stanza of the hymn "Bring Many Names," theologian-poet Brian Wren expresses his sense of a God who is both mystery ("never fully known," "far beyond our seeing") and at the same time close to us, with whom is the place of human belonging ("closer yet than breathing, everlasting home"). The phrase "joyful darkness" combines words that we ordinarily see as contradictory. How can darkness be joyful? With these two words, Wren conveys the notion that God is the source of joy and yet, to us, impenetrable, like darkness. He combines two words not ordinarily found in association in order to speak about God as truly God. Before we can begin speaking about God, we need to become aware that it is impossible to speak about God, because God eludes our words and understanding.[2]

This is where we start: with the acknowledgment that in talking about God, we are trying to do the impossible. Scripture, as we know, is a record of the experience of God's presence in the faith community. The Bible speaks in numerous ways of God's nearness and does not shy away from using terms for God that are ordinarily applied to human beings. God is said to have hands, feet, eyes, a mouth; God walks, marches, sits, dwells; God laughs, is angry, is sorry. By contrast, the Bible also speaks of God in ways that express God's mystery and otherness.

In this chapter, we study a portion of Isaiah 40–55, a text that more than any other in the Bible insists on the incomparable nature of God. This text, so full of the closeness and nearness of God, also states repeatedly and elaborately that God is not to be compared to anything or anyone. I bring this second aspect of God to the foreground to guard against the view that we might capture God's nature in any language, be it of the past, the present, or the future. In our search for language about God that is other than masculine, we look first for models in Scripture that emphasize a God who transcends male and female.

Exile and Crisis

Significantly, the concepts about God in Isaiah 40–55 were formulated at a time of great crisis. Although there are many dissimilarities between our situation and that of Ancient Israel in the sixth century B.C.E., we may experience our faith and identity as a covenant community under threat in a similar way. The momentous changes envisioned today in moving from patriarchal existence to a new way of being have precipitated urgent questions about God's nature that are not unlike those to which Isaiah 40–55 responds. It is to the response found in this text that we look for a starting place in terms of the present need for new formulations of our traditions, especially a reimagining of God.

According to common understanding, Isaiah 40–55 dates back to a prophet who lived during the time of the Babylonian exile. Because there is no record of the proper name of this person and in order to maintain the link with Isaiah 1–39, we indicate this prophet by the name Second Isaiah. To know what was going on at the time of Second Isaiah, what the concerns and the questions were of the community to whom these words were addressed, we need both information and imagination, for exile is an experience that is foreign to many of us.

The historical reality is that the Babylonian exile took place in the small kingdom of Judah in the first two decades of the sixth century B.C.E. There were three attacks over a number of years by the reigning empire of the day, Babylon. During the course and as a result of these assaults, the Davidic dynasty came to an end, the state lost its independence, the Temple was destroyed, and the land was deprived of significant habitation. Deportations, although never total, usually removed all significant leadership and left behind a people in miserable physical and mental condition. They were without resources, without spiritual and political leadership; broken fragments of a once-flourishing community.[3]

These facts are necessary, but they are not enough in themselves to attune us to the situation behind the words of Second Isaiah. Another biblical text may help us on the way with our imagining. The short book Lamentations is a loud cry of anguish over the devastation brought about by the exile and its aftermath. Listen to these words:

My heart is in tumult,
My being melts away
Over the ruin of my poor people,
As babes and sucklings languish
In the squares of the city.
They keep asking their mothers,
Where is bread and wine?
. . . .
    As their life runs out
In their mothers' bosoms.
                        (Lam. 2:11, 12)[4]

Better off were the slain of the sword
than those slain by famine,
who pined away, wounded,
for lack of the fruits of the field.
With their own hands, tenderhearted women
have cooked their children;
such became their fare,
in the disaster of my poor people.[5]
                        (Lam. 4:9, 10)

These texts sharply and painfully evoke the persisting violence and disintegration of community brought about by war. They speak about the most defenseless victims of war and its aftermath: women and children. Such images of extreme violence are not alien to us who watch them daily in our newspapers and on television. The recent destruction in former Yugoslavia and in Rwanda, for example, has made us aware once more of the reality of war.

To make things even worse for the Judahite community, many people interpreted the events of exile and war as a punishment from God because of their shortcomings. The language of Lamentations is permeated with statements that witness to this conviction: "The LORD has made her suffer for the multitude of her transgressions," declares the poet about the fate of Jerusalem (Lam. 1:5, NRSV). And the lamenter contends:

"Look and see
if there is any sorrow like my sorrow,
which was brought upon me,
which the LORD inflicted
on the day of his fierce anger."
                        (Lam. 1:12, NRSV).

Ancient Israel understood the land in which it lived to be a direct gift from God. The Davidic house by which Judah was ruled had a special place within God's design for Israel, and from it would come forth the Messiah who would complete Israel's redemption. The Temple in Jerusalem was seen as the sign of God's presence in the midst of the covenant people. At the time of the Babylonian exile, these had been taken away and destroyed, in spite of God's promises, in spite of a history of God's activity on behalf of God's people. One way for the people to explain the events was to interpret these losses as God's doing, a divine response to the people's failure to live up to the demands God made of them. Had not the prophets warned that destruction would come? Thus, fear, anxiety, and guilt predominated in the shattered community.

By the time Second Isaiah came on the scene, a generation or more had passed since the Babylonian conquest.[6] The exiles who had survived the deportation had been able to settle in southern Mesopotamia and from all accounts were not in the same desperate straits as those left behind in Judah. By 540 B.C.E., the time in which we place Isaiah 40–55, we may assume a fairly stable and somewhat prosperous community of Judahite refugees in and near Babylon. The Babylonian Empire was then in the process of being conquered by King Cyrus, whose policies toward conquered ethnic groups were enlightened and liberal. Eventually, in 538 B.C.E., Cyrus gave the Judahites official leave to return to their homeland. Although not everyone took this opportunity, the return to Judah made possible the reestablishment of Jerusalem as a cultural and religious center; Israel would not be an independent state again, however, until twenty-five hundred more years had passed.

We can envisage two communities at the time of Second Isaiah: one at home in Judah, the other in Babylon. About the group in Judah we know almost nothing. We can only surmise that the people there in 540 were somewhat less besieged and not as immediately threatened as Lamentations depicts them. Yet this must have been a community that eked out a living on a subsistence level and that continued to be deprived of its political and religious center. The community in Babylon, in exile, had no doubt originally contained the political and religious leadership of the people. This community was able to maintain itself and even experienced some prosperity. Yet in Babylon there was a sharp awareness of the loss of homeland. Psalm 137, with its fervent expressions of loyalty, provides a glimpse of the anguish that tormented the exiles:

> If I forget you, O Jerusalem,
> may my right hand forget its grip,
> my tongue cleave to its palate.
>   (Ps. 137:5–6)

The psalm concludes with a hair-raising cry of hatred:

> Fair Babylon, you predator,
> happy are they who repay you in kind
> the work you completed on us!
> Happy are they who seize and smash
> your small ones on the stones.
>   (Ps. 137:8–9)

Feelings of guilt and doubt were present in both groups. How could God let this happen? Was God not powerful enough to prevent the loss of land and Temple? Were other gods more powerful? If their loss was their own fault, what did it mean now to be a covenant people? What kind of God was their God? Questions such as these preoccupied the community.

There is a great distance in time and place between us and the world of the Babylonian exiles. There are, however, also connections, bridges that may span this gap. In my earlier book *Reformed and Feminist,* I argued that the community's questions about its identity and life, about God and God's presence, predominate especially in times of crisis.[7] During the Babylonian exile, the continued existence of the people Israel and its faith was seriously threatened. There was no certainty that anything would survive the disaster.

As a church, we may be nearing a similar time of crisis. Although what has befallen us is not identical to what befell Israel, our questions are as urgent and the continuance of the Christian community may be as much at stake. A significant sector of the Christian community asks about our identity, our life together, and about God and God's presence "in the light of women's newly cherished human dignity and equality."

When the Temple in Jerusalem came down, Israel's faith could have disappeared with it. If patriarchy may be compared to a temple, then that temple is now in the process of coming down. While our patriarchal temple is coming down, so also is much of the tradition of our faith. Second Isaiah's response to the community's questions was at least one important factor in the survival of the people's spirit and their faith. In studying this response, we may find the elements that will foster the survival and regeneration of our own faith.

Speaking of God (Isaiah 40-55)

Who meted out in his hollow hand the waters,
and measured the heavens with the span?
Contained in a third cup the dust of the earth,
and weighed in the scale the mountains,
heights with balance weights?
. . . .
To whom then will you liken God?
And to what likeness will you compare him?
. . . .
To whom shall you liken me and I shall resemble?
—Says the Holy One—
Lift your eyes on high
and see who created these,
bringing out their numerous hosts
by name he called them all
in great abundance of wondrous power;
and no one is missing.

(Isa. 40:12; 18; 25, 26)

Isaiah 40 introduces the themes and motifs that are worked out in the subsequent chapters and, with chapter 55, forms a framework around the text. In chapter 40, the urgency of the questions about the community's identity and about God is clear from the repeated assurance of the opening lines: "Comfort, comfort my people, . . . cry to her . . . that . . . her sin is paid" (40:1–2). The community's very identity is henceforth marked by being a forgiven people. The prophet wastes no time in arguing whether the community's sense of guilt is appropriate or not. The people are simply addressed on the point of their experience, which is one of guilt.

After this opening call, the focus shifts to God's imminent arrival. So close is God's advent that the herald cries, "Here is your God!" (40:9). In the course of this announcement, three divine aspects are identified and underlined: endurance, strength, and tenderness. Humanity is ephemeral and its loyalty quickly gone; not so God's word, which "endures in time" (40:8). Strength is depicted in God's coming as a warrior leading the vanguard of a conquering army:

> . . . God coming in strength.
> His right arm rules for him. (40:10)

Then, in a shocking reversal of the warrior image, God is compared to a shepherd who is most concerned for the weakest of the flock, the mothers and the babies:

> Like a shepherd he grazes his flock,
> with his right arm he gathers the lambs;
> to his breast he lifts them.
> The mother sheep he guides. (40:11)

Second Isaiah's initial description of God states what God is doing rather than who God is. God is indicated simply as "your God," to emphasize the close relation between the people and God. What God is doing and how God is doing it are at the center of attention. Although the focus, initially on the people, is now on God and stays there for the rest of the chapter, the people and their identity, their questions, and their worries are not left behind. They are fragile and in pain, the lambs and mother sheep of the text, and as such, they may count on God's loving care and protection. The image of God carrying the people in their distress occurs in the Bible especially in relation to the time of the Exodus. Both the Exodus story itself and the prophetic material that refers to this period use such imagery (Ex. 19:4; Deut. 32:10, 11; Hos. 11:1–4). Second Isaiah uses and reshapes these Exodus images. The people must be declared forgiven and God's arrival must be announced before the prophet can turn to an elaborate evocation of God's nature.

In 40:12–26, the issue is God's incomparable nature as it serves God's creative and redemptive attention to all creation, not only to Israel. This issue is close to the center of Second Isaiah's concerns (see also 44:7, 8; 45:9–19; 46:5–11; 48:12, 13). Of all the texts in Isaiah 40–55 that address this subject, chapter 40 is the most detailed in its description of God's incomparable greatness. The text is bound together by a series of rhetorical questions. The scenes joined to the questions are set on a wide canvas: the whole creation is the theater of God's activity. Heaven and earth, the nations, idols, and the stars of heaven come into view as the prophet attempts to speak of the incomparable nature of God.

Three rhetorical questions introduce the subject of the discourse: "Who meted out . . . ? Who regulated the Spirit . . . ? Whom did he consult . . . ?" Rhetorical questions have obvious answers. The answer to the first question is "God" and to the next two, "Nobody." God, and nobody else, is the focus of the community's concern. Alongside this concern, the babble of voices

and powers that buzz in Israel's ear becomes insignificant. Twice
the question is asked: "To whom will you compare God?" (40:18,
25). Twice the understood answer must be "God cannot be compared to anyone or anything." Even the stars, worshiped as divine
powers in Babylon, are the recipients of God's care: God calls
them all by name.

God is above and beyond the human capacity to understand
or frame adequate models for comparison. Yet all of Scripture is
a speaking about God, about God's interaction with the community, and about the community's perceptions of this involvement.
Second Isaiah, who is concerned above all with the relationship
between God and people and with the restoration of this relationship, needs to establish this point first: God transcends human
comprehension and the human capacity to render God in human language.

It is most important that we, who study Isaiah long after its
original composition, do not lose sight of the context in which
these statements about God were made. The context is what you
might call a crisis of confidence. The covenant community has
lost confidence in God as Israel's savior and in itself as God's
beloved people. Second Isaiah reassures them on both points.

Indeed, the need of the community is never far from this
prophet's concern. Another set of rhetorical questions runs
through chapter 40: "Have you not known? Have you not heard?
Do you not understand?" (40:21, 28). God's covenant community
knows "all this" about God, that God exceeds the limitations of
human imagining and speech. At least, they should have known
this, and this particular question may be somewhat ironic. Verse
27 also asks a question; it is not rhetorical but rather an almost
reproachful query:

> Then why do you say, Jacob,
>   and speak, Israel:
>   "My way is hidden from the Lord
>   and from my God my right slips away"? (40:27)

The text implies: If you know "all this" about God, then why
charge God with ignoring your plight? Then the text once more
reiterates God's endurance, strength, and incomparability. The
speech culminates in 40:28–31, verses that make clear the point
of the whole description:

> Do you not know?
> Have you not heard?
> An enduring God is the Lord,

> creating the ends of the earth;
> who does not grow weary or falter;
> unfathomable his insight.
> Giving to the weary strength
> and to those who lack vigor
> increasing their power.
> Young fellows grow weary and falter,
> and lads stumble and totter.
> But those who wait on the Lord
> gain new strength.
> They rise on wings of eagles,
> they run and do not grow weary,
> they walk and do not falter. (40:28–31)

The prophet has described God's incomparable nature for a purpose, showing no interest in depicting God's transcendence for its own sake, in a vacuum, as it were. The insights offered into God's incomparable nature have led up to a clear statement of God's empowering nature. Thus is God's incomparable nature put at the service of God's love. The ones who were carried like babies, held aloft on God's pinions, will be able to stand on their feet and come to God. In a descending image, from flying to running to walking, the chapter closes with a people capable of movement toward a God who is moving toward them.

"Your Ways Are Not My Ways"

With the insight of God's incomparable nature that is at the service of God's love, we arrive at the greatest mystery of all. The New Testament states unequivocally that God is love (1 John 4:8, 16). The Bible is a long reflection on what God's love means for the creation and how it plays itself out in the world. The assumption of all Scripture is that humanity on its own, without God's involvement, is left to destruction and self-destruction. As New Testament scholar George Edwards observes, "The real story of the Bible is the deliverance of humanity from the pit by the God of the Bible."[8] To this end, God is engaged in the human community. While, according to Scripture, the love of God embraces all of creation, it goes out especially to the ones excluded by human oppression and hatred. In the words of Luke, the special recipients of God's care are the "lowly" and the "hungry" (Luke 1:52, 53); as found in the company of Jesus, they are the "tax collectors and sinners." (See, for example Matt. 9:11; 11:19; Luke 5:29; 15:1. Matthew 21:31–32 adds "prostitutes.") In terms of the Hebrew

Bible, they are the "widow, the orphan, and the stranger" (Deut.
16:11; 24:17–22; 26:12; 27:19, for example). Speaking of God is
deeply interwoven with speaking about ourselves, and speaking
of God's love always implies a call to the human community to
make this love present, visible, real, especially to those who are
excluded.

The community of Ancient Judah in the latter part of the sixth
century B.C.E. needed to be convinced that they were the beloved,
forgiven community, who would be led into a new existence in
the presence of God. This new existence included the promise
and the call to be a loving, forgiving, inclusive community, according to the text of Second Isaiah. In Isaiah 40–55, the people
are asked to accept the inclusion of all the nations and, indeed,
all creation in God's redemptive action. They are told that the
means to their deliverance will be a non-Israelite, nonbeliever
king: Cyrus. Cyrus was to be the means of the people's deliverance, and the text names him as God's servant and God's Messiah. In Isaiah 45, the people are told that arguing about this
would be as ridiculous as a pot arguing with its maker (see
pp. 56ff.). Finally, the community is invited to the great banquet
that God has spread, they and others with them.

Chapter 55 brings to resolution what was announced in Isaiah
40. In the opening lines, an empowered people is invited to walk:

> Hey, all thirsty ones,
> walk to the water!
> And those without money,
> walk!
> Buy and eat,
> walk, buy,
> without money
> without pay
> wine and milk. (55:1)

The only requirements to be invited are need—"thirsty ones"—
and lack of resources—"those without money." These people are
invited to walk to the water, the symbol of life and of the presence
of God in Scripture. The beloved community is invited, of course,
but "nations" will also run to it, to become a part of the great
homecoming feast.

Isaiah 55:7, in an unexpected turn, mentions a specifically invited group: "the wicked." The return of the wicked to God will
be the occasion for God to make a lavish display of divine pardon. In this context, the prophet makes a new statement about
the incomparable nature of God:

> Let the wicked forsake their ways
> and the evil ones their deliberations.
> Let them return to the Lord
> who will have compassion
> and to our God
> who will abundantly pardon.
> For not are my deliberations your deliberations,
> nor your ways my ways,
> —says the Lord—
> For as high as the sky above the earth
> are my ways higher than your ways
> and my deliberations than your deliberations.
>
> (Isa. 55:7–9).

In this text, often adduced as evidence of biblical witness to God's transcendence, the prophet speaks indeed of God's incomparable nature, as in Isaiah 40. But this concluding chapter provides even more strongly than chapter 40 the insight that God's power serves God's love. Here the focus is on God's forgiveness, God's wild inclusiveness and abundant compassion, as compared to human forgiveness. God's compassion is literally "womblike compassion." This compassion is as abundant as much-needed spring rain, as sure as its effectiveness and as successful in what it sets out to do.

Ancient Israel, Ancient Judah, God's model covenant community, had fallen far short of the promise of what it could become. The people had domesticated God, made of the God of all creation an ally who would get them out of all the trouble they would find themselves in. They had made of land and Temple idols, securities for the presence of God with them and for their place with God. The Temple had come down around their ears, just as the prophets had foretold. It had to come down around their ears in order for there to be something to continue out of the mess they had made. The promise to them of God's love and forgiveness and the call to reflect this love in their life as a community with God had not ceased. Their God was not domestic; their land was always a gift, not a security; and the Temple was a human institution, always in need of reformation, of breakdown and restoration.

As interesting as it may be to speak about the sins of other people, we must bring the focus back to ourselves. We need to ask ourselves if we are as aware of our shortcomings as were the Judahites of the exiled community in Babylon, the broken community in Judah. Do we know that we have failed in our task of reflecting God's love and compassion? Are we ready to admit that we have not lived the call to a new humanity in Jesus but have let patriarchal and hierarchical ways of existing together in sexual and racial inequality dominate our lives? Have we made the Church into an idol—a guarantee of the presence of God? Are we ready to confess that we have made God a bulwark in defense of patriarchal ways of existing? Are we ready to repent and accept the word of forgiveness? Gentile Christians especially should be aware of the "abundance" of God's compassion and pardon. Are we able to begin with the response of Second Isaiah?

Are we able to admit also, with this prophet of exile and crisis, that no matter what our position—feminist, traditionalist, or in between—in speaking about God we are going to have it wrong? Are we able to entertain the whisper of "It is and it is not"?[9] Are we willing to say that whether we call God "father" or "mother," "he" or "she," we are both right and wrong, for as we speak we know that our words are only a stammering approximation of the reality that is God? If we are able to do this, then we may be capable of proceeding, going on with both the uncertainty and the certainty. The uncertainty of our human naming of what is divine, mysterious, and far beyond us will not provide us a resting place. The certainty that God's loving motherly compassion embraces us as we walk will keep us going. What counts is not our proficiency in God-talk but our need, our thirst and hunger for the divine presence. For that need, God has abundant response.

For Reflection and Response

1. Read Isaiah 40–55 through entirely two or three times. Note words and phrases that strike you as strange, beautiful, unhelpful, or otherwise remarkable. Try to obtain a sense of the main themes of the book.
2. Can you find an experience in your own life or that of your community that is like "exile"? How would you describe it?
3. Do you agree that "we do the impossible when we speak of God"? Is this evident in hymns or in other liturgical language?
4. What questions does Isaiah 40–55 raise for you in terms of speaking of God in the light of women's newly cherished human dignity and equality?

3

Names and the
Gender of God

Tell me, I pray, your name.
Genesis 32:29

I make a distinction in this book between biblical names of God and designations or titles. In the first category I include words that are closest to proper names, such as "God" and "El Shaddai." These names are discussed in this chapter. In the second category I include words that are more descriptive, such as "king" and "father"; these I review in chapter 4. The word "Lord" is a hybrid, since it is a title in English that is based on a name in the original language. I have therefore discussed it under both categories.

Scripture names God in a variety of ways, a diversity not apparent in most English translations. The names indicate shifts in the experience and perception of the covenant community of Ancient Israel. In this chapter I examine four names for God found in the Hebrew Bible, and I discuss whether these names are appropriately rendered with masculine-gendered pronouns alone.

Elohim

Unlike English, Hebrew assigns to all nouns a gender classification, as does Greek; nouns are either masculine or feminine in Hebrew. The word that is rendered "God" in English translations is most often *Elohim* in Hebrew; it is actually a masculine plural noun, literally meaning "gods." In the Hebrew Bible this is not the most frequently used word for the God of Israel, but it occurs quite often, and its Greek equivalent predominates in the New Testament. God is what we call a *generic* name, used in the Bible not only for the God of Israel, the God of Jesus Christ, but for deities of other religions also. Most often in the Hebrew Bible, Elohim indicates the God of Israel, and therefore the translation "God" is not inaccurate since Israel conceived of God as one being, not a plurality of beings. We can only speculate as to whether the original users were conscious of the plural form of Elohim or whether the familiarity of usage had worn this awareness away.

In the Hebrew Bible, the verbs coupled with Elohim, when it is used to mean the God of Israel, are almost always singular, with one notable exception.[1] Genesis 1:26 announces God's intention to create humanity thus: "Then God said: Let us make humanity in our image and our likeness." In this verse God speaks in the plural—let *us* make, *our* image, *our* likeness—and in the lines following, the created human beings are referred to with the plural pronoun "they." In Gen. 1:27, the text hastens back from the precipice of reading plurality in God and reverts to the singular in describing the act of creation:

> Then created God humanity in his image.
> In the image of God he created it;
> male and female he created them.

In Gen. 1:26, at the point of the announcement of the creative act, God's speech transcends gender because the verbal we-form has no gender connotation in Hebrew. In verse 27, the verbs return to the masculine singular, "he," but what is created is a plurality, "them." What is one in God comes out in the reflection of God as two differentiated human beings: male and female.

Genesis 1:27 is uniquely important among all the biblical texts that have God as subject. It is one of two texts that describe the creation of humanity in terms of the image of God (see Gen. 4:1–2). Its three lines are constructed as poetry. Hebrew poetry is characterized by repetitions and variations of words and phrases, by word order and reversals of this order. To highlight the word order in Hebrew, I have translated as literally as possible. In Gen. 1:27, the verb "created," with God as subject, is repeated three times, the first two times in contrasting order: it stands one place from the beginning in line one and one place from the end in line two. This threefold repetition, combined with the reversal, highlights the act of creation. The Hebrew verb "create" that is used here occurs elsewhere in the Bible in reference to God's action alone, as distinct from a shaping or forming activity in which humans engage also (Gen. 2:7, for example).

"Humanity," *adam* in Hebrew, is repeated at the end of the second and third line, as "it" and "them" respectively, moving from singular to plural. "In his image" reoccurs as "the image of God" in line two and for the third time as "male and female." In Genesis 1, God is in charge of the creative act without assistance, and God's action is unique, not comparable to human activity. Humanity's origin goes back directly to God. Humanity, first two singulars, ends up as a plurality. This movement, coupled with the movement from "the image of God/his image" to "male and female," could not say more clearly that the image of God, a singular image, in God's unique, creative act issues in plurality in humankind. Together, not one more than the other, male and female are in God's own image. In her landmark study on this text, biblical scholar Phyllis Trible observes, "Sexual differentiation does not mean hierarchy but equality. Created simultaneously, male and female are not superior and subordinate. Neither has power over the other; in fact, both are given equal power."[2]

As I observed, the Bible was shaped in a patriarchal context (p. 10). All the more remarkable, then, is this word about the human creature, male and female, equally created in God's image. Genesis 1:27 is surely a witness to the way the biblical text transcends its limitations. In fact, more still can be said. What does this verse say or imply about God? Interpreters of Scripture are careful to point out that the image of God in humanity may not be read back into God. As Phyllis Trible observes, "Sexual differentiation of humankind is not thereby a description of God."[3] Does the text say nothing about God, then? Image and likeness are words that may ward off assumptions of identification, but they do point to something or someone.

What can we say, on the basis of Gen. 1:27, about how to speak of God "in view of women's newly cherished dignity and equality"? That dignity and equality are guaranteed by the text, according to my interpretation. What more can we say? God is, by common agreement, neither male nor female; God transcends sexuality. But the Bible speaks of God in words that are, nonetheless, sexually differentiated, and so do we. The biblical narrators refer to God as "he." Having to choose when speaking of God in personal terms, they chose the masculine singular verb form over its feminine counterpart. Is this masculine reference intrinsically more appropriate than the feminine? If God indeed transcends sexuality, as is generally inferred from this text, the answer to the question must be no. God is referred to no more accurately with "he" than with "she." Positively stated, on the basis of Gen. 1:26–27, God can be referred to with feminine as well as with masculine pronouns. Both are equally accurate and inaccurate.

Both feminine and masculine pronouns for God are accurate because the image reflects the original. Because God is one, humanity's sexual differentiation is held together in God. Feminine and masculine pronouns for God are also equally accurate because sexual differentiation is not present in a hierarchical fashion in humanity: male and female are equally created in the image of God and equally reflect God's image. This absence of hierarchy points to the same absence in God's nature, which includes male and female equally, not one more than the other.

At the same time, feminine and masculine pronouns for God are inaccurate because the image must be distinguished from identification with the original. What exists in human beings as two sexes cannot be read back into God literally. God transcends sexuality. Finally, these pronouns are inaccurate insofar as all speech about God is inaccurate, because human beings operate within the limitations of human language and in speaking about God are always wrong as well as right.

The writers and compilers of the biblical creation stories were convinced that humanity had not kept the image of God inviolate. The opening chapters of Genesis tell of the disturbance of the harmony that God had created and intended, harmony between creature and creature, on the one hand, and the creature and God, on the other. Henceforth, humanity would live a flawed existence. Our questions addressed to the text arise out of our recognition of patriarchy as a major expression of humanity's flawed existence. Ancient Israel's perspectives did not allow for a recognition of patriarchy as a distortion of the image of God. The writers of Genesis opted for male imagery in verbs and pronouns, as if God were more male than female. The limitations of the unquestioned patriarchal context are clearly at work in the biblical text.

Even so, a text shaped by the concerns of Ancient Israel may transcend the limitations of these concerns. Out of our engagement with Gen. 1:26–27, we have found that male and female are created equally in God's image and that what is not held hierarchically in humanity points to an absence of this hierarchy in God's nature: God is not more appropriately named with male than with female designations. Nor does Genesis 1 offer the only text in the Bible that takes us in this direction, as we shall see.

El Shaddai

Other words in the Hebrew Bible that translate into English as God are *Eloah* and *El. El* occurs alone or in a number of combinations: El Elyon (God Most High; Gen. 14:18–19); El Olam (Eternal God; Gen. 21:33); and El Berith (Covenantal God; Judg. 9:46). These names most likely have direct roots in Canaanite religion, where El was the head of the pantheon. Outside of Canaan, among Israel's neighbors, El was a common name for a deity. The Hebrew Bible uses El, alone or in combination, more than two hundred times. English translations commonly obscure the multiple forms that underlie the translation "God."

The name El Shaddai is of particular interest to us because of its possible implications. This combination is traditionally translated as "God Almighty" (see Ex. 6:3, for example), with a note in the NRSV on the Hebrew original. The designation occurs most often as a single word, *Shaddai*, rendered "Almighty" in the NRSV, again with a note referring to the Hebrew (see Gen. 49:25, for example). Thirty-one of the forty-eight occurrences of the name are in the book of Job. It can also be found in texts as ancient as Gen. 49:25, Num. 24:16, and Ps. 68:14.

The English translation "almighty" comes from the Greek rendering of the Hebrew as *pantokrator* and gives only one of the possible meanings and derivations of *El Shaddai*. The most likely grammatical derivation of *Shaddai* is from the Hebrew word *shad*, meaning "breast," mostly occurring in the dual form *shaddayim* (breasts). A literal translation of *El Shaddai* may be "God of the breasts" or "breasted God." That the connotations of the name El Shaddai are with offspring and fertility is clear from Gen. 49:25 and also from the book of Ruth, where Naomi complains that God has brought her back to Bethlehem "empty" and accuses "Shaddai" of having done her injury (Ruth 1:22). So interpreted, the name El Shaddai, or Shaddai, has obvious female characteristics. This connection was obscured by the Greek translators of the Hebrew Bible and by most subsequent translators and interpreters. A typical comment in a contemporary wordbook of the Bible offers the Hebrew word for breast as the most likely root for Shaddai, raises no grammatical objections to this derivation, but considers this derivation of Shaddai not worth much attention because the name concerns a "male Deity."[4]

In spite of such protestations, it seems most likely that *shad*, "breast," indeed provides the proper derivation for Shaddai, a name originally connected to a deity specifically tied to birth and fertility. By the time the texts that use this name found their final shape and were translated, the root and meaning had become obscure or were deliberately obscured by editors and translators of the Bible, for fear of applying female characteristics to the God of Israel.

Although it may at first feel strange and unfamiliar, Shaddai is perhaps best left untranslated.[5] The following prayer, composed by feminist theologian Miriam Therese Winter, offers an example

of possible ways of using this name of God. Note the different
characteristics that Winter assigns to God Shaddai:

> Wide are the windows of Your compassion,
> warm are the wings of Your protection,
> eternal, maternal Shaddai.
> I run to You in my pain and fear
> and am comforted to know
> You are near
> in trial and tribulation,
> lifting me up to new heights of hope
> in the circle of Your mercy.
> As I walk with You
> through uncertainty,
> I feel at home in the ambience
> of Your never-failing love.
> May I never fall out of favor.
> May I never lose hold of hope.
> Keep me close to You, Shaddai,
> now and forever.
> Amen.[6]

The Unpronounceable Name

Names are words loaded with power. Many modern commen-
tators mark this understanding of names as a point of disjunction
between contemporary and ancient experience. A remark by biblical scholar Bernhard Anderson may be considered representative: "In modern usage, names are convenient labels by which
we differentiate one thing from another, one person from another. . . . In the ancient world . . . a person's self was expressed
and contained in his name."[7] Yet the difference between the experience of ancient times and our own may be one more of degree than of essence. I know few people today who enjoy having
their name mispronounced or used as a joke. We may recall how
many women change their nicknames or shortened names back
to their full Christian names. Why do women keep or retrieve
their paternal name or other family name if names in our culture
are so unimportant and for information only? Children are well
aware of the power of naming when they mock someone's name.
The self-protective chant "sticks and stones . . ." flies in the face
of the evidence; name mocking and scolding *do* hurt. Our names
are far more than pieces of information; they are signs and symbols of our very selves and are bound up with our identity.

I had occasion to experience this connection between my name and my identity most strongly. It happened about twelve years ago, just before the funeral of my father, who had died as a result of a traffic accident. His death came as a great shock, for at almost eighty-three years, my father was a very healthy man who still worked full time. I had received the news of his instantaneous death by telephone from the other side of the Atlantic Ocean. I had made my plane trip and was occupied, together with my siblings, with the complications of winding up the family estate, my mother having died some years before. While we were dividing personal belongings, I asked my sister whether she knew the whereabouts of my father's tiepin, a monogram of his initials that I had given him for his eightieth birthday. She did not know but suggested that it might still be on the tie he had been wearing when he died. "It must be in the bag with all his other clothes on the back porch," said my sister. "I was too scared to look at them."

I decided not to be squeamish and at the earliest opportunity rummaged through the bag to find the tie and especially the pin. There were the clothes my father had worn on his last trip on the motorcycle: his jacket, ripped at the shoulder, the sleeve almost torn off; his helmet, the strap gone; and yes, the tie.

It was a good tie, with the pin I was looking for still on it and a smear of blood across the dark blue fabric. As I lifted the tie out of the bag, the phone rang and I went inside to pick it up, the tie still in my hand. It was the solicitor in charge of handling my parents' estate, who wanted to know the children's full Christian names. I began by reciting the three names of the oldest, my brother. In the family order, I came next. To my horror, my mind stopped working, and I could not remember any of my names, first, middle, or last, full or short. I was staring into an abyss. I mumbled something about shock into the phone and went to find my sister, whose name I had no trouble remembering. She went to take care of the business for me, and my memory returned very soon after that.

It is not difficult to understand the reasons for my memory lapse: tiredness, shock, and grief. What is more striking is the complete loss of identity that I experienced when I forgot my own name. I truly lost myself for a moment when I faced my father's absence through the touch of his torn and bloodied clothes, to which were pinned the letters of his name.

What is true for human names is also applicable to a divine name: identity and power reside in a name. Israel used a proper name for God, *YHWH,* more than six thousand times in the Bible.

Initially used by one group of biblical writers, this name gained predominance and is also found combined with Elohim. The four letters usually are translated as "LORD" in English translations and as "LORD God" when found combined with Elohim.[8] The biblical text connects the revelation of this name with the exodus from Egypt (e.g., Ex. 3:15; 6:3).

The derivation of the four consonants in YHWH is not clear; there may be a connection to the verb "to be" in Hebrew, or the name may be rooted in an ancient emotive cry of worship, "O, That One!" Ancient Israel's practice was to write the name with consonants only. At some time, the covenant community of Ancient Israel stopped pronouncing the name of God and only the consonants remained in the holy writings. No one knew exactly what the original pronounciation had been. Eventually, the vowels belonging to the word *Adonai* were added to YHWH and Adonai was read. The Greek translation of the Hebrew text rendered it *kurios,* the basis for the English reading "Lord." In contemporary Christian scholarship, it is often customary to insert hypothetical vowels between the consonants of the name YHWH and to pronounce it accordingly. The Jerusalem Bible follows this practice.

Christianity might do well to learn at the feet of Judaism in respect to this name of God. Jewish believers would not entertain the notion of trying to pronounce the sacred name and find it deeply offensive and blasphemous when others attempt to do so. The insight that the name of God must not be pronounced arose not out of superstition but out of an appropriate understanding of the power of naming and of the impossibility and inappropriateness of humanity's pretending to exert this power over the Holy God. Christians, indeed, like "fools rush in where angels fear to tread" when they reclaim the pronunciation of YHWH. The Christian community in so doing both misses an important theological insight and traps itself in a false sense of superiority in relation to Judaism.

What is one to do with an unpronounceable name? We can follow the practice of a great part of Judaism and read *Adonai,* a form of the word "Lord" in Hebrew; or we can read *Hashem,* the Hebrew word for "The Name." If we opt for the "Lord" of most English Bible translations, we are some steps removed from the original, which was intended as a name rather than a title. A serious problem with the word "lord" is that the unpronounced and unpronounceable name of God has become located in a male term that speaks of power in traditional, patriarchal, hierarchical terms. I return to this discussion in the next chapter (see p. 36).

The Holy One of Israel

That God is unknowable and cannot be named may be summarized in the word "holiness."[9] Because this is a complex concept about which volumes have been written, it may help to begin with a description from biblical scholar Baruch Levine:

> Holiness is difficult to define or describe; it is a mysterious quality. Of what does holiness consist? In the simplest terms the "holy" is different from the profane or the ordinary. It is "other." . . . The "holy" is also powerful or numinous. The presence of holiness may inspire awe or strike fear, evoke amazement. The holy may be perceived as dangerous, yet it is urgently desired because it affords blessing, power, and protection.[10]

"Holy" is combined with God as an adjective but can also stand alone and be translated "the Holy One." In the latter case, the expression comes close to being a name. I treat it here as a link to chapter 4, in which I discuss God's titles and designations.

The word "holy" in connection with God points, then, first to the otherness of God. In Ancient Israel, this otherness was frequently the occasion for praise (e.g., Ex. 15:11; Pss. 77:13ff.; 89:7; 99; 111:9), as in the familiar proclamation of the seraphim in Isaiah's vision:

> Holy, holy, holy!
> YHWH of Hosts!
> Filled is the earth with his glory.
> (Isa. 6:3)

Typically, the contemplation of God's holiness causes both adoration and, at the same time, a consideration of human shortcomings in the face of God's splendid perfection. Isaiah therefore cries out that he is unclean and his people are unclean (6:5). The perception of human flaws causes fear or awe in the face of God's holiness.

Since God is "other," is God then unreachable and out of touch? For the Ancient Israelite community, God was the Holy One, but this did not mean that God was remote. God was with the people precisely as the Holy One. As the prophet Hosea announces on behalf of God:

> For I am God and not a man
> in your midst the Holy One;

I will not come in anger.
(Hos. 11:9)

This saying points to the two things to be grasped about God's holiness: (1) God is not like a human being (literally, the text has "a man"); and (2) precisely as the "other," God is in the midst of the people. Note that the point of unlikeness between God and the human being is forgiveness, as it was in Isaiah 55 (see p. 21).

In the book of Isaiah, God is called not just the Holy One but "the Holy One of Israel." In addition to what we have observed so far, this expression underlines for Gentiles that God resides as the Holy One not just with any community but in the midst of this particular community: Israel. As the unknowable, holy mystery, God is known in Israel and through Israel. For the Christian community, this name of God focuses the attention not only on God and God's holiness but also on Israel as the holy people of God. With gratitude we acknowledge our debt to God and God's people Israel of the past and of today.

God's holiness relates directly to the community. Because God is, as the Holy One, in our midst, God's holiness issues a call.[11] The covenant community created at Mount Sinai was termed a "holy nation" (Ex. 19:6). The most familiar statement may be Lev. 19:2: "You shall be holy, for I, the LORD your God, am holy" (NRSV). According to Baruch Levine, God's holiness is not intended to describe God's essential nature but rather how God is manifest. In Hos. 11:9, God's holiness resides in God's forgiving activity. As Levine says, "The statement that God is holy, means . . . that God acts in holy ways: God is just and righteous."[12] This insight helps to overcome the distinction interpreters often make between holiness in worship and holiness in the social sphere. Leviticus 19, assumed to be centered in the concerns of the priests, contains an entire ethical code. There we find the commandment to love the neighbor as the self (Lev. 19:18) and to love the stranger in the same way (19:34).

If God's holiness means primarily that God acts in just and righteous ways, then the community in covenant with God is required to act in the same way in following its call to holiness. To return to our starting point, the community as a holy community is required to be other as God is other, different from the ordinary. This apartness manifests itself when the community emulates God's passion for justice. The prophets of Israel articulated above all the conviction that worship, no matter how devoted and constant, is not acceptable to God when justice is absent from the life of the community. Within the framework of my concerns in this book, we could rephrase this belief thus: The naming of God and our concern for justice must be all of a piece.

Justice is always specific in the Hebrew Bible and means God's concern for the downtrodden, those who are on the margin, those who are squeezed out. The covenant community should be holy and set apart in its passionate embrace of God's care for those very same people. It should be unlike the rest of the world that steps on those who are already on their way down and victimizes further what has been wounded. No, this community, in imitation of the Holy One it worships, shall not quench the smoldering wick, and the bruised reed it shall not break (Isa. 42:3). When this passionate love for the marginalized is evident in the midst of the community, the community will have a sense of what it means to claim the Holy One of Israel as the One it worships.

The ascription "Holy One," or "Holy One of Israel," provides something of a transition between a name and a title for God. This naming of God highlights the connection between language about God and human identity. While the holiness of God points to God's otherness, it also lays claim on the human community in whose midst God is present as the Holy One. God's holiness issues a call to the community that names God holy, to mirror God's justice and righteousness in caring for the most vulnerable among them.

Blessing Song

> May the blessing of God go before you,
> may her grace and peace abound;
> may her spirit live within you,
> may her love wrap you round.
> May her blessing remain with you always,
> may you walk on holy ground.[13]

For Reflection and Response

1. Think about the word "God." Do you associate it with a male image? If it is not a masculine word, then why is God always referred to as "he?"
2. Think of the power of names and naming in your life. Write a paragraph about yourself beginning with "I am . . . ," using your own name and other names to which you are connected.

3. Write a paragraph about God, beginning with "God is . . . ," making use of names discussed in this chapter.

4. Can you think of a holy place you have visited, a holy thing you have seen, or a holy event you have experienced? What made them holy?

4

To Whom Does
Scripture Compare God?

For I am God and not a man.
Hosea 11:9

If all speaking of God is flawed, then how do we speak of God? How does the Bible speak of God? Unlike its neighbors, Ancient Israel made no visible images of its deity. The covenant community had to rely on the presence of God without visible, tangible, humanly created models of God. The prohibition of visible representations of God testifies to an understanding of the danger of idolatry: the identification of divine reality with human representation.

Words also create images, and in so doing, they are open to the same danger of idolatry, of identifying the unseen with the seen, the creator with the created, the unnameable with a name. All speech about God, including biblical speech, is rooted in human experience. In being so connected, language for God works as a comparison. In calling God a judge, for example, God is compared to a familiar figure of society. We need to be aware always that language for God is language of comparison and not of identification.[1]

The danger of idolatry that exists in language creates a need for diverse and abundant images and names for God. Drawing on a vast array of sources, the Bible gives evidence of the necessity for many titles and images for God.[2] The entire created world, animate and inanimate, was available and useful to those who spoke of God and God's interaction with the creation in biblical times. Among many other creatures and things, God is compared in the Bible to a ruler, a judge, a shepherd, and a potter, but also to a bear, a lion, a rock, a brook, and a wall. Some of these comparisons occur only once or a few times; others predominate at certain times and not at others. A great deal of flexibility and fluidity is present in designations for God in the biblical text.

How does the process of comparison work? One can discern three steps or movements in this process. An example may help

35

to explain the dynamics. When God is called "king," God is compared to a human ruler known by a community. Then, as soon as the comparison is made the flaw in it also becomes apparent. Yes, God is king; no, God is not like a human king. God does not abuse power and violate justice as human kings do all too often. Finally, the image of kingship itself undergoes change and moves closer to the ideal.[3] Kingship is submitted to the criterion of divine rule, once it has been applied to God. I call this entire movement, from agreement to negation to reaffirmation, the "yes, no, and more so" dynamic.

Does a comparison remain effective once it has been made? I have described the threefold movement in the way it is *supposed* to work. Comparisons for God are in trouble when their "yes, no, and more so" dynamic malfunctions. Such a malfunction may occur when the human reality from which the God-language has been drawn is no longer known and familiar. Or the human experience may be so negative that the entire comparison begins to suffer from a negative coloring.

In this chapter, I explore biblical titles or designations for God, words that can be used both to describe and to address God. I evaluate these designations in terms of their resonance with contemporary experience and hence in light of the threefold movement of the comparison dynamic. Then, in reimagining and searching for alternative language, I look for language for God that is rooted in Scripture and that also keeps the threefold dynamic intact.

Speaking of People — Speaking of God

A few weeks after I had begun my first course as a new teacher, I was met after class by a delegation of students. They were nervous but came straight to the point: They were shocked, they said, that I referred to God with masculine pronouns in the classroom, and they requested that I stop doing so. Because I was not very familiar with the issue at that time, I proposed to spend some time talking about it outside of class and agreed that in the meantime I would not use "he" for God in my courses unless I was directly quoting Scripture. The students were not very polite, and they might have chosen more tactful ways to deal with my inexperience. But perhaps because they were somewhat lacking in finesse, their distress moved me deeply. I changed to a different practice and reconsidered language as it pertains to God. For years, I avoided using any pronoun for God in class or in worship services. It was not difficult to do, and I did not feel I had lost a great deal by ceasing to name God "he," but it always seemed a provisory solution. The absence of a word was only the prelude to finding more satisfactory God-language.

During those years, many congregations and institutions developed policies on inclusive language in reference to people. In my academic community, it was made clear that these policies did not pertain to language about God. Some of us had abandoned referring to God as "he," others had not. All of us kept traditional male titles for God, such as "Lord" and "Father," and for Christ, such as "Lord" and "Son," even if we avoided the pronoun "he." The practice, then, for God-language became in effect a choice between exclusively male language, on the one hand, or male and neuter language, on the other.

When speaking of people, inclusivity was seen as so important that policies had to be made. But speaking of God was another matter. The split troubled me, for it seemed to separate God-language from human experience. The words "man" and "he" were no longer understood to be inclusive of both male and female human beings and, according to many researchers, had never been inclusive.[4] Finding alternative words for people was not difficult, and we lost nothing in the process. But something happened to the "old" words. Because language not only is an expression of concepts but also has an influence on our thinking, words such as "man" and "he" were more exclusive in their reference after it became common to use them for males only. Today, when we come across the word "man" in literature that predates concerns for inclusivity, it is often not clear whether humanity or a single male is indicated. The word does not communicate well. Our thoughts get hooked on "man," and we may need to read a phrase a few times to understand what the writer has in mind. Awareness and usage have cast words such as "man" and "he" in a different frame, so that they now stand in the sharp light of maleness.

This being so, the word "he" has become more problematic in relation to God, for it creates an understanding of God as male. Male designations and titles for God produce the same effect. In the case of the biblical text, this may not have been what the writers had in mind. Nevertheless, masculine pronouns and male titles for God take on the burden of maleness today because of the development these pronouns and titles have undergone in the course of our search for inclusive people-language. Human experience and the naming of God are intricately connected.

Is God a Man of War?

As a community delivered from life and soul-crushing bondage, Israel rejoiced in the defeat of its former oppressors. The people sang and danced to celebrate the occasion of the drowning of pharaoh's army in the Sea of Reeds. Because they credited God with this success, they sang God's praise:

> Adonai is a man of war,
> Adonai is his name. (Ex. 15:3)

The experience of the Israelites was one of freedom after slavery, light after a long time of darkness, heaving a great sigh of relief when a burden is lifted, and breaking out in shouts of excitement. God was the one who led them to this place, to God be the praise and the glory!

But to call God "a man of war" sounds crude to us today. That God would be a man stands in sharp contradiction to the notion that God is God and not a man at all (cf. Hos. 11:9). That God would be a man of war is particularly repugnant, creating as it does an image of masculine violence.

This poem in Exodus 15 closely reflects a particular experience. The title "man of war" as used for God was applicable in only a limited way and occurs just one other time in the biblical text (see Isa. 42:13).[5] Clearly, as experience changes, designations for God change. The title "king" for God, for example, does not occur in the first five books of the Bible. This may have been because the Hebrew word for king, *melek,* was too close to the word "Moloch," the name for the god of Moab, particularly abhorred by the Israelites because of the Moabite rite of child sacrifice; or it may have been natural not to use a title for God with which the community had no firsthand experience, apart from its negative experience with pharaoh.

God as Male Authority:
King and Lord

"King" and "lord" as biblical designations for God draw from a similar field of experience.[6] Broadly speaking, both words indicate a male who is one's social superior and exercises power over his environment. "King" carries the greater power of the two and is a more specific word, indicating both an administrative office and status. The appellation "king" for a deity was common in the world of the Ancient Near East, and Israel shared with its neighbors the attribution of royal power to its God. Yet "king" is not a dominant image for God in the Hebrew Bible, although it is not as limited as "man of war." Of the roughly forty occurrences of "king" for God, over half are clustered in a group of psalms that celebrate God's kingship in a general and cosmic sense (see, e.g., Psalms 93; 95; 96; 97; 98; 99; 145; 149). God is said to be "a great king above all the gods" (Ps. 95:3), and God's kingship is over the entire earth (Psalms 96; 97; and 99). In prophetic material, the designation may be more specifically oriented to Israel, and God is called Israel's king in several texts (cf. Isa. 43:15; Jer. 8:19; Zeph. 3:15; Micah 2:13).

The threefold dynamic of king imagery for God can be analyzed as follows. The resource for the reference is the human king, whose power and splendor provide the points of reference with which to compare God. Then the "no" of the dynamic enters in, because God's kingship is unlike human rule. It is more extensive, including the entire creation. Above all, God's rule is marked by attention and care for those in need, "satisfying the desire of every living thing." (Ps. 145:16, NRSV). In the midst of the praise of God as king, the psalmist recalls God's special care for those "who are falling" and that God raises up "all who are bowed down" (Ps. 145:14, NRSV). Human rulers are often characterized by the opposite traits: they "crush" people, they "kill the widow and the stranger, they murder the orphan" (Ps. 94:5, 6, NRSV). "Wicked rulers . . . band together against the life of the righteous, and condemn the innocent to death" (Ps. 94:20–21, NRSV).

Finally, in the process of applying the imagery of kingship to God, the idea of kingship itself is reshaped. The ideal king of Psalm 72 is described in a mirror image of divine rule:

> May he judge your people with righteousness,
> and your poor with justice.
> May the mountains yield prosperity for the people,
> and the hills, in righteousness.
> May he defend the cause of the poor of the people,
> give deliverance to the needy,
> and crush the oppressor.
> . . . .
> For he delivers the needy when they call,
> the poor and those who have no helper.
> He has pity on the weak and the needy,
> and saves the lives of the needy.
> From oppression and violence he redeems their life;
> and precious is their blood in his sight.
>
> (Ps. 72:2–4; 12–14, NRSV)

This description gives a fair idea of the properties of ideal kingship and provides a standard by which earthly rule must be measured.

"King" as a designation for God or Christ is infrequent in the New Testament, where the dominant title is *kurios,* "lord." "Lord" is used in the text in three ways: for God; for Jesus, as a title of respect during his ministry on earth; and for Jesus as the risen Christ. *Kurios* initially referred to any lawful owner of property (including people), the master of a household. Naturally, such persons were male. Eventually, *kurios* came to mean any male of higher rank and authority than oneself. A socially superior male could be addressed as "lord" and spoken about as "lord." At the time of the Roman Empire, the time of Jesus and the early Church, the title "lord" was also applied to the Roman emperor.

Both titles, "king" and "lord," not only render an image of God but also create an image of the human community in relation to God as king and lord. Where God is king, the human community constitutes the realm of God's rule, under God's care and protection. The citizens of this realm respond to God as their ruler and are directly responsible to God for their actions. This ethos operated with special force for the early Christian Church at the time of the Roman Empire. The first covenant community had constituted itself as a "kingdom of priests" (Ex. 19:6) and, for the first centuries of its existence, had done without an institutional monarchy. It is no coincidence that the writer of 1 Peter applies to the early Christian community terms borrowed from the Exodus and wilderness period of Israel's history: "a royal priesthood, a holy nation, God's own people" (1 Peter 2:9; cf. Ex. 19:3–6).

Both "king" and "lord" are problematic God-titles today. They refer clearly to males without opening up the equivalent possibilities of "queen" and "lady," and thus they create a skewed male picture of God. In addition, the connection with contemporary experience is lacking. The context from which the comparisons were drawn is long gone, and the images malfunction in the comparative dynamic. If we want to know how the images functioned in reference to God and human beings, we need information about kings and lords of the remote past. This information then helps us understand the biblical text and engage it, but it does not make anachronistic designations relevant. "Lord" and "king" as titles for God operate in a religious world only, cut off from actual, lived experience. Worse, the malfunction in the dynamic of the comparison robs the image of its comparative force and pushes the imagery into literalism. In view of the long tradition of God as king and lord, an attachment to the terms is under-

standable; in view of the problems that are attached to them, they
need to be reconsidered.

What are our alternatives? Are there designations for God in
Scripture that are not so encumbered by exclusive male roles and
that retain the points of the comparison made in the text?

God as Teacher

One important point of the comparison, as I noted, is that believers are directly responsive to God and God's guidance and
direction for their lives. Thus, believers under God's rule are expected to become responsible to God and to one another. A dominant term for Jesus in the New Testament that gradually lost
its place in the early Church in favor of *kurios* was *teacher.* In
Hebrew the word was *rav,* or *rabbi* as it is sometimes found in
the Gospels; in Greek, *didaskalos.* Teaching was one of the most
prominent functions of Jesus in his public ministry (cf. Matt. 4:23;
9:35; 11:1; 12:9ff.; 13:54; Mark 1:21; Luke 4:15; John 18:20; etc.).
The teaching of Jesus was "with a view to the ordering of life with
reference to God and to one's neighbor" (Matt. 22:37ff.; cf.
19:16ff.).[7]

"Teacher" is obviously a term that lives in contemporary experience. It is not a function of a particular culture and will not disappear as cultures come and go, although the function will
undergo change. "Teacher" does not belong to males only; both
women and men are and have been teachers. The threefold dynamic of the comparison can operate freely. Yes, God is our
teacher, but God does not teach as humans teach. And in the
process of applying the image to God, the concepts of "teacher"
and "teaching" have been enriched and changed.

Jesus' favorite mode of teaching was the parable. A parable
draws on the knowledge of the listeners and pulls them into a
world they recognize. Parable teaching does not assume the lis-
tener to be an empty space, a know-nothing, to be filled by
a teacher who knows all. Most of all, parable teaching calls on
the listeners to respond in ways that are life-transforming. The
teacher demonstrates authority in ways that call forth the authority of those who learn. The teaching of Jesus does not put the
community in a passive position but rather asks it for a decision.

The word "teacher" as a designation for God is rare in the Hebrew Bible, yet the concept of God as teacher is present wherever
the people receive torah, God's instruction for their life. Instruction is necessary for the human community because the assump-

tion in the Bible is that without it, people would live in destructive and self-destructive ways. Torah, God's guidance and instruction, is viewed as God's gracious gift and the sign of God's presence to the community. When the Israelites were taken into the covenant with God in the wilderness and received God's instruction, they promised to *act* and to *listen* (Ex. 24:7).

In all respects, then, "teacher" is a term that can be reclaimed and used to address and describe God. It is rooted in Scripture and keeps the threefold dynamic of the comparison intact. I offer the following prayer as an example of drawing on the understanding of God as teacher and setting believers in a posture of eagerness to learn.

> God, our good teacher,
> open our ears to your direction and guidance.
> Forgive our laziness,
> our unwillingness to learn new things.
> Blow through the fog in our minds
> with the wind of your passion
> and love for the creation.
> Teach us, good and merciful God,
> to be good and merciful.
> Teach us with your unending patience
> to be your community,
> full of patience, forgiveness, and grace,
> in the spirit of Jesus our teacher. Amen.

God as Kinsman: Father

A common title for God in Christian usage is *father.* "Father" is rare in the Hebrew Bible, both descriptively and in terms of address, but is prevalent in the New Testament. The reason that "father" occurs so seldom with relation to God in the context of Ancient Israel may be that the god of Canaanite religion, El, was called "father" and understood as progenitor of other gods and of humanity.[8] It may be that to avoid the danger of idolatry, Ancient Israel rarely used *av,* the Hebrew word for father, to speak of God or to God. Of the more than one thousand times *av* appears in the Hebrew Bible, it is used for God only a dozen or so. When *father* occurs as a title for God, it is a part of a cluster of images that are taken from family life.

When the biblical storytellers, poets, and prophets wanted to express the deepest, most intimate relationship of God with the covenant community, they drew on the human experience of the entire family. For example, God is compared to a lover who is forsaken by his bride (Jer. 2:1ff.), to a husband whose wife has left him (Hos. 2:14ff.), and to a father whose children have been faithless (Deut. 32:6; Jer. 3:19). Ancient Israel called God "father" as an expression of trust in God's liberating and creative activity (Isa. 63:16; 64:8; 1 Chron. 29:10; Mal. 2:10). Or the term may appear in a somewhat tentative self-declaration on God's part: "If I am a father" (Mal. 1:6); "you would call me father" (Jer. 3:19); or, more assuredly, "I have become a father" (Jer. 31:9). Finally, God is said to be "father" in specific relationships: to the fatherless (Ps. 68:6) and to the king (2 Sam. 7:14; Ps. 89:26).

In the New Testament, this *network* of family imagery for God has, for all practical purposes, disappeared, and father has become the dominant image for God. God is called "my father" and "our father" by Jesus and is described as "the father" in the Gospels and as "the father of our Lord Jesus Christ" and "the father" in the rest of the New Testament. Elizabeth Johnson and others see this usage as dominant in the early Christian church rather than typical for Jesus and his entourage.[9] This may well be the case. Nonetheless, we must acknowledge the predominant use of "father" for God in the New Testament, arising, no doubt, in the early church out of a need to define the relations between God and Christ as well as those between God and the community.

Even though the use of "father" to refer to God is not common in the Hebrew Bible, the use of family imagery is extensive. Biblical writers drew on imagery of family affection to express the emotional and vulnerable nature of God's loving relation to Israel. God as husband and lover has a faithless female as human partner who is being wooed back by God. There are, in addition, references to the human community as "children" who behave rebelliously and self-destructively.

Parental and spousal images of God are rooted in the experience of patriarchal social relations. Today, these relations are revealed in all their violent and abusive potential. The problem with these images is not that they lack a connection to contemporary experience but that this experience is shot through with negativity. Brian Wren correctly observes that "Jesus knew and named God as Abba/father in such a way that the patriarchal order itself was called into question."[10] He is also correct in stating: "That name no longer has the power, *in our context,* to subvert patriarchal norms; indeed it is angrily invoked in defense of them."[11]

A related problem with the paternal image for God is the assignment of a childlike posture to the believer, particularly damaging for women, who need to free themselves from such stereotypes. In addition, we recall that the impossibility of speaking of God necessitates many names and images (see p. 35). In reducing the variety and number of names and images to one, we risk idolatry. As feminist theologian Sallie McFague observes, "By excluding other relationships as metaphors, the model of father becomes idolatrous, for it comes to be viewed as a description of God."[12]

Thus, the exclusively male referencing of God as a parent suffers from a triple weakness: it draws on experiences that today are found wanting; it runs the risk of keeping women in a child-like posture vis-à-vis a father figure; and third, the reference is at risk of being idolatrous. In reviewing Scripture's use of the paternal image for God, we found that the Bible reserves language of family life for the expressions of God's deepest and tenderest love for the people and of God's vulnerability in the face of this love. Both as a parent and as a daughter, I view the parental image of God as essential in the sense that it is the locus of God's love for the creation. Here, too, it is important that the "no" of the dynamic resonates. If we know the love for or of a parent, then we know something of God's love for the creation, for us. But God is both like and unlike the human parent, does not assert total control, and is not abusive; God loves as tenderly, wholeheartedly, and defenselessly as the human parent, only more so:

> When Israel was a child, I loved him,
> and out of Egypt I called my son.
> The more I called them,
> the more they went from me;
> they kept sacrificing to the Baals,
> and offering incense to idols.
> Yet it was I who taught Ephraim to walk,
> I took them up in my arms;
> but they did not know that I healed them.
> I led them with cords of human kindness,
> with bands of love.
> I was to them like those
> who lift infants to their cheeks.
> I bent down to them and fed them.
>   (Hos. 11:1–4, NRSV)

This text from Hosea testifies to the image of God as mother as well as father. If, as I believe, parental language is essential to express the nature of God but father-language is encumbered with the problems I noted above, then the natural movement is to equivalent language and the use of mother as well as father;

for it is not in its exclusively male character that parental love is valid. God's parental *love* is father- and mother-love both, God's parental *relation* is both that of father and mother. Certainly, God's authority is like that of both parents; it proceeds out of love and desire for the child's shalom. I return to these issues in chapter 5, when we consider biblical texts that speak about God in female images. At this point, let us be reminded by Sallie McFague that "God as mother does not mean that God is mother (or father). We imagine God as both mother and father, but we realize how inadequate these and any other metaphors are to express the creative love of God, the love that gives, without calculating the return, the gift of the universe."[13]

God as Rock

An inanimate image for God that occurs more than forty times in the Hebrew Bible is *rock*. In the Christian liturgy, this comparison remains in a prayer used occasionally before the sermon: "Let the words of my mouth and the meditation of my heart be acceptable to you, O LORD, my rock and my redeemer" (Ps. 19:14, NRSV). Sometimes "rock" is changed to "strength" when used in this contemporary setting.

The original word in Hebrew (*tsur*) indicates a hill or cliff, rather than the single stone that comes to mind from the English "rock." In the context of Ancient Israel and its neighbors, a rock was more often than not associated with a sense of holiness, divine revelation, and the miraculous. In fact, a purely secular use of *tsur* is rare in the Bible. A rock can be a place of miraculous provisions (see Deut. 32:13; Ps. 81:16; and Job 29:6); a place where God is made manifest (Ex. 33:21, 22); or a place of sacrifice (Judg. 13:19). Hence, God is both described as "rock" and addressed in this manner. The imagery at work is quite complex and certainly indicative not only of strength, although solidity and strength are a part of the image. More particularly, God the rock provides safety and protection, engages in saving action, and shows abiding loyalty to the faithful community (Pss. 42:9; 62:2, 6, 7; 73:26; 78:35; 92). God as rock is the place of refuge for the innocent who are unjustly accused (Pss. 31:1–3; 71:3; 94:22; 144:1ff.).

In addition, consideration of God's incomparability enters with the mention of God as rock (1 Sam. 2:2; Ps. 18:31). In Deuteronomy 32, "rock" is a guiding metaphor throughout the poem and is used as a synonym for God. The rock is said to be the worker of salvation and the origin of Israel's existence, among other things (Deut. 32:4, 15, 18). Listen to Ps. 42:9 for the intensity with which the believer addresses God as rock:

> I say to God, my rock:
> Then why do you forget me?
> Why do I go in darkness
> while my enemies sneer?

There is great richness in rock imagery, if we care to recover it. Although we may have lost the sense of the sacredness of rocks today, our experience is not entirely disconnected from this comparison. We recognize the awesome quality of rocks in the presence of the Rocky Mountains or the Grand Tetons. We use "rock" as an image for solidity and safety. Conversely, rocks can present danger; they are not cozy presences.

We may try the image of God as rock in the following prayer.

> O God, our rock,
> our high and holy place,
> our safe retreat,
> Presence of Power,
> take us in your shelter.
> Be a provider of wonders
> in our sere lives;
> let water flow
> and honey sweet appear.
> You, rock, our God,
> protect us with the cool
> shadow of your granite peaks,
> guide our wandering feet
> like wild goats on your flanks
> where we find surcease from our sorrow. Amen.

God as Maker and Mender

Designations that point to a foundational activity of God are *maker/creator, redeemer,* and *savior,* of which only the last survives in the New Testament in a significant way. "Maker/creator" and "redeemer" occur approximately twenty times in the Hebrew Bible, "savior" thirteen times. In the New Testament, "savior" refers sixteen times to Jesus Christ and a handful of times to God. "Redeemer" has disappeared, although the verb "redeem" and the noun "redemption" are present.

"Maker/creator" designates a God with whom the creation, in particular the covenant community, Israel, originates. The world, with all that grows and lives on it, comes from God; God is its home. God is, in particular, understood to be the origin of God's people, who bear special responsibilities because they are created by God. With this in mind, consider the following text:

> For your husband is your maker,
> Adonai of hosts is his name;
> and your redeemer the Holy One of Israel;
> the God of the whole earth he is called. (Isa. 54:5)

In the first and third lines of this passage, images of God's power and majesty, "maker" and "Holy One of Israel," are combined with terms of intimacy and kinship, "your husband" and "your redeemer." Second Isaiah identifies Israel's creator and Holy One as the one who has the closest, most intimate relationship with the covenant community. The second and fourth lines point beyond God's bond with Israel to the widest arena of God's concern—"Adonai of hosts," "God of the whole earth"—that is to say, the whole creation.

"Redeemer" and "savior" both point to God's liberating activity. The distinction between the two is that the word "redeemer" evokes the concept of cost. Redemption was a social custom of Ancient Israel, by which a kinsman who had the means to do so took responsibility for someone in the clan who was without resources. Redemption involved a price. When "redeemer" is applied to God in terms of Israel, it conveys the idea that God pays a price for taking on the responsibility for this covenant community. Later, the Church applied this same idea to the person of Christ.

"Savior" can also be translated as "liberator." God is Israel's savior/liberator in that God frees the people from the burden of their oppression. In traditional Christian terms, Jesus Christ is the savior in that Christ liberates believers from the burden of their sins. God's liberating and saving action was always seen as concrete. The oppression in Egypt and Babylon was real and life-threatening. From this precipice of death, God saved the people. The goal of God's freeing action is always to bring the people to God's presence; this can be said for the Exodus from Egypt, the return from Babylonian exile, and God's liberating action in Jesus Christ.

"Maker/creator," "redeemer," and "savior" are words that express the biblical beliefs that God makes, shapes, creates the world and God's people; that the world belongs to God and is responsible to God; and that it needs God's freeing action to engage in a response that produces health, wholeness, shalom. A fundamental assumption of the Bible is that humanity cannot do it on its own, that it dooms itself and the entire creation if it chooses to live outside of God's presence. Although "redeemer" is not a word with obvious male connotations in English, redemption could be achieved only by males in Ancient Israel's society. Theologian Letty Russell suggests another image of God: "mender of the creation," for God's engagement is always on behalf of the mending of creation.[14] I offer the following prayer to bring together images for God as maker and mender.

> Mender God,
> we bring to you
> torn and ragged lives,
> our communities fraying at the seams,
> the cuffs and collars.
> Won't you take your hand to us?
> Won't you look us over,
> see what can be done?
> Mender, maker, seamstress God,
> shake us out, straighten those crooked hems,
> mend the ragged, gaping tears.
> Mender, maker, seamstress God,
> Make this garment whole again. Amen

In Summary

We have looked in this chapter at familiar images of God in light of the "yes, no, and more so" dynamic of comparative language for God. The "yes" part of the movement assumes familiarity through human experience. Some designations for God, such as "king" and "lord," falter in this first part of the comparison, since they no longer resonate with contemporary experience. In addition, the maleness of these designations has become burdensome in view of the increased emphasis on inclusive language for human beings. Because language is a part of our experience, male pronouns and titles for humanity and God are experienced today by many as emphasizing maleness. The title "father" for God, although not divorced from experience, is inadequate in the sense that it sets up an image of a God who is more adequately named as male than as female. In chapter 3 we reviewed the inadequacy of this perception.

In view of these considerations, "teacher" and "mother" are appropriate designations for God and have substantial support in the Bible. A third title, biblical but somewhat lost to our imagination, is God as "rock." Rock imagery connotes safety, strength, protection, loyalty, and source of life. Finally, God as creator and savior of the covenant community and the world may be reimagined as maker and mender. The comparison of God to maker opens up to imagery that draws on women's experience. In chapter 5 we turn to texts that speak of God as mother.

For Reflection and Response

1. From this discussion arise the designations "teacher," "father," "mother," "rock," "maker," "redeemer," "liberator," and "mender" for God. Can you think of other images that arise from the ones offered in the discussion?
2. Do the words "maker," "redeemer," and "liberator" have an exclusively male connotation for you? Can you think of equivalent alternatives?
3. Compose a short prayer, making use of one of the designations suggested in this chapter that are unfamiliar to you.
4. How is "mender" an appropriate image for God? How does the threefold dynamic work with this image? What are potential problems of this designation?

5

God—Maker and Mother

A religion which seeks to convey the Teaching
of God who is above and beyond both sexes
cannot succeed in conveying that Teaching, if
it seeks to do so in a manner which implies that
a positive divine value is attached to only one
of the sexes.[1]

Ancient Israel saw itself as a people liberated by God. The first
and foundational liberation was from Egypt, the "house of
bondage"; the second, in the biblical text patterned after the first
in concept and imagery, was the liberation from the Babylonian
exile. God was celebrated by the believing community as the One
who "brought the people out."[2] The liberating event constituted
freedom from oppression and had as its most obvious goal life in
the land of the promise. In an even more profound sense, the
people were freed from oppression in order to live in God's presence. In the Exodus narrative, the people are told that they have
been brought to God's very self (Ex. 19:4); and Second Isaiah
closes with the invitation to the people to come to God (Isa. 55:3).

It is not coincidental that female images for God occur in texts
that speak of God as freeing the people from their enslavement
in Egypt or Babylon. As recounted in the book of Exodus, in the
course of God's liberating activity, God created the people as a
community, bound into covenant with God. Second Isaiah cast
God's freeing action even more explicitly in terms of creation
than the writers of Exodus. Second Isaiah emphasized that God,
the creator of the entire world, is in particular the *creator* of Israel,
Israel's *shaper* and *maker,* who *formed Israel in the womb* (cf.
Isa. 43:1, 7, 15; 44:2, 24; 45:9, 11; 51:13; 54:5). Within these two
contexts, exodus from Egypt and return from Babylon, creation
imagery is connected with the image of God as giving birth to
the community.

The female images discussed in this chapter are all connected
to God's maternal nature but not all to birth-giving. Different aspects of motherhood and mothering are highlighted in the texts.
Those I discuss here offer a remarkable diversity of perspectives
on what constitutes motherhood. Their number is small but their

power is great.[3] Together with the arguments made so far, the
texts with female imagery for God support the thesis that it is as
appropriate—or inappropriate—to refer to God with the pronoun "she" as it is to refer to God with "he," as appropriate to use
female as it is to use male titles. I explore this biblical terrain in
the hope of freedom from our Babylonian captivity to exclusively
male language for God.

A Woman in Childbirth
(Isa. 42:13–14)

Isaiah 42 is an announcement of God's impending action on
behalf of the community, called a "people robbed and plundered,
. . . trapped in holes, hidden in prisons" (42:22). The central part
of the chapter contains a section of jubilant praise to God, praise
in which nature and peoples participate: the sea, the coastlands,
and the desert are all exhorted to "sing praise" (42:10–12). Then
in 42:15–17 follows a description of God's powerful action and
intervention in order to lead the people home. The lines that concern us occur between these two sections:[4]

> Adonai like a mighty hero goes forth,
> like a man of war stirs up fury;
>
> he yells, even roars,
> against his foes shows his might.
>
> I have been silent for a long time,
> kept still and restrained myself.
>
> Like a woman in labor I scream,
> I gasp and strain all at once. (Isa. 42:13–14)

Scholars disagree on the unity of Isa. 42:13 and 14. For some
translators and interpreters, verse 13 ends the preceding section
of praise. Understood in this way, the jubilant praise of the preceding passage culminates in the image of God as the mighty
warrior, who goes out with a battle cry against the enemy. (The
image may strike us as peculiar, but we recall that the same comparison can be found in Exodus 15, a celebratory song at the victory over pharaoh's armies. In fact, the words "man of war" as
applied to God are found only in these two texts.)[5] Isaiah 42:14,
according to this arrangement, then opens a section that is entirely in the first person and announces the actions of God, who
makes a road to safely lead the people, here called "the blind" (v.

16). For other scholars, the two verses together (Isa. 42:13–14) introduce the section that depicts God's intervention and thus are more of a unit.[6] Although we consider the verses as a unit, keep in mind that the different approaches reflect the tension that occurs when two such disparate images for God are presented together.

I have provided as literal a translation as possible to give a sense of word order and repetitions. By the rules of Hebrew poetry, an expression used in one line receives a corresponding expression in the next line.[7] This correspondence is a type of repetition and has the effect of providing a double image. Such repetitions may occur many times, thereby enriching and enhancing their effect. For example, in Isa. 42:13–14, "mighty hero" is repeated in the following line as "man of war." A third, more subtle repetition is made with the Hebrew verb for "shows his might," one word in Hebrew, which is closely connected to the word for "mighty hero," also one word in Hebrew. Many of the terms have a double correspondence in these lines. For example, in verse 14, "shows his might" corresponds to both "stirs up fury" and "goes forth"; "have been silent" is repeated as "kept still" and "restrained myself." The woman in labor "screams, gasps, and strains." These variations create a multidimensional image and modify one another. In verse 14, "to be silent" is modified by "keep still," a more intentional action than silence. With "restrain myself" the text adds the notion of deliberate self-control, an idea that is not necessarily a part of silence and stillness, which could be imposed from outside. The overall effect of repeating terms or phrases is to intensify and focus meaning. The "mighty hero" is more clearly drawn with the words "man of war," a more specific term with a historical reference.

Most of the time, correspondence of terms does not mean a literal repetition of words or meaning. Both equivalent and contrasting images may be used. The contrasts in our text are between the noise of the opening lines and the silence that follows in verse 14. This silence is then contrasted anew with the sounds of the woman giving birth. The two types of sound are contrasted also: the screaming warrior (fury) and the screaming woman (birth pains). The absence of sound, itself a contrast, connects the two contrasting sounds.

Words or word groups can also be left without corresponding terms, with the effect that they "stick out" and draw special attention to themselves. This is the case with the "foes" of the fourth line of our text.

Word order is also important, for it is possible to emphasize words by giving them a different place in the sentence each time or, conversely, by leaving them in the identical spot. The poetry can do this because Hebrew is very flexible compared to English, for example, about word order in a sentence. The images for God in Isa. 42:13–14 are in first place, following the name Adonai in verse 13: Adonai (is like) a mighty hero, a man of war, a woman in labor. I look more closely at the effect of this triple image further on.

The intensity of the passage is due to the frequency of verbs and their nature. We read the lines carefully and ask three questions: What do we hear? What do we see? What do we feel? We listen, we look, and we experience.

What do we hear? The first sounds are the cries of the hero striding forth to battle with the enemy, stirring up his war craze and the foe's fear with his yelling. Then, instead of sounds of fighting, which we might expect, there comes a silence; not a silence of peace but an intense one, a held-in, pent-up, forced silence, building to an explosion. The three verbs "have been silent," "kept still," and "restrained myself" make this very clear. Last, the sounds we hear are not those of explosive anger or grief but the screams and panting breath of a woman in labor. Each time, the poet surprises us, sets up an expectation that is answered in a way different from what was anticipated.

What do we see? God as a valiant fighter strides to the battlefield "against his foes" and, we assume, on behalf of God's people. The word I have translated as "mighty hero," *gibbor,* is used for God especially in a context of praise rather than in reference to actual battles. God is *for* the people and fights on their behalf, a notion that Israel shared with its neighbors. But there are other kinds of might, and Israel's God is "mighty" in other ways, in particular in the care lavished on orphan, widow, and stranger (Deut. 10:18, for example). God's might shows itself in God's loyalty and devotion to the community of Israel (Neh. 9:32). This particular aspect of God's might seems lost when the words "man of war" focus and intensify the image. There is now no doubt as to what we are seeing: God, the mighty hero, is the warrior. We see, perhaps, the open mouth of the fighter as he utters his battle cry.

Next is the woman in childbirth. We see her open mouth as she screams or pants, straining with the birth pains. The shift between the warrior we saw first and this last image is radical, so that we may have difficulty getting the woman clearly in view. Is she screaming? Panting? Gasping?[8] We would like to know more, but the text leaves ambiguity. There is pain, as there is most always in the birth process; anticipation also, for life about to arrive; and effort, strain, to make new life come forth from its confinement.

The images have in common that neither warrior nor woman is passive; they share strength and active participation in what is going on. Furthermore, the outcome for themselves may, in both cases, be death. The hero may die in battle, the woman in childbirth. In contrast, the intended impact of their actions on the outside world is radically different. On the warrior's side, there is destruction; on the woman's side, there is the creation of life. The power of the two figures thus serves contrasting ends. The warrior who goes out yelling against his foes is powerful in that he may deal death to his enemies. The woman who screams in labor is powerful in that she may enable life. Another contrast is that the woman is more vulnerable and more dependent than the warrior. The foes disappear from the text for a good reason, since the woman in labor is not in a hostile position toward her community but rather depends on its help. If we think in terms of the process of intensification of the images, then a mighty hero becomes a man of war, who in turn becomes a woman in childbirth. The cries that herald death become the cries that announce life. One who went out against the world is turned into one who is dependent on the world for help with the birthing.

What do we feel when we let the imagery work on us? The hero is frightening in his intensity, his battle rage, his singleness of purpose. He is also alien. There is a great distance between ourselves and this fighter. The third-person description helps to increase our distance from him, so that we remain curiously unaffected in our feelings in spite of the warrior's noisemaking. The woman in labor, by contrast, is close to our experience. The change from the third to the first person draws us into the scene directly: *I* scream, *I* gasp, *I* strain. Although the danger to her life in sixth-century B.C.E. Palestine would have been far greater than it is today, we know there is still a risk in childbirth. There is pain and strain, screaming, gasping, and groaning. None of these feels alien to us.

Let us review what these images convey about God. The warrior image is familiar; it is an old, traditional image in terms of God, for Israel and us. Even if we are uncomfortable with it, the male image of a strong God who intervenes is not alien. This is how we know God as king, lord, and father.

Paradoxically, the image of the woman in childbirth, while putting us on far more familiar terrain as far as our experience goes, is much less familiar as an image applied to God. It is a shocking image. It was probably shocking in Second Isaiah's time too. It shocks both because of the explicitly female imagery and because of its implications. The picture of God as a woman in labor puts God in the position of sharing in the pain of creation; it shows God as vulnerable and as powerful as a woman about to have a baby.

The multiple images, hero and warrior and woman in labor, do not permit us to sentimentalize or stereotype the woman. There is power and risk and energy at work in the woman in childbirth, even as there is for the warrior about to do battle. Both have a singleness of purpose, which is the cause of the battle rage in the warrior and the straining of the woman. The intensifying or focusing feature of the poetry drives the hero and warrior images toward the image of the woman and forces us not to ignore or underestimate the importance of the image of God as the woman in labor.

Biblical scholar Elizabeth Achtemeier has protested that female terminology for God inevitably produces birthing images. These images, she maintains, are not warranted by the Bible, which understands God to be totally other than the creation and in no way bound up with it.[9] Contrary to Achtemeier's opinion, the birthing image is indeed used for God, as we have just seen; that it is not the only female image available from Scripture we shall see. As Second Isaiah spoke of the redemption and re-creation of God's people, the prophet reached for old images, reshaped them, and added new and unexpected ones, linking creation and birth-giving. Isaiah 42:13–14 paints a unique picture in providing a close-up, as it were, of God as a woman in labor. Yet this text is not the only one where God is compared to a birth-giver. The life to which God gives birth is the community freed by God, brought into God's presence, and taken into covenant with God. This covenanted community was brought into new life with God during the period of the Babylonian exile. The storytellers and poets of the Bible compare this process with birth-giving.

A Child's Protest
(Isa. 45:9–13)

Isaiah 45 is to a great extent about Cyrus, the ruler who conquered the Babylonian Empire and eventually allowed the Judahite exiles to return to their homeland. For most of us, Cyrus is just a name from the Bible. From the history books we may learn that he was an enlightened ruler who gave a good deal of freedom and autonomy to the different ethnic groups in his realm. Yet Cyrus was also a warmonger, a man of violence who gained his realm not by peaceful negotiation but by bloody conquest. God appointed this man of violence, according to Second Isaiah, as God's "anointed," a title reserved especially for Israel's kings in their relation to God. God included Cyrus as a participant in God's plans for exiled Judah. Not only Judah was of concern to God, moreover, but the entire world comes into view with its relation to God in Isaiah 45. The chapter closes with an invitation to "all the ends of the earth" to be freed and turn to God (v. 22).

It is one thing to honor the deeds of an individual. It is altogether different to accept this individual as having a place in God's redemptive activity for God's people and the creation. The opening lines of Isaiah 45 leave no doubt:

> So says Adonai to his anointed,
> to Cyrus whom I seized by the hand . . ." (45:1)

The text continues by outlining the part Cyrus will play in relation to Israel and in relation to God. Because the survival of the people is God's concern, Second Isaiah links Cyrus directly to God and God's activity. This prophet who knows God's nature also knows the nature of the people, however, and therefore has laid the groundwork carefully. Israel has been assured and reassured of God's forgiveness and love, God's interest and care. Sure of their place in God's love, the covenant people can afford to look beyond the narrow confines of their own group, to the world and to individuals who are outside the covenant circle, who are also under God's care.

Such widening of horizons is not always welcome, and Isa. 45:9–13 functions as a reply to an actual or a realistically anticipated protest. "Hey, wait a minute," people might have objected, "who is this Cyrus? We haven't heard much good about him. Where does he fit in? If anyone can be a part of God's work all of a sudden, then who are *we* as God's people? We will lose all sense of identity. What does the covenant mean, if this outsider, this nonbeliever, can be given appointments that we reserve for our very own?" To these protesters comes the reply "Listen! *You* wait a minute!"

> Listen, those who argue with their maker,
> potsherds with their potter.
> Shall the clay say to its potter:
> "What are you doing?
> Your work has no handles!"

Listen, those who say to a father:
"What are you begetting?"
and to a mother:
"With what are you writhing in labor?"

So says Adonai,
the Holy One of Israel, its maker:
Will you question me about my children?
About the work of my hands command me?

I myself made the earth
and humanity upon it I created.
My own hands stretched the heavens
and all its host I commanded.

I myself roused Cyrus in righteousness
and all his ways I make straight.
He himself will rebuild my city,
and my exiles he will send home,
without price and without pay,
—says Adonai of hosts. (Isa. 45:9–13)

The image of the people in verse 9 is of potsherds or clay, broken or unformed matter, with the nerve to argue with the one in charge of shaping them, of making them into something. A less-defined second image, introduced with a renewed "Listen!" points to those who would question a father or mother. What are you doing? What are you begetting? With what are you in labor? That the questions are asked critically is clear from the last line in verse 9: "Your work has no handles!" The three questions are summarized in God's reply in verse 11: "Will you question me about my children?" The assumption is that no pot and no child would ask such a question. Not that it is unacceptable to question God; the entire Bible witnesses to the fact that God is repeatedly questioned by believers, receives protests and complaints from everyone, and that this is never a cause for reproach. The point made about the potsherds' or children's questions is not that they are not allowed but that they are absurd. The pot, as well as the children's very being, depends on the potter and the parent; the pot would not become a pot without one to shape it; the child would not have life without one to beget and give birth to it.

But of course, the people are not questioning their own existence and value, they are critical of God's relation to other creatures, other "pots" and "children." The text, in fact, declares that it is as absurd to question the One who created them about the worth of other creatures as it is to question their own value. The argument opens with the attitude of potsherds and clay toward "their" maker and potter. That these potsherds stand for Israel is clear from verse 11, where the Holy One of Israel is called "its" maker. In verse 10, a lack of personal relationship is reflected in the wording as the protesters question "a" father and "a" mother. Just so is God a father and a mother to more than Israel. Three protests find a response in God's two questions of verse 11: "Will you question me about my children, about the work of my hands command me?" That "my children" and "work of my hands" refer to all of life is clear from the subsequent verse, in which the entire creation is named. God is maker of more than Israel.

The imagery for God in Isa. 45:9–11 moves from that of maker/ potter (v. 9) to father/mother (v. 10). In verse 11, this correspondence is achieved by "maker" in the one line and in the next, "my children," which implies God's image as parent. The people are correspondingly compared to "potsherds" and "clay" (v. 9), and the "work of my hand" (v. 11), on the one hand, and to "children," on the other (implied in v. 10, explicit in v. 11). Two images are at work for God and for human beings. First, the maker/potter is in control of the work he or she creates; the degree of control may depend on the potter's skill and the quality of the clay, but he or she is nevertheless in control. The clay does not contribute actively to its own shaping. The second image, that of parent in the process of begetting and giving birth, is one of taking part in a process of creation. Moreover, there needs to be a degree of cooperation from the life that is brought forth. A child has a far more active role in its becoming than a pot in its production. Thus, the images qualify one another and focus on the less control-oriented image: father/mother and children. The people are more than pots; God is more than a potter. God is father and mother to the people Israel and, finally, to the world. Total control on God's part may be as much wishful thinking as total control on the part of a human parent.

Qualified as it is by the imagery of making and shaping, the comparison of God to a mother in this passage is not built on a stereotype of motherhood limited to nurture. The parent has the right and the obligation to care for and supervise more than one of its offspring. By elaborating on the extent of God's creative activity, the text indicates not only the area of God's authority but the extent of God's responsibility.

A Mother's Responsibility
(Num. 11:11–12; Ps. 90:2)

Numbers 11:11–12 emphasizes God's responsibility toward the covenant community in having given it life. In Numbers 11, the people who have been freed from slavery in Egypt are once more cantankerously complaining about the deprivations of their present condition. They actually refer to all the good food they used to eat in Egypt. God's anger is roused twice, and Moses has finally had enough. He rails at God:

> So Moses said to Adonai: "Why do you treat your servant badly and why have I not found favor in your eyes, that you lay the burden of this whole people on me? Was it I who became pregnant with this whole people? Or did I give birth to them that you should say to me, 'Carry it on your breast as a nurse carries an infant?'" (Num. 11:11–12)

The clear implication of Moses' speech to God is that Moses did not do any of these things but that God conceived "this whole people" and gave birth to them, so that the responsibility to care for them, to "carry" them, rests with God. That this notion is taken seriously by God is proven by the sequel, in which God responds positively to Moses' predicament (see Num. 11:16–17, 24–30).[10]

Although it is usually Israel to whom God gives birth, this comparison is not limited to the relationship between God and Israel. In Isaiah 45, discussed above, the "children" mentioned include those outside Israel. An even clearer statement, and a more inclusive one, is made in Psalm 90:

> Before the mountains were brought forth
> and you writhed in labor with earth and world,
> from of old and forever you are God. (Ps. 90:2)

The NRSV obscures the expression "writhed in labor" by translating it with "formed." This translation neutralizes the birth imagery and is certainly not faithful to the Hebrew original, which uses the same verb as Deut. 32:18 and Isa. 45:10. Interestingly enough, here the birth image is extended to all creation, not just human beings.

Can a Child Forget?
(Deut. 32:18 and Hos. 11:3-4)

The imagery in Deut. 32:18 is similar to that of Isaiah 42 and 45. This poem, notoriously difficult to date, is essentially an account of Israel's special benefits that result from God's care, its rebellion, its punishment, and its final vindication. The term "rock" is a constant reference to God throughout the poem. Verse 18 concludes a passage that describes in detail God's loving care for the chosen people and is followed by a section describing their faithlessness. They are said to have "abandoned" Adonai and to have "scoffed" at the "rock of their liberation" by turning to other gods, called "no-gods" and "idols" in subsequent verses (Deut. 32:20). In verse 18, the text summarizes the people's faithlessness:

> The rock that gave you birth you paid no mind
> you forgot the God who writhed in labor with you.
> (Deut. 32:18)

In this verse of two lines, each expression is repeated and thus given a double image: "the rock that gave you birth" becomes "the God who writhed in labor with you," a more graphic and intense image. "You paid no mind" and "you forgot" draw attention because they are positioned last and first in their lines, respectively, thus emphasizing the people's disloyalty. The words for God, with their modifications, surround the people's act of forgetting. The imagery is maternal, and the word choice leaves no doubt as to what birth-giving entails. The God whom Israel has forgotten is the God who bore pain for the people, as a mother bears pain in bringing forth her child. The focus of Deuteronomy 32 is on the faithless acts of the people, at times sharply emphasizing their treachery as that of children toward a parent who spent lavish care on them, a care that included the pain of giving them birth.

The theme of the people's faithlessness in the face of God's motherly care is also present in Hosea 11. After indicting the people for abandoning God, the prophet Hosea speaks for God:

> Yet it was I who taught Ephraim to walk,
>   I took them up in my arms;
>   but they did not know that I healed them.
> I led them with cords of human kindness,
>   with bands of love.
> I was to them like those
>   who lift infants to their cheeks.
>   I bent down to them and fed them. (Hos. 11:3–4, NRSV)

The imagery in this passage reflects strong motherly activity, including traditional notions of nurture but also going beyond them in the mention of teaching and healing and leading.

A Mother's Protest
(Isa. 49:14-17)

Isaiah 49 opens the second part of Second Isaiah (Isaiah 49–55), in which there is less emphasis on Israel's sins and more on hope for the future. God's salvation will be "to the ends of the earth" (49:6). The return of the exiles is described in verses 7–13 as a journey, with God as compassionate guide. This passage ends with the words:

> Sing, heavens, and shout, earth,
> break out, mountains, into singing!
> For comforted has Adonai his people
> and on his oppressed he has compassion.
> (Isa. 49:13)

The verb "to have compassion," *raham* in Hebrew, is directly related to the word for "womb," *rehem*.[11] If this connection is made, then what may be intended is a word that draws its meaning from a female organ that protects and sustains life. In translating the word "compassion," it is difficult to render this reference in a meaningful way. I point out the derivation here because the idea of "womblike compassion" prepares for what is to follow.

Directly following the exhortation to praise, we read:

> And Zion said: "Abandoned has me Adonai,
> and my God has forgotten me."
>
> Can a woman forget her infant?
> A compassionate mother the child of her body?
> Yes. Even these may forget;
> but I will not forget you.
>
> Look, on my hand-palms I have engraved you,
> your walls are before me constantly.
> They hasten to you, your builders,
> while your destroyers and devastators from you depart.
> (Isa. 49:14–17)

Zion raises an objection and God answers. In Zion's complaint, the verbs "abandon" and "forget" are set around the names of God. Israel, here indicated with "Zion," sees its God through a haze of feelings of abandonment. A question is turned on this cry: "Can a woman forget her infant? A compassionate mother the child of her body?" There is only one question but it is asked twice, in the double image of two lines. At each point, the second line intensifies the first: "woman" becomes "compassionate mother," "infant" becomes "the child of her body." The word "forget" drops out and thus leaves an echo in the second line. The word I translate with "compassionate mother" is from the same root as the word "compassion," discussed above.

One of the most difficult things for me to face about my mother's death was that the person was gone for whom everything I did held interest, whose concern extended even to my family. For years after her death, I would still tell her about the little details of our life in my mind. That is what a mother's attention to a child means to me. When a question is asked such as this one in Isaiah 49—"Can a woman forget her infant?"—we would like to return a horrified No! But not everyone's experience with a mother is as positive as mine; also, the continuing interest of a mother is experienced by some as interference and a burden.

The double question "Can a woman/compassionate mother forget?" is rhetorical: The assumed answer to it is no. A logical sequel to the question would be "Should I then forget Zion?" adding another rhetorical question; or, in a positive reply, the sequel to the question could have been "So will I not forget Zion." Instead, the text allows the reality of human mothers to intrude: "Yes, even these may forget." The voicing of this acknowledgment makes the statement about God all the stronger: "But I will not forget you." The use of the second person, "you," in the place of the third person, Zion, also has the effect of strengthening the affirmation.

Next, the text spells out what God's remembering means for Israel. The city is engraved on God's palm as a tattoo; the broken walls, standing as a part for the entire broken city, are always on God's mind. In the second half of verse 16, Zion/Jerusalem receives the emphasis by the constant repetition of the pronoun "you" or its possessive, "your." God, as a compassionate mother to the broken community, desires its restoration and guarantees the rebuilding of the city. In the section following this passage, Isa. 49:19–21, this theme is elaborately worked out with the promise of the regeneration of the people. A dwindled and depopulated city will become too small for its inhabitants, and in amazement, those deprived of offspring will look around and ask, "Where have these come from?" (Isa. 49:21).

A Mother Comforts
(Isa. 66:13)

Isaiah 66 is the last chapter of Isaiah 55–66, which is considered to be from a slightly later period than Isaiah 40–55. It is full of graphic images of the restored community as an infant being carried by its mother, Jerusalem:

> Rejoice with Jerusalem, and be glad for her,
> . . . .
> that you may nurse and be satisfied
> from her consoling breast.
> > (Isa. 66:10–11, NRSV)

The image of mother Jerusalem, carried through verse 12, switches to God in verse 13:

> As a mother comforts a man
> so will I myself comfort you,
> and in Jerusalem you will be comforted.
> > (Isa. 66:13)

God as comforting mother takes the place of mother Jerusalem. Moreover, the image for the human community has moved from infant to adult, a change that advances the relationship from the mother–infant stage to one of greater maturity. The male adult, not an image immediately springing to mind when we think of a human being in need of comfort, is here the recipient of exactly that comfort, and in abundance. The male image stands, of course, for the community under God's care, Israel. "Comfort" is the key word in these lines, three times repeated with identical words. How does God comfort as a mother?

I remember my own mother as not particularly "comforting." As children, my sister and I would joke among ourselves about her shortcomings as a nurse when we were ill, for example. I remember sharply, however, one thing my mother did that I identified with comfort. On my long bicycle trip back from high school, it was often dark in the wintry afternoons in The Netherlands. The ride home always seemed long when doing it alone. It could be boring and dreary. When it became dark, I was sometimes afraid; I was cold too, the weather being often extremely inclement. There was little traffic on the long, poplar-lined road that took me home: some late cyclists, no cars.

Then, far off, I would see a bike's headlamp; and I would wonder who else was on the road, hoping it was my mother, who sometimes rode out to meet me part of the way. On coming closer, she would call out, "Is it you?" There was then, at those moments, nothing so comforting as my mother's presence, a presence that spelled home for me.

So, I imagine, was God's motherly comfort intended for the community of Ancient Israel; so it is intended for the human community that is covenanted to the God of Israel today. God's motherly comfort is essentially a presence, a presence that is our home.

In Summary

The biblical image of God as mother, far from being one-dimensional and confined to birth-giver or nurse, gives rise to a rich diversity of imagery. In this diversity, the image of giving birth is significant, for it includes the connectedness of God to the creation of the new community, the pain God bears on its behalf, and the responsibility God has for its care. Although extended to the entire creation, this responsibility is relevant in particular for the community that is in covenant with God. In addition, God as mother holds the people in constant remembrance and regenerates their brokenness. God also guides the people, heals them, and teaches them. Finally, God as mother is the presence that symbolizes home for the human community.

For its part, the community that relates to God as mother owes God its loyalty and trust. In its life, the community is expected to reflect the values taught to it by its mother. Sallie McFague remarks that God as maker and mother "is involved in 'economics,' the management of the household of the universe to insure the just distribution of goods."[12] Injustice, narrow-mindedness, limiting the circle of God's love—these are not acceptable in the community. For the human creature, the point of the comparison of God to mother is not childlike dependency. Rather, the love of God as mother creates an arena within which the creature may act and where human beings are held responsible for their acts, individually and especially as a community.

There are words whose relation to mother imagery is not immediately apparent in English translation, such as "compassion," the Hebrew *rahamim*. Such words allow us to expand the mother image of God, encompassing a larger field than one would assume by identifying simply the number of times the comparison of God to mother is made explicit in the Bible. It is important to become aware of such possible references, for it would be unfortunate if we remained locked into overwhelmingly male imagery for God with some added "maternal" characteristics. Such characteristics more often than not are stereotypes and, when applied to God, reinforce a stereotypical concept of human females and femaleness. As Elizabeth Johnson observes, "Given the patriarchal construction of motherhood, there is a danger that the mother image in speech about God, especially if it is the only female symbol used, may subtly undermine women's search for identity in their own whole person apart from the relationship and role of mothering."[13]

It is important, then, to emphasize the diversity of the image of God as mother in Scripture. But we inquire also about female images that are not confined to that of mother. We look now for a direction in which to enrich female imagery for God beyond the maternal.

For Reflection and Response

1. Read Isa. 42:13–14. Describe things you *hear, see,* and *feel* that have not been described in this chapter.
2. What is the significance of keeping God separate from the creation?
3. What difficulties do you see in parental images for God, be the image of father or mother?
4. Put together a list of verbs that are linked to God as mother in the biblical passages discussed in this chapter. Discuss what they mean to you. Do the same for the image of the child.

6

God—Eagle and Spirit

You I carried on wings of eagles and brought
you to myself.

Exodus 19:4

On occasion, the biblical text compares God's activity on behalf of Ancient Israel to that of an eagle. This image has
parental implications and is both protective and educational in
nature. An extension of this comparison occurs where the Bible
speaks of God's protective "wing." In the New Testament, the
protective aspect of this image takes over in the "mother hen" of
Jesus' words about Jerusalem.

Eagle imagery leads naturally to a consideration of God's
Spirit, since the biblical text draws on a network of bird and wing
images when it refers to the divine Spirit. It is not by coincidence
that all the Gospels depict the Spirit as descending on Jesus at the
time of his baptism in the form of a dove.[1] As the eagle of Scripture "hovers" over its young, so the Spirit "hovers" over the waters
at the dawn of creation.[2] As Christians, we are accustomed to
think of God's Spirit as one of the persons of the Trinity. Rather
than imposing this Trinitarian framework on our understanding
of the Spirit of God in the Hebrew Bible, I suggest that we let the
process work in reverse and learn about God's Spirit from Hebrew Scripture, without explicit reference to the Trinity. We may
then apply what we have learned to our understanding of the
Trinity.

"As an Eagle . . . as a Hen"[3]

As it is today, the eagle was a symbol for strength and power
in ancient times. Of the twenty-seven times the Hebrew word for
eagle appears in the Bible, it refers only twice to the actual bird;
all other times the usage is figurative. Sometimes an enemy nation
is depicted as coming down on Israel with the speed and strength

of the eagle (Deut. 28:49; Jer. 4:13; Hab. 1:8; Lam. 4:19). Sometimes God threatens to come down on Israel's enemies, "swoop-
ing down like an eagle" (Jer. 48:40; 49:16, 22; Obad. 4). The
imagery alternately emphasizes strength and speed; another
animal image may be added to embrace both characteristics, as
when David laments over Saul's and Jonathan's deaths and calls
them "swifter than eagles, stronger than lions" (2 Sam. 1:23).

The image in these passages is of the eagle coming down on
its prey with ferocious speed and singleness of purpose. The pro-
verbial vigor of the eagle provides the picture for the revival of
the depleted community in Isa. 40:31: "They shall rise on wings
of eagles" (cf. Ps. 103:5: "Your youth is renewed like the eagle's").
Mystery and awe naturally surround a creature of such splendor
and power. The Wisdom writers thus ponder the mystery of the
eagle's "way in the sky" (Prov. 30:19), and in the visions of Ezekiel, one of the four heavenly creatures has the face of an eagle
(Ezek. 1:10).

The connotations of swiftness, strength, and mystery lend richness and depth to the image of the eagle wherever it occurs in the
Bible. While these qualities are significant for the two passages
I discuss here, Ex. 19:3–6 and Deut. 32:10–13, these texts also
move the image in a different and unique direction.

Exodus 19:3-6

The first twenty-four chapters of the book of Exodus consist
of two main parts. Chapters 1–15 tell of the misery of the people
in Egypt, the exodus from that country, and the victory over Pharaoh's military power at the Sea of Reeds. Chapters 16–24 concern
the journey to Sinai and the founding of the covenant between
God and the people in that place. We noted already that Israel
saw itself as a people liberated by God and that it was set free for
the purpose of living as a community in the presence of God. To
give shape and definition to this goal, God and the people are
tied in the covenant bond, and the people receive divine instruc-
tions for their conduct as a community in special relationship with
God. The act of covenant making is narrated in Exodus 24 with a
unique and binding blood rite and solemn promises on the part
of the people. Moses acts as mediator between God and people,
taking on the role of priest and prophet. It is Moses, then, who at
the outset is commissioned by God to speak the great declaration
of Exodus 19 to the people who are about to be taken into the
covenant:

And Moses went up to God.
Then called to him Adonai from the mountain:
"This you will say to the house of Jacob,
and tell to Israel's children:

You yourselves have seen what I did to Egypt,
and you I carried on wings of eagles,
and brought you to myself.

Now, listen, listen to my voice,
and keep my covenant.
And you will be to me
a treasure out of all peoples.

For mine is all the earth,
but you, you will be to me
a royal realm of priests,
and a holy nation.

These words you shall speak
to Israel's children." (Ex. 19:3–6)[4]

At the introduction to the events at Sinai stand these lines with their momentous statements about the people's past, present, and future with God. The goal of God's action in freeing them from domination is their arrival in God's presence: "I brought you to myself." Verse 4 recites God's past actions and their results. Verses 5 and 6 endow the people with both promise and charge. It is Israel's great commission to be ever alert to God's voice, which is the manner of God's presence among them, for in so doing they will keep the covenant. If they proceed from this foundation, they have it in them to become God's treasured people, living closer to God than any other nation. The entire earth is under God's care; Israel is not the only nation of concern to God. But they, Israel's children, will be the mediators with God on behalf of others, a realm of priests; they will be dedicated to a life of mutual shalom, a holy nation, a showcase of justice in the world.

It is important to note this context in order to understand the words about God's activity as eagle. First, there is the image of Egypt: the enslaving nation, itself enslaved to its pride and ferocity, which fell finally into the sea. What befell Egypt and Israel is contrasted by implication: Egypt sank, Israel rose. Both falling and rising are ascribed to God's activity: "I did to Egypt/you I carried . . ."

The implications of the eagle-wing imagery are multiple. We recall the strength, speed, and ferocity that mark the image when used elsewhere in the Bible. Here are added the components of protection and education. The comparison of God to the eagle is parental in nature, rather than maternal or paternal. Both mother and father eagle teach the young birds to fly. They do so by rousing the nest, by flapping their wings and stirring the young ones to flight. When the young birds are in the air, the parents fly under them, showing by example and at the same time ready to catch and carry the young ones when they fall. Young Israel had been stirred out of Egypt and, in its weak and immature state, had to be carried by God as fledgling offspring are by the eagle. The people have been safe; they have been cared for and protected by God's love. God fended off the marauders as fiercely as a parent eagle defends its young.

But the people must not stay baby birds forever; indeed, they cannot. Now, brought into God's presence, they are ready to receive the charge for their adulthood. They must move on their own wings, in God's presence, in the manner to which God charges them. The parental image of Ex. 19:3 is not only one of protection but also one of preparation. The image does not bind the people into a perpetual childlike posture. Martin Buber observes about this text, "Here we have election, deliverance, and education; all in one."[5]

Deuteronomy 32:10-13

Referring to the same period in the wilderness and God's care for the people, Deuteronomy 32, the so-called Song of Moses, spins out the image of God as eagle in greater detail:

> God found them in a desert land,
> in a waste of howling wilderness,
> surrounded them and cared for them,
> guarded them as the apple of his eye.
>
> As an eagle stirs its nest,
> over its young hovers,
> spreads its wings, takes them up,
> carries them on its pinions,
>
> so Adonai alone guided the people,
> there was with them no foreign god.
>
> He set them on the heights of the land,
> and gave food from the produce of the field;
> suckled them with honey from the cliff,
> and with oil from flinty rock. (Deut. 32:10–13)

The lines with the eagle imagery are surrounded by emphatic statements about God's intense guarding care for the people. This care is elaborated in the verses that follow, especially in terms of feeding (32:14). The poet seems unable to stop, piling one symbol of abundant sustenance on top of another: honey, oil, milk, butter, fat, and wine are all provided. The emphasis on the nature of God's care as providing over and above what is necessary for sustenance sets the stage of Israel's rebellion in sharp relief (32:15–18).

When God "found" Israel in the desert, the people were in great need of care. Israel was like the baby bird in the nest, in need of all it must learn to become self-sustaining. The eagle is pictured as the bird who stirs the young into action, probably by flapping its wings over the nest. Then the parent takes the young up on its wings, carrying them, presumably to show by example. In these verses, the eagle image is sustained from verse 11 through the beginning of verse 13, where God is said to have set the people on "the heights." Eagles build their nests high on the rocks in inaccessible places, to keep the young safe. Just so was Israel put out of reach, so that it could grow in safety.

As I have pointed out, the picture of the eagle parent caring for the young and teaching them to fly is parental rather than fatherly or motherly. Deuteronomy 32:13, however, pulls the comparison in the direction of the maternal. A shift of images takes place in the middle of verse 13, since eagles do not "suckle" their young. Yet here God is said to have "suckled" the people, nursing them as a mother nurses her children. As I have already shown, this poem does not shy away from maternal comparisons for God (see p. 60).

God's wing is not an uncommon symbol for protective shelter in the Bible. Wings, when used in language of comparison, may be assigned to supernatural beings or to the wind, for example. When assigned directly to God, wings are always accompanied by the word "shadow." The "shadow of God's wings" is a hiding place from terror, a safe place of being guarded and protected. The believer prays:

> Guard me as the apple of the eye,
> hide me in the shadow of your wings,
> from the wicked who despoil me.
>
> (Ps. 17:8, NRSV)

There is refuge under God's wings, as there is in "God's tent" (Ps. 61:4). This place of individual and communal safekeeping is also a place of joy (Pss. 57:1; 63:7; 91:1).

Wings are also a familiar feature for creatures that move between the human and the celestial realm. Divine messengers or angels are endowed with wings. In the Christian tradition, God's Spirit takes on the form of a bird. I suggest that we understand the symbol of God's wings as an extension of bird imagery for God and view it as parental in nature, with a slant to the maternal.

In the New Testament, Jesus' "lament over Jerusalem" uses bird language with a significant change. In addressing Jerusalem, the Gospels of Matthew and Luke report the following words of Jesus:

> Jerusalem, Jerusalem, the city that kills the prophets and stones those who are sent to it! How often have I desired to gather your children together as a hen gathers her brood under her wings, and you were not willing!
> (Matt. 23:37; Luke 13:34, NRSV)

In comparing himself to a mother hen, Jesus lets go of the strength and ferocity of the eagle. The awesome aspect of the bird image is entirely gone, replaced by a far more familiar sight and sound: the clucking domestic bird that gathers her chicks for protection from danger and the elements. In addition, the image is clearly maternal.[6]

The Presence of God
in the Spirit

The Hebrew word *ruach* means primarily "breath," "wind." Both the Hebrew *ruach* and its Greek equivalent, *pneuma,* indicate the elemental, natural, and vital force that one associates with breath and wind.[7] When the word is linked to God, *ruach* is translated as "spirit," pointing to God's vitality and power as they affect the creation. Hebrew thought about God, as we find it reflected in Scripture, shows little interest in the existence of God apart from God's contact with the creation. Many times in the Bible, the means of this contact is God's Spirit. The German scholar Hermann Gunkel has said that all that is powerful and awesome in human life, that which exceeds human capacity, is ascribed to the working of the Spirit in the Bible.[8]

The word *ruach* has feminine gender most of the time in Hebrew.[9] My discussion here focuses on the presence of God's Spirit in the Hebrew Bible as a female, life-giving, empowering, and educational disclosure of God's self. The Spirit cannot be manipulated; it comes and goes as it wills. God's Spirit is unpredictable, autonomous, and powerful, as the wind seemed to be to the ancient world. The Spirit can draw human beings into the sphere of the Divine and is then associated with prophecy, as it presents itself in spontaneous and occasional forms. Prophecy was, in origin, probably like a frenzy, expressing itself in uncontrolled movement and unintelligible speech (Num. 11:24–29; 1 Sam. 10:6, 10; 1 Kings 22:10; Joel 2:28). There is little mention of the Spirit in the major prophetic writings before the Babylonian exile, such as Isaiah 1—39, Jeremiah, Hosea, Amos, and Micah. This absence may be due to an uneasiness with the linkage between the Spirit and ecstatic prophecy. Finally, in Ezekiel, a renewed and particular emphasis on the work of the Spirit occurs.

Although we cannot know the effect of the feminine gender of *ruach* on the awareness of the hearer in ancient times, we are conscious that today gendered pronouns receive sharp focus. In my translations, I have left intact the biblical custom of referring to God in masculine forms. By the same token, I read the feminine pronoun for the Spirit when the text warrants it. At the least, this may raise our awareness that in the Hebrew text, God's self-disclosure as it occurs through the Spirit receives a female reference, in noun, pronoun, and verb form. By contrast, within Trinitarian thought and speech, female referencing of the Spirit while adhering to an exclusive male naming of the two other persons of the Trinity would hardly be helpful. Such divisions run the risk of enhancing female stereotyping and subordinating the feminine "dove" to the masculine "father and son." [10] I advocate here a naming of the Spirit insofar as it advances a reimagining and naming of God in terms that are no more male than female and no less female than male.

She Who Gives Life

> When God began to create,
> the earth was a trackless waste;
> darkness on the face of the deep,
> and the Spirit of God, she was hovering
> on the face of the water. (Gen. 1:1–2) [11]

The opening lines of Scripture describe the situation at the moment of the beginning of the creation. The earth, not shaped yet, was a formless blob; darkness covered the threatening waters of chaos; and the Spirit of God was present, "hovering" on the surface of the water. The verb "hovering" is the same as the one encountered in Deut. 32:11 describing the activity of the eagle toward its nest. Of greater significance yet, this particular verb occurs only in these two texts. Because of the recurrence of this unusual term, a linkage of meaning between the two passages may be established. When we considered the hovering eagle, it became clear that the bird's activity was for a purpose: this was not an aimless fluttering or merely an agitated movement but rather a movement to agitate, to stir up. At the very beginning of things, when God is about to give shape to what is shapeless, the Spirit is actively present, moving to stir. The same verb also anticipates the protective action of the parent bird on behalf of its young. Thus the "hovering" of the Spirit in Genesis 1 announces its future protective presence on behalf of the creation.[12]

The connection between the imagery in Deut. 32:11 and in Gen. 1:2 has been observed by others. The ancient Jewish commentaries on Gen. 1:2 note, "And the Spirit of God . . . hovered like a bird flying and flapping with its wings, its wings barely touching the nest over which it hovers."[13] The German scholar Hermann Gunkel remarked, long before a concern over language for God was present, "The Deity who develops the chaos into a world, was imagined originally as a brooding female bird."[14]

The verb I translate as "she was hovering" has a feminine form. Because English translations do not need to repeat the subject (Spirit) with a pronoun, they obscure the femaleness of the Spirit; the smoother translation of the phrase is "the Spirit of God was hovering." Yet I suggest that we read the more clumsy, literal version. Such a reading has the advantage of highlighting the point that the Bible from the outset refers to a major manifestation of God's presence with a feminine reference. This is congruent with our conviction that equivalent usage of pronouns, both female and male comparisons for God, reflects an appropriate biblical understanding of God.

The Spirit in Gen. 1:2 is the presence of God as it creates and gives and sustains life. We find this same notion in Psalm 104. This psalm describes all types of life, human and animal, animate and inanimate, in their dependence on God for life and sustenance: "These all look to you, to give them their food in due season" (Ps. 104:27, NRSV). Verse 30 of the same psalm highlights the role of the Spirit in this process:

> You send your Spirit and they are created;
> you renew the surface of the ground.
> (Ps. 104:30)

That the Spirit is equivalent to God's life-giving and all-encompassing presence is also made clear in two additional psalms:

> Do not cast me from your presence,
> and your holy Spirit do not take from me.
>
> (Ps. 51:11)

> Where shall I go from your Spirit,
> and where from your presence shall I flee?
>
> (Ps. 139:7)

In each of these verses, the word "presence" corresponds to "Spirit." In Ezekiel also, the Spirit is the giver of life: in the vision of the "dry bones," the reassembled bones are not alive until the Spirit enters them (Ezek. 37:1–14).

She Who Empowers

In the New Testament, the presence of the Holy Spirit signals God's creative, empowering action on two important occasions. The first is the Spirit's role in the birth of Jesus. The "Holy Spirit," according to Luke, "will come upon you [Mary], and the power of the Most High will overshadow you" (Luke 1:35, NRSV). The Holy Spirit is here equated with the power of God. The second occasion is the presence of the Spirit at the birth of the Christian community, as described in Acts 2 (Acts 2:1–4).

This view of the Spirit as a specific and effective power in the lives of individuals or groups is especially in line with the activity of the Spirit toward judges and prophets in the Hebrew Bible. The Spirit of Adonai, the God of Israel, empowered several judges to save the beleaguered tribes from their distress. These military leaders, in one of the most dangerous periods of the young nation's life, received the energizing power of God's presence in order to fulfill their task. At another critical juncture, when the fledgling monarchy almost foundered on competition in the ranks of leadership, the young upstart David received God's Spirit to equip him for his task. Many times the verb that is used of the Spirit's activity in connection with Israel's leaders conveys a complex notion of strength, success, and effectiveness. Translations render variously "the Spirit possessed" or "the Spirit came mightily upon" or "the Spirit rushed upon" for the expressions in Judg. 14:6, 19 and 15:14 and in 1 Sam. 10:6, 10; 11:6; and 16:13. In Hebrew, the verb denotes an action that is healthy, vigorous, efficient, and successful. This complexity is not easily rendered with one word in English, however. It is helpful to keep in mind that the biblical verb is not simple and combines all of these characteristics when the Spirit is said to "come upon" Samson, Saul, and David.

Each time the empowering Spirit appears in the texts cited above, feminine verb forms are used. Literally, the texts read, "The Spirit, she came upon/was strong upon . . ." In such a literal translation, the restatement of the subject may overburden the phrase to the point of obscuring its meaning. In these cases, we may want to leave the traditional translations intact and keep in mind the presence of the feminine verb forms in the original text.

It is clear that the presence of the Spirit is not described in the Hebrew text in stereotypically maternal terms. The life-giving, empowering presence of the Spirit infuses the recipient with life and energy. The Spirit enables and energizes to specific action, also of a political and military type. At times, it appears as if the Spirit of God represents a special, divine energy field, into which she draws human beings. In being so drawn into the divine sphere, humans partake of the mystery and awesome aspect of God, which may express itself through prophecy.

Prophecy, before it became intelligible utterance as we know it through the prophetic books of the Bible, was probably first akin to ecstatic frenzy: "prophesying" meant to carry on in a prophetic state, finding expression in movements and, perhaps, unintelligible and repetitive chant. Saul "becomes a prophet" through the activity of the Spirit (1 Sam. 10:6, 10), and the elders prophesy temporarily during the trek through the wilderness (Num. 11:25, 26). The Spirit, then, can be said to "inspire" prophetic speech (see, for example, Num. 11:25; 1 Sam. 10:10; 19:20, 23). This connection between the Spirit and a state of ecstasy may have become difficult as time went on, prophetic frenzy causing mistrust and discredit rather than awe (see 1 Kings 22 for an example). Mention of the Spirit is virtually absent in prophetic texts before the Babylonian exile, perhaps in order to create distance between the prophets and ecstatic prophecy. It is not until the period beginning shortly after the exile and beyond that the Spirit makes a strong reappearance in the text (cf. Isaiah 40–66 and Ezekiel).

She Who Educates

The word "educate" is derived from the Latin root *educare*, meaning "to lead out." In Ezekiel, the Spirit has precisely this task of bringing Ezekiel out to show him and teach him something. If the earliest prophets were those drawn into the divine sphere by the Spirit "filling them" or "possessing them," the prophet Ezekiel is "carried," "led," or "lifted" by the Spirit. A physical manipulation of Ezekiel takes place through the Spirit. The Spirit enters him and "she sets him on his feet" (Cf. Ezek. 2:2). In almost all the Ezekiel texts, the feminine can be represented with a pronoun in the translations:

The Spirit carried me and she took me away. (Ezek. 3:14)

The Spirit carried me between earth and sky and she brought me to the East Gate. (Ezek. 11:1)

The Spirit carried me and she brought me to Chaldea of the exiles in a vision. (Ezek. 11:24)

The activity of the Spirit in Ezekiel is truly educational. The Spirit leads Ezekiel out through visions to see the future of his defeated people. Ezekiel lived closer to the exile than did Second Isaiah and had perhaps witnessed the destruction of his people and land. The Spirit teaches Ezekiel through visions that the future is not closed and that God's engagement with the people is not a thing of the past. There is yet a community to be, a center of worship to be created.

In Summary

What have we learned? In the Bible, God as eagle defends, protects, and educates the human community that is especially under God's care. The eagle provides a father/mother image, although at times maternal traits receive the most weight. In the network of bird images, human beings are the recipients of this care but are also put at a certain risk by God's "stirring up" of the nest. In the parental comparison that is embedded in comparing God to a bird, humanity is in the process of moving out and growing up rather than being positioned in a static child–parent relation to God. Wing images provide the symbol of God's ongoing protective presence, pulling the comparison to the maternal.

The Spirit of God in the Bible is a female, life-giving, empowering, and educational presence, implicitly or explicitly depicted as a bird at times. She is protectively and creatively present "when God began to create," stirs people to action at crucial times in the history of the covenant community, infuses them with divine presence to the point of ecstasy, and teaches them hope for the future.

Brian Wren has captured the connections between bird imagery and God's Spirit with powerful attendant images in his hymn "Great Soaring Spirit":

Great soaring Spirit,
sweeping in uncharted flight
beyond the bounds of time and space,
God's breath of love,
you fill the outflung galaxies
and move through earth's long centuries
with aching, mending, dancing grace.

Great eagle Spirit,
crying from the tallest crags
to all discarded and distressed,
glad gusting love,
come, scatter trivialities
and raise envisioned ministries
to hear and honour earth's oppressed.

Great nesting Spirit,
sheltering with mighty wings
your chattering, demanding brood,
deep, restless love,
come, stir us, show us how to fly,
till, heading for tomorrow's sky,
we soar together, God-renewed.

For Reflection and Response

1. Is it shocking to think of God in terms of animal imagery? What animal is habitually used as an image of Christ? Is that shocking? What are other animal images of God in the Bible?
2. Think of a time that you were especially aware of the presence of the Spirit, in both a private and a communal setting. Describe your experience.
3. Do you perceive a great deal of "Spirit awareness" in your faith community?

7

The Paths of Wisdom

Her ways are ways of pleasantness, and all her
paths are peace.

Proverbs 3:17, NRSV

Sophia is one name used for God today by many Christian feminists. New Testament scholar Elisabeth Schüssler Fiorenza
speaks of Sophia/God as proclaimed by Jesus.[1] Theologian Elizabeth Johnson calls Sophia "a female personification of God's own
being."[2] At the Re-Imagining Conference in Minneapolis, Sophia
was invoked during ceremonies and the blessing sung to each
presenter. The first question I address here is: Who is Sophia?

Then, I move to the concerns of wisdom as a school of thought
and the setting of the book of Proverbs, in which we find the
greater part of the texts that concern us. In these texts, we encounter wisdom in the form of a female figure, Woman Wisdom.
I address the identity of this figure, her relation to God, and finally, her significance for women today.[3]

Who Is Sophia?

Sophia is the Greek word for wisdom (Hebrew, *chokhmah*);
she appears as a female figure in the Hebrew Bible in Proverbs
and Job 28. Her role is expanded in the Wisdom of Solomon and
the Wisdom of Sirach, books that are part of the Bible for the
Roman Catholic and Orthodox branches of Christianity.[4]

In the New Testament, *sophia* is implicitly or explicitly identified with Jesus in many places. One of the most striking texts
makes the following statements:

> But we proclaim Christ crucified, . . . Christ the power of God
> and the wisdom *[sophia]* of God. (1 Cor. 1:23–24, NRSV)

> . . . Christ Jesus, who became for us wisdom *[sophia]* from God.
> (1 Cor. 1:30, NRSV)

Other significant passages from the New Testament include Matt.
11:25–27, 28–30; 23:34–39; Luke 7:31–35; 10:21–22; John 1:1–3,
14; 8:23–24; 12:44–48.

In a recent work on Sophia, the authors argue that "almost
every major New Testament portrait of Jesus depends on the
implicit combination of the Messiah and Sophia figures."[5] Long
before feminist theology arrived on the scene, however, New Testament scholars maintained that the earliest interpretation of Jesus
was Sophia Christology.[6]

Somewhere along the way, the identification of Sophia with
God or with God incarnate in Jesus lost its meaningful place in
Christian belief and doctrine. The reasons for this loss are complex, some of them highly speculative, and a discussion of them
lies outside the scope of this book. Suffice it to point out here that
the identification of Sophia with the Divine is deeply rooted in
Christian traditions. These traditions, as reflected in the New Testament, themselves arose from previous articulations about
sophia/chokhmah. Wisdom as a female figure, Woman Wisdom,
appears in the Hebrew Bible predominantly in the first nine
chapters of Proverbs. To these first formulations we now look
for clarification about the context and significance of Woman
Wisdom.

What Is Wisdom?

Proverbs and Job belong to a collection of biblical books
called wisdom literature. What defines wisdom in this context?
What were its concerns and aims? Since Proverbs is at the center
of this discussion, it is important that we understand the time of
composition, the social conditions of the time, and the major concerns of the community. Only after a brief survey of these important questions do we turn to Woman Wisdom.[7]

Simply put, wisdom concerns itself with the proper management of life in all its aspects, social and religious, private and
communal. The purpose of wisdom is educational, and sayings
such as those found in Proverbs were most likely designed for
the education of young males, as is evidenced by the recurring
address "my son" ("my child" in the NRSV). The form in which
wisdom is expressed is the short saying. These sayings function
both as models and as explanations. Wisdom addresses both the
"ought" and the "is" of life. A short, typical wisdom saying is:

> Hatred stirs up strife,
>   but love covers all offenses. (Prov. 10:12, NRSV)

The saying explains in two lines why disharmony occurs, on the one hand, or peace, on the other; it also advises, indirectly, how one situation may be avoided and the other enhanced. Some wisdom sayings may be explicitly advisory or educational, others more explanatory (compare Prov. 24:28 and 25:19, for example).

To address multiple situations and avoid unhelpful rigidity, wisdom approaches life from a variety of perspectives. One text first explains what might cause friendly behavior or its opposite:

> The poor are disliked even by their neighbors,
> but the rich have many friends. (Prov. 14:20, NRSV)

Then it goes on to describe a more fitting attitude, by declaring judgment:

> Those who despise their neighbors are sinners,
> but happy are those who are kind to the poor. (Prov. 14:21, NRSV)

At times, wealth and prosperity may be assigned to hard work and poverty to laziness (Prov. 10:4–5, for example); but wealth is also viewed as a gift from God and a reward for a proper attitude (Prov. 22:4).

Different contexts may call for different behaviors, and thus contradictory sayings may occur:

> Do not answer fools according to their folly
> . . . .
> Answer fools according to their folly. (Prov. 26:4–5, NRSV)

The "wicked" and the "fools" and their ways are contrasted with the "righteous" and the "wise" throughout Proverbs. The first group creates conditions of life that are ruinous, the second manages its life in such a way as to produce health and hope. Generally, tact and prudence are prized over loquaciousness and hastiness. Laziness is viewed consistently as a cause for disaster.

In her work on wisdom, biblical scholar Claudia Camp suggests a division of Proverbs into two main parts.[8] The first, chapters 1–9, outlines the role and importance of Woman Wisdom and the dangers of her opposites, the "strange/other/foreign" woman, the evil woman, the seductress, and the stupid, or foolish, woman. The second part, Proverbs 10–30, contains collections of short wisdom sayings. Camp points out that writing down and codifying wisdom sayings has a rigidifying effect on them. Codification undermines the vitality and effectiveness of the sayings.[9] Proverbs 31, Camp suggests, should be viewed, with chapters 1–9, as the framework around the collected sayings, in effect providing them with an appropriate context. If we agree with this proposal, as I do, then Woman Wisdom becomes essential not only for the texts in which she appears but for the entire collection of sayings in Proverbs. Woman Wisdom supplies the sayings with an overall theological theme and guidelines, liberating them from fragmentation and inflexibility.

Israel was not alone in its interest in wisdom, and wisdom literature shares many features with the same type of writing found, for example, in Egypt and Mesopotamia. Yet the community in which the book of Proverbs originated, as we now know it from the Hebrew Bible, faced its own unique situation that is reflected in the text. Although many sayings in Proverbs may well be older, the book itself probably dates from the first part of the fifth century B.C.E. At this time, more than a generation after the period of Second Isaiah, Judah was under Persian rule, with a degree of religious and political autonomy. Certainly, the Judahite community was trying to reestablish itself with a sense of purpose, belonging, and identity. Kingship and the glory of the Solomonic Temple were a memory, and although conditions were not as desperate as those of the period of Lamentations, Ezekiel, or Second Isaiah, the community faced enormous difficulties and struggles.

One of the main concerns of the time was family structure. With the disappearance of the royal house as the representative of the covenant bond between God and the community, the family regained its importance in a theological as well as a social and economic sense. Claudia Camp has argued that the authority of women increased within this context of resurgence of the family.[10] Not only the reproductive and nurturing roles of women were valued but also their managing and counseling skills. Proverbs 31:10–31 provides a picture of the qualities and activities that constituted the "ideal" wife; nurture of the young is not explicitly one of those qualities. The woman of Proverbs 31 is a hard worker; she is a merchant, she is a teacher, and her most notable qualities are dignity, prudence, and charity. Woman Wisdom, then, fits well into this social and religious context.[11]

Who Is Woman Wisdom?

Chokhmah (occasionally *chokhmoth*), *sophia*, and *sapientia*— these words for wisdom in the three languages of the Bible's earliest translations all have feminine gender. More important, as I have noted already, wisdom appears as a female figure in the Bible. A great deal is said about her in a relatively small number of texts. She strides onto the scene abruptly:

> Wisdom cries out in the street;
> in the squares she raises her voice.
> (Prov. 1:20, NRSV)

One can only speculate about her origins. Many scholars seek a background in goddess worship, in Egypt, for example. Others, like Camp, see her firmly rooted in her own sociological and religious context. Rather than lose ourselves in speculations of her origin, we turn to the main texts where Woman Wisdom is found: Proverbs 1–9. What do these texts say about Woman Wisdom, about her relationship to God and to humanity?

Woman Wisdom has a unique relationship to God. She is said to be the firstborn, conceived by God:

> YHWH conceived me at the beginning of his way,
> the first of his acts of old.
> Ages ago I was woven in the womb,
> at the first, before the beginning of the earth.
> When there were no depths, I was brought forth;
> when there were no springs abounding with water.
> Before the mountains had been shaped,
> before the hills, I was brought forth.
> (Prov. 8:22–25, trans. Claudia Camp)[12]

It is clear from these lines that Woman Wisdom is perceived as having been present before anything was made. Also, God is portrayed in this passage as the mother of Wisdom. As Claudia Camp observes, "The process of YHWH's conception, bearing and birth of Wisdom is here depicted without reservation."[13] Proverbs 8 goes on to state Wisdom's relation to the created world, as well as to God:

> I was his delight day after day,
> playing in his presence at all times,
> playing in his inhabited world,
> and my delight was with human children.
> (Prov. 8:30b–31)

Wisdom is here the mediator, she in whom God delights and who, in her turn, delights in God's creation, including humanity.

Particular activities of Woman Wisdom are equivalent to God's activity. When she first appears on the scene in Proverbs 1, Woman Wisdom calls and, on receiving no response, announces:

> Then they will call upon me, but I will not answer;
> they will seek me diligently, but will not find me.
> (Prov. 1:28, NRSV)

Strikingly similar language can be found in prophetic texts that describe God's call to Israel, Israel's refusal to respond, and God's reaction to this refusal (see, for example, Isa. 65:2, 12; 66:4; Jer. 7:13, 24–27; Hos. 2:14–15; 11:1–2). Woman Wisdom also "keeps" and "guards" those who heed her (cf. Psalm 121). Significant also is the banquet spread by Woman Wisdom, to which she invites in order that those who respond may "live":

> Come, eat of my bread
> and drink of the wine I have mixed.
> . . . and live. (Prov. 9:5–6, NRSV)

In the opening lines of Isaiah 55, God issues the invitation to eat and drink, with the intended result of "life" (Isa. 55:1–3). That the presence of God and the pursuit to be in God's presence equal life is a theme throughout the entire Bible. Woman Wisdom also gives life to those who seek her and heed her (Prov. 1:33; 3:18, 22; 4:13; 8:35; 9:6). "Whoever finds me finds life," declares Woman Wisdom, and "all who hate me love death" (Prov. 8:36, NRSV). Like the God of Israel, Woman Wisdom is a purveyor of justice:

> By me kings reign,
> and rulers decree what is just. (Prov. 8:15, NRSV)

Other parallels between Woman Wisdom and God reside in who she *is* rather than in what she *does*. Woman Wisdom, like God, affects life by her very presence. In clinging to Woman Wisdom, human beings will learn "understanding," "prudence," and "insight," which in turn will lead to a secure and stable life "without dread of disaster" (1:33, NRSV). Proverbs 3:13–18 describes most eloquently the rewards of life lived in the presence of Woman Wisdom:

> Happy are those who find wisdom,
> and those who get understanding,
> for her income is better than silver,
> and her revenue better than gold.

She is more precious than jewels,
and nothing you desire can compare with her.
Long life is in her right hand;
in her left hand are riches and honor.
Her ways are ways of pleasantness,
and all her paths are peace.
She is a tree of life to those who lay hold of her;
those who hold her fast are called happy. (Prov. 3:13–18, NRSV)

Is Woman Wisdom God?

The answer to the question "Is Woman Wisdom God?" is not simple. As we have seen, there are a number of clear equivalents between God's actions and those of Woman Wisdom, between God's presence and her presence. Woman Wisdom also has a unique relationship both to God and to the creation. What is said about Wisdom is not said about anyone or anything else in the Bible. Proverbs 1–9, rather than providing a full-blown picture of a "female personification of God's own being,"[14] outlines a divine aspect disclosed in female form. Insofar as wisdom is a divine characteristic, Woman Wisdom is a personification of an element of the Deity. Proverbs, then, opens the door to the possibility of female personification of God's being. Indeed, such a development took place over the course of time.

The books Wisdom of Solomon and Sirach witness to this development.[15] Although these texts are not a part of the Hebrew or the Protestant canon, they are a part of the Bible for the Roman Catholic and Orthodox branches of Christianity. Above all, these books testify to the natural direction taken by the writers of the sacred texts once the concept of Woman Wisdom as divine disclosure was set in motion. In these texts, especially in the Wisdom of Solomon, Woman Wisdom, at times referred to simply as "she," is the savior and deliverer of Ancient Israel. Wisdom rescued, protected, saved, guided, and delivered the community, all activities ascribed elsewhere in the Bible to God. In short, Wisdom

guided them along a marvelous way,
and became a shelter to them by day,
and a starry flame by night. (Wisd. Sol. 10:17, NRSV)

Along another line of development, Wisdom became identified with the Torah. The books of Sirach and Baruch make this identification. Wisdom/Torah is given by God to Jacob/Israel as a way to knowledge:

She [Wisdom] is the book of the commandments of God,
the law that endures forever. (Bar. 4:1, NRSV)

The identification of Jesus with Wisdom in the early Christian
community was thus a natural one, given all the considerations
outlined here. To summarize the most important of the characteristics that connect Wisdom and Jesus: Wisdom "comes" from
God, existed before anything else was created, mediates between
God and the creation, calls folk to come to her, and gives life to
those who accept her. We may remember also the obvious association of Wisdom with teaching and thus with the understanding
of Jesus as teacher.

Elizabeth Johnson argues cogently for an inclusive understanding of Jesus, who assumed one nature in which the female
was included. Jesus was human in solidarity with suffering humanity. "The intent of the christological doctrine was and continues to be inclusive," Johnson states.[16] She finds the most
appropriate symbolism for this inclusive humanity represented in
Jesus in the identification of Jesus with Sophia: "As Sophia incarnate Jesus . . . can be thought to be revelatory of the graciousness
of God imaged as female."[17]

It is clear that one possible avenue is to follow Johnson's analysis to continue appropriating the significance of Woman Wisdom. Returning to what is stated of Wisdom in the Hebrew Bible,
I am reminded of a statement by biblical scholar Roland Murphy,
who calls Woman Wisdom "a communication of God."[18] Murphy
writes of Wisdom as speaking "in the accents of God." We must
perhaps be as vague as this to underline that *chokhmah* is not a
finished concept in the Hebrew Bible and that different possibilities of continuing to understand her are legitimate and in line with
the biblical tradition. One avenue for reappropriating *chokhmah*
that I have not yet touched on I now pursue.

Woman Wisdom and Women

If the value of women's participation in rebuilding the postexilic Judahite community is reflected in the role of Woman Wisdom in Proverbs, Woman Wisdom in her turn may have worked
as a symbol of empowering presence for those very women. As
the formulation of Woman Wisdom took place in the context of
women's new dignity and revaluing of their place in postexilic
Judah, women could reimagine themselves in terms of Woman
Wisdom. Since that time, much has happened to women and

Woman Wisdom both. Woman Wisdom was interpreted and rein-
terpreted and finally became co-opted and forgotten by the patriarchal voices of the tradition. She whose voice was raised with
such authority was finally silenced. As she was silenced, women's
voices, perhaps once a part in the articulation of her essence, disappeared as well. Today, women's voices sound with a new clarity and authority. It is, then, not so surprising that *chokhmah/
sophia* is receiving new honor in this process. I approach our
connections to Woman Wisdom through three questions: What is
the significance of her speaking? What does she speak about?
Where does her speaking take place?

The first thing to note about her is that she *speaks*. Not only
does she speak, she *cries*. In Prov. 1:20–21, for example, four
verbs occur in the span of four lines about her speaking activity:
"she cries," "she raises her voice," "she cries out," "she speaks"
(NRSV; see also Prov. 8:1–3). When she speaks, she is far from
soft-spoken or gentle. She cajoles and reproaches, threatens and
promises. She is her own authority.

Women's voices are heard today in a manner perhaps fore-
shadowed by Woman Wisdom. One of the overwhelming impres-
sions left by the Re-Imagining Conference was of the diversity of
voices, which came from all corners of the globe, from different
cultures and backgrounds, all speaking to women's understanding of God in light of their newfound dignity. One of those understandings was God's presence as Wisdom, Sophia. Not only do
we need to trust our own speech as women but we need to "listen
one another into speech," as feminist theologian Nelle Morton
put it.[19] We listen Woman Wisdom into speech.

What does Woman Wisdom speak about? I noted earlier that
she is her own content. She speaks about herself: wisdom. Wisdom is not a set of rules or a set of abstractions or a certain way
of logic but rather a way of being. As the writers of *Sophia—The
Future of Feminist Spirituality* put it, the commitment to wisdom
is a "commitment to the task of learning constantly. . . . Sophia
calls people to be learners. . . . She is in fact the learning process itself."[20]

The only thing we need to worry about in respect to our learning, our wisdom, is the danger of thinking that we have arrived
at the full extent of our knowledge and that nothing more needs
to be learned, nothing needs to change. Reimagining God is an
effort to learn new things about God, to believe new things can
be learned even from "old books," to believe that God has new
things to reveal, even about the complexities of God's own
nature.

Where does Woman Wisdom's speaking take place? She moves

between outside and inside, between market and house. Woman's power exercised outside of the house is an anomaly within the patriarchal system. As much as things have changed with respect to women's roles, negative views of Hillary Clinton and her activities make clear how strongly such convictions are still held today. Yet Woman Wisdom is equally "at home" at the street corner and the city gate as she is at her banquet table. She is at home in heavenly spheres as well as with the "children of humanity." There is no sphere to which she is restricted, no region from which she is banned. Trust in the presence of Woman Wisdom can thus empower women to speak with authority of a wisdom that is not abstracted from the way we live, to speak our wisdom in the place that we choose, be it a lectern, a pulpit, a kitchen table, or a conference platform.

This is not all that must be said. The positive image of Woman Wisdom has a set of negative parallels in the text, perhaps generated by her positive presence. The strange/alien/foreign (NRSV, "loose") woman, the seductress, the wife of another man, and the foolish or stupid woman provide counterparts to Woman Wisdom (Prov. 2:16–19; 5:3–6:5; 6:24–35; 7:6–27; 9:13–18). A view of women as either superior or inferior, saints or prostitutes, is a typical patriarchal portrayal. Dividing one category of women from another, approving of one type while disapproving of the other, has been and is a politically effective strategy to keep things going as they are.

How should we respond to these negative images? First, the negative images of women in the first chapters of Proverbs may help us to stay aware of the cunning and deviousness of patriarchy. We need to maintain an awareness that our reimagining of God and ourselves is only a step, albeit an all-important one. Theologian Linda Mercadante, in her illuminating study of the Shakers and their images of God, points out that inclusive God imagery did not necessarily accompany inclusive, "depatriarchalized" practices in the Shaker communities. As she observes, "Imagery must emerge from, confirm, and relate to changes in experience, and be encouraged, and reinforced by changes in social structure."[21] That warning should keep us on guard, for the dismantling of patriarchy needs to take place on all levels of church and society, and our reimagining is significant only insofar as it accompanies such a dismantling.

Second, the negative presence of women in Proverbs may help us to face the reality of women, who are human and have all the faults that come with being creaturely. Claudia Camp has argued especially for understanding the combined portrait of Woman Wisdom and her negative counterpart as a unity that embraces the paradox of being human.[22] There is something positive to be learned from the negative portrait of women who exercise their influence especially through their sexuality. As women, we have a right to our sins. Facing the stereotypical view in Proverbs 1–9, we may be free to reject the exclusive association of carnality and sin with women, which is typical for some parts of Scripture and the Christian tradition. And we may be free to accept this connection together with men as a part of the broad spectrum of sin in which we all participate. As we speak in the company of Wisdom, our "sister and intimate friend" (Prov. 7:4), we speak also our sins, instead of letting them be spoken to us and for us by others.

In Summary

Woman Wisdom comes to us from the text of Proverbs as a personification of a divine element. From the images articulated in Proverbs, direct lines lead to an identification of Woman Wisdom with God, Torah, and later, Jesus. For a long time lost to the eye of the believer, she has come into view with renewed significance in recent feminist theological discussions and liturgies.

I leave open the question of whether we should use the image of *chokhmah/sophia* in speaking of God. An openness and an unfinished quality to this figure as we meet her in the Hebrew Bible allow for various possibilities. In the meantime, her presence in Scripture engages women at the point of their authority and ability to speak their reality and the reality of God.

For Reflection and Response

1. Read Proverbs 1–9 and 31:10–31 again and make a deliberate effort to read them as a woman speaking to her son(s). Write down your observations.
2. What subjects would you address that are not discussed in these chapters, speaking as a mother to your son(s)? Write down such subjects.
3. Read the chapters as a mother speaking to her daughter(s). What subjects would you address in that case? Compare with the lists you made for questions 2 and 3.
4. How would you use Sophia in a prayer or a hymn?

8

"I Will Be Who I Will Be"

This you shall say
to Israel's children:
"I will be"
has sent me to you.
Exodus 3:14

How do we speak rightly of God? We are not the first to ask this question. A profound exchange about God's name takes place in the book of Exodus. When Moses is appointed to lead the children of Israel, slaves in Egypt, into freedom, he, too, inquires about God's name. We will end our inquiry by joining in this question of Moses. The response of Ex. 3:14 presents both an enigma and a revelation, safeguarding at the same time the freedom "to be" according to God's nature and the guarantee to be present according to God's promise.

Moses asked a question and he received an answer. The answer may not have been entirely to his satisfaction, for it is an answer only in part. It is, after all, God he has asked about. We, too, have asked questions and received some answers. At the same time, the answers have raised new questions; they are answers only in part. It is, after all, God we have asked about and reimagined. The truth of God also eludes; we began with that insight, and we end with it.

Exodus 3:14 assures certain things about God. First, God has made a promise to be present—with God's people Israel, with the world. That promise stands. It is up to Moses, to the escaped slaves, to us, to live faithfully with that truth. Second, God's presence may be counted on, though the manner of God's presence is not predictable. God will be present as God wills it, not as is dictated by history or even by sacred texts.

The identity of the community is bound up with God's identity. God goes forward with the escaped slaves into the wilderness, where they will find both God and themselves. They will find a God who promises ongoing presence and themselves as a people transformed into a new way of being by this presence. Moses' identity is bound up with God's identity. When Moses asks, "Who are you, what is your name?" he asks at the same time, "Who am I, what is my identity?"

As we have asked about God's name, we have asked about ourselves also. As we reimagine God, we reimagine ourselves as a community that holds fast to the promise of God's presence. These issues we now examine.

A Conversation in the Desert

The first two chapters of Exodus tell of the oppression in Egypt experienced by the descendants of Jacob and of the miraculous survival of the hero under whose leadership the slaves will escape. Once the hero, Moses, has grown up, his violent protection of a slave necessitates his flight from Egypt. He finds a new home in Midian, where he marries and works for his father-in-law. There is an entire story embedded in Exodus 1–2 that could have ended there. Moses' story, however, is only part of a much greater narrative, albeit an essential part. At a crucial point, when it seems that events will go on forever as they have and that the hero's mediation has come to nothing, God enters the tale. The last verses of Exodus 2 note that God has heard the cry of the enslaved people in Egypt and takes notice. (Ex. 2:23–25) This is the beginning of a radical turn of events for Moses and the slaves in Egypt.

Exodus 3:1–4:17 is the account of a conversation between God and Moses. It is a long text, and we cannot analyze it here in full detail. Our focus is on the first fourteen verses of chapter 3, especially verses 13–14. This portion of the text is presented in this chapter in my translation. Before proceeding along the path that I attempt to trace, it will be helpful to read Ex. 3:1–4:17 in its entirety in a modern translation, such as the NRSV. The text as it stands now in Exodus is the product of a long writing and editing process that occurred after the events of which it speaks. Different speakers and writers had a hand in the composition. We cannot assign it, therefore, to one particular period of Ancient Israel's history.[1] I propose that we enter this narrative with our imagination. Although we are not Moses and do not face a task of identical hardship and magnitude, we may imagine ourselves involved with the same type of questions that occupied Moses. We, too, in our way, stand on holy ground as we seek to name the Holy One. We, too, in our way, involve ourselves in questions of our own identity, even as we inquire about God's nature.

Now Moses was tending
the flock of Jethro, his father-in-law
—a priest in Midian—
and he led the flock
beyond the wild
and reached the mountain of God, Horeb.
Then an angel of Adonai appeared to him
in a fiery flame out of the bush.
And he saw and, look,
the bush was burning bright with fire
but it was not consumed.
Then Moses said:
Let me turn aside
and look at this marvelous sight,
why the bush is not burning up.

God saw that he turned to look,
and called to him out of the bush:
"Moses, Moses!"
Moses answered:
"Here I am."
He said:
"Do not come closer;
slip your sandals off your feet,
for the place where you stand
is holy ground."
He said further:
"I am the God of your father,
the God of Abraham,
the God of Isaac,
and the God of Jacob."
And Moses hid his face,
for he was afraid to behold God. (Ex. 3:1–6)

The curtain opens on a quiet rural scene, into which intrudes an unexpected sight. So Moses turns off the path to take a look, for he is curious. It sounds almost leisurely: "Let me turn aside . . ." A hint that what he sees is most likely not a curious natural phenomenon is provided with the place indication, "the mountain of God, Horeb." Here, strange events may be expected to happen. And so they do. For a short while, all stays more or less as could be expected. Introductions are made, and Moses shows the proper awe by not only taking off his sandals but covering his face, thus, ironically, no longer able to see what he came to behold. He behaves as a good religious person should, and God behaves as God should.

Moses, as we may imagine, has settled down quite a bit after his tumultuous youth. He is, perhaps, like some of us who devoted ourselves passionately to what we saw as just causes in our youth but who have "come to our senses." Moses still sympathizes with the plight of his people, but he realizes that there is very little he can do to change things. He has a steady job, and if his life is not as grand and exciting as it once was, so be it. He has made a good exchange: stability, a family, and a steady income in the place of the fear and anguish of his younger days. Yet we may suppose that he has not forgotten his sisters and brothers in Egypt and is, at first, glad to hear of God's intended intervention in the state of affairs. Perhaps he hopes for a heart-to-heart talk about what has been keeping God from doing anything for so long.

> Adonai said:
> "Oh, how I have seen
> the misery of my people in Egypt
> and have heard their cry
> from before their slave drivers;
> yes, I know well their woes.
> I have come down to rescue them
> from Egypt's hand,
> and will lead them from that land
> to a land, wide and good,
> a land flowing with milk and honey;
> to the place of the Canaanite,
> the Hittite, Amorite, Perizite, Hevite, and Jebusite.
> For, look, the cry of Israel's children
> has come to me.
> Also have I seen
> the oppression with which
> Egypt oppresses them.
> Come, I will send you to Pharaoh
> to lead my people,
> Israel's children, from Egypt." (Ex. 3:7–10)

At first, all is still as it should be. God, identified as the God of the ancestors—literally, the God of "your father"—anchored in past promises, will take a hand in the miserable circumstances of Jacob's descendants. Who would not be glad at such news? "I have come down to rescue them!" (3:8) Finally! Now Moses can go on with his job without worrying.

Except that is not at all how it turns out; for as soon as God has announced the intended rescue, it appears that Moses will play a major part: "Come, I will send you to lead . . ." (3:10). From this point on, the conversation becomes difficult. Moses has no intention of involving himself in this enterprise and throws out one objection after another. Each time Moses objects, God has another task ready. Moses becomes more blunt, until he finally pleads, "Send someone else" (4:13). Literally, his last objection reads, "Send, please, by a hand you will send"; that is, send whomever you will send, anybody but me! Moses never accepts his assignment in so many words. It seems as if he acquiesces quietly, finally, his resistance worn down.

> Moses answered God:
> "Who am I,
> that I should go to Pharaoh
> and lead Israel's children
> from Egypt?"
> He said:
> "But I will be with you.
> And this will be for you the sign
> that it is I myself who sends you:
> when you lead the people from Egypt,
> you shall worship God on this mountain."
> (Ex. 3:11–12)

Moses begins his protest with questions. First he asks, "Who am I?" The implication is that he is not worth consideration for such a grand assignment. A possible reply to this type of objection could be reassurance that the person is indeed capable. Of course you can do it! Instead, God counters with a promise: "I will be with you." Twice more God repeats this promise of presence (4:12, 15), a promise central to the entire textual unit. Moses has spoken in real or false modesty, either pretending lack of self-confidence or indeed lacking trust in his capacities. Whether a real question or not, he has asked a question about his identity, and he receives an answer. The answer reveals that Moses' identity as a leader is tied to God's presence, and this is true not only for his individual identity but also for that of the community yet to be, which will be in the presence of God at this very place.

Moses is in trouble. To be in God's presence is awesome but still manageable as long as he knows where he is with God. God, the God of his father, he knows about. Not entirely safe, but known enough that he can handle it. Now, his old definitions are crumbling, and he gropes in a fog.

> Moses said to God:
> "When I come to Israel's children

and tell them:
the God of your fathers
has sent me to you,
and they ask me:
What is his name?
What shall I tell them?"

God said to Moses:
"I will be who I will be."
And again he said:
"Thus you must say it
to Israel's children:
I will be has sent me to you."
(Ex. 3: 13–14)

Moses' question is wrapped up in a hypothetical question, for
he hides his own question behind that of the people. It is a sin-
cere question nonetheless, and one that again receives an answer.
The "Who am I?" is bound up with the "Who are you?" Ostensibly
a question for a name, Moses gets more than a name and less
than a name: "I will be who I will be."

The Impossible Name
(Ex. 3:14)

The "name" appears as three words in Hebrew: *ehyeh asher
ehyeh*. The early Greek translation of the Hebrew Bible is translated into English as "I am who I am."[2] There is a long tradition
that understands this phrase to speak to the unchangeable, mysterious nature of God's being. The Hebrew verb forms used here,
however, would be translated ordinarily with a future tense: "I
will be" rather than "I am."

Also, as Martin Buber, among others, has pointed out, the
Hebrew verb for "to be" does not "carry a meaning of pure existence. It means: happening, coming into being, being there, being present, being thus and thus; but not being in the abstract
sense."[3] It appears, then, that Greek grammar and philosophy influenced this translation in a direction that was not intended by
the Hebrew, an influence that was readily acceptable in the world
of the early Church. In the context of Hebrew language and
thought, God's being is talked about as God relates to the creation. Apart from this relation, consideration of God's being is of
no interest to the writers of the Hebrew Bible. The statement

about God in Ex. 3:14, "I will be who I will be," is a statement about both God's being and God's relating. To split these two creates too narrow an understanding of what the text attempts to convey. What, then, is contained in these words about God?

We begin with the most obvious: the answer that Moses receives to his question does not provide a name at all. It is not possible to speak about or to pray to God by his name. This is also the only place in the Bible where God is so named. Is God playing with Moses, teasing him? Or does "I will be who I will be" indicate annoyance, anger, even, that Moses dares to ask such a question? It is not possible to be sure in this regard, but I assume that the answer to "what is his name" is a serious and profound one that responds on different levels to the question. The impossibility of this name means to say exactly that: it *is* impossible to name God. The "I will be who I will be" escapes all attempts at naming. Speaking of God begins with the recognition of that impossibility and moves toward the same insight. The proper name provided in this text, YHWH, in the end turns out to be unpronounceable.

Moses is at a juncture. From now on, things will not be the same, not for him and especially not for the slaves he is to lead out of Egypt. From a group of slaves, a community will grow under God's guidance, with God's help, in God's presence. To that end, they will need to trek through the wilderness, trusting in the presence of this God whom they cannot tame with title or name. To say farewell to enslavements is not as easy as one might think, and many times the people will long for the predictable discomfort of Egypt. At least there they knew what was what and who was who and were not stepping into this impossible, uncertain future with a God no one had ever seen.

I have suggested that patriarchal systems and concepts are comparable to enslavement. In our attempt to break with this enslavement, we have asked our questions about naming God. We began by pointing to the mystery of God, who cannot be captured in a name. It was, for Moses, a good beginning point; it is a good beginning point for us. It is also a point of which we need to be reminded constantly; the only "wrong" naming of God is that which is sure of having it "right." As we recognize the truth of the impossibility of naming God, we recognize also our need to do so. In Exodus 3, the statement "I will be who I will be" is surrounded by names for God. "God" occurs (3:1 and throughout), as well as "God of the fathers" (3:6, 13, 15, 16; 4:5); above all, one finds here "YHWH." The search for the proper way to speak about and to God does not take place in a vacuum. We have therefore looked to the Bible for clues and possibilities in our reimagining God.

Promise of Presence
(Ex. 3:14)

The name that is not a name in Ex. 3:14 holds a denial, but it also affirms something. Buber, who wrote eloquently about this text, translated the phrase as "I will be present as I will be present."[4] God is saying: The manner of my being present is as I will it, not to be caught in one image or manipulated by one name. I will be to you a mother, a father, a kinsman, a kinswoman, a warrior, a shepherd, a teacher, a healer, a friend, a mother bird, a rock, a woman in labor. I am She; I am also He. I am none of these. But I will be present. I was present in the past, I am present now, and I will be in your future. The God of Scripture, the God of Jesus Christ, is above all a God who promises presence. It is in this presence and because of it that transformed existence becomes a possibility.

The slaves in Egypt had a long way to go, from their enslavement into freedom, from being a crowd into becoming a community. The road was by no means always a straight one; there was a constant falling and getting up. First, they had to face their enslavement: see it for the bondage it was and say farewell to it. Bonds, though they cause pain, may yet feel familiar, may be more difficult to shed than one might suppose. One thing was sure: without God's presence and the vision it provided, they would not make it.

We, too, have a long way to go. Enslavement to patriarchal ways of being and acting has to be seen for the destructive bondage it is, so that we can say farewell to it and go into freedom. We face a long trek in the wilderness, where old, familiar patterns will have to disappear. Even though they are oppressive patterns, we may cling to them, as Israel clung to the "fleshpots of Egypt." One thing is sure: without God's presence and our mindfulness of that presence, we will not make it.

The people freed from slavery in Egypt had to learn new ways of being together, so that they could be a community that mirrored the passionately loving justice of God. The Eagle who had brought them thus far was ready to let them go to try their own wings, anxiously, as a parent who is ready to let go of a child. Yet as the people moved into a new existence, they went accompanied by a presence, "a shelter to them by day, and a starry flame at night" (see p. 84)

But what kind of presence could Ancient Israel expect, can we expect? In this book, we have explored many aspects of God's presence. We began with the ineffable nature of God, its refusal to be tied down to one title, one name, a one-gendered perspective. We explored the comforting, sheltering, nurturing nature of God's presence and also its empowering, enlivening, teaching character. All of these aspects can be and are indicated by female imagery in the Bible. The presence of God, above all, involves us in God's work with the creation. Moses found out that God wanted more from him and needed more from him than agreement, a religious nod of approval to the God of the past and to divine plans for rescue. God's enterprise with Israel involved Moses, because God's enterprise with the creation always involves human agency.

Our objections may sound much like those of Moses. Who are we? Who are you? Suppose no one listens and no one believes us? We are not capable; please let someone else do it. All the protests receive essentially the same response: I will be with you. I will be who I will be, but I will be there.

The God of the Future
(Ex. 3:14)

When *ehyeh asher ehyeh* of Ex. 3:14 is rendered as "I am who I am," perhaps the most important aspect lost is the dynamic quality of this revelation and its openness to the future.

Like Moses, we may recognize the God who is anchored in past promises, who in the text is called "the God of your father(s)" (Ex. 3:6, 15, 16; 4:5) This acknowledgment is by no means unimportant. The ancient covenant community of Israel engaged itself constantly in reflection on the presence of God in its history. It articulated in story, song, prayer, and precept the conviction that God had always been the God of their deliverance. Looking to the past, Ancient Israel renewed constantly its trust in God's ongoing liberating presence. In so doing, they recaptured old images of God and reshaped them. When Second Isaiah reimagined God the warrior man into a woman in childbirth (Isa. 42:13–14), past and present images were woven together to signal new possibilities for the future in God's presence.

We, too, look to the past, to the history of God with Israel and the world as it is reflected in the Bible. It can be seductive, how-

ever, to look for God in the past only, to lock God into old images. "I will be who I will be" also means that the manner of
God's presence with the community and the world is to be named
anew, again and again, as the community's experience changes
and God's presence needs to be reimagined. "I will be who I will
be" means that the discussion about speaking of God is never
closed. The past will always guide and inform the discussion; the
biblical text awaits our questions, so that God's word can come
into being for our time.

For Reflection and Response

1. Name the most important characters in the story of Exodus 1–2
   from memory. Read the story and name the characters again, in
   order of appearance. What strikes you about the list?
2. Why would the slaves in Egypt not know God's name?
3. What connotations do you make with "I am who I am?"
4. How does patriarchy create "destructive bondage"? Which of
   these bonds are ones we might cling to?

Conclusion

In considering how we may speak rightly of God, the discussion can never be closed, for as we are right about God's name we are wrong at the same time. God exceeds our designations, even our wildest imaginings. With that point I opened this exploration in the Bible for alternatives to exclusively male language and imagery for God. We are accustomed to think that the biblical text speaks of God in male terms only. Our search was for images of God that offer realized alternatives as well as those that open up possibilities for such images.

The search began with a recognition of God's incomparability and Scripture's way of dealing with this issue. As it is expressed in Second Isaiah, God's incomparable power and greatness are at the service of God's love for Israel and for the entire creation. The beginning point for reimagining God is the trust that God's holiness does not put God at a distance but brings God terribly close.

The Bible speaks of God in many ways. At the second step of our search, we found that the God of the biblical witness is not male. God's equal image in male and female human beings speaks also to the nature of a God in whose one being this duality is held in equality. The choice by the biblical writers to refer to God for the most part as male was determined culturally rather than theologically. In Jesus Christ, the oneness of male and female is reaffirmed (Gal. 3:28), a oneness that speaks also to both male and female nature being held as one in Jesus.[1]

Moreover, the Bible's witness to God in names and comparisons is not uniformly male. One of God's names, El Shaddai, has clear female connotations. The sacred name of God, YHWH, transcends male and female and points again to God's holiness and mystery.

We found that imagery of God as creator of the covenant community, Israel, and of the world is shaped by the comparison to God as a mother. The title "Father" for God by biblical principle and textual witness, then, needs to have beside it the equivalent image of "Mother." Parental imagery for God is a key theme in the Bible, speaking above all to the intimate, vulnerable, and loving qualities of God's relation to the creation. In Scripture, this imagery does not lock the human partner in a static childlike posture but rather calls on the partner's responsibility.

Biblical images of God as father/mother eagle and as life-giving, empowering, educating female Spirit have opened up avenues to reimagine God. Woman Wisdom, as a communication from God, leads us down a path where women find authentication and authority in naming their reality and naming God. Finally, the revelation of Ex. 3:14 embraces past, present, and future, including what has been said about God and what yet remains to be said.

Patriarchal relations in principle are built on the inequality of female and male. These relations are a violation of God's image in the creature. They are a flagrant trespass against the commandment to love the neighbor as the self (Lev. 19:18; Mark 12:31). Patriarchal relations foster a network of oppressive attitudes and behaviors, in which sexism, racism, classism, militarism, and homophobia work together to create masses of marginalized people.[2] This system of oppression crushes the life out of all that is weak and vulnerable and wounds further what is already wounded. The patriarchal way of life violates not only the prescriptions of love for neighbor and self but, in addition, sins against the commandments not to oppress the stranger (Ex. 23:9), to love the stranger as oneself (Lev. 19:24; cf. Deut. 10:19), and to execute justice for the downtrodden (Ex. 22:23; Deut. 1:16; 16:19; 19:19; 24:17; Isa. 1:17; Jer. 7:1–15, for example).

Insofar as the Christian community participates in patriarchal relations, it is guilty of these violations. Insofar as the Christian community is silent in the face of such violations, it participates in them. The community in covenant with God is called to responsibility and guardianship of relations of *shalom,* a word essentially indicating wholeness. Wholeness is absent from a faith and its institutions that support and advocate patriarchy by silent consent or active participation. One step on the way to wholeness is to restore the word-images we use of God to full inclusivity.

We have looked for clues in our reimagining God in a text of the past because we believe that this text is not only a text of the past. Were it so, it would be meaningful only insofar as a search of our past is significant and meaningful. The community that accepts this text as the Bible believes that the Bible, as the Word of God, addresses us at the point of our present questions; that is to say, the Bible is not a static text, appropriate for one time and one context only, because the God of the Bible is not a God who is locked into one mode of being. God is "I will be who I will be."

In our reimagining, we considered the biblical image of God as a woman in labor. A birth-giver participates in the pain of the new creation. Chapters 2 and 3 of Exodus emphasize the familiarity of God with the suffering of the people by the verb "to know": Ex. 2:25, "God saw the children of Israel and God knew"; Ex. 3:7, "Yes, I know well their woes." The Hebrew verb for "to know" always implies more than having information. "To know," *yada'* in Hebrew, is to have intimate acquaintance with, to know from the inside out. That God knows the suffering of Israel's children means not only that God has observed and heard their misery but that God knows this misery from the inside. For Christians, Jesus is *the* manifestation of God's presence through whom God knows our misery from the inside. The apostle Paul commands the community that confesses Jesus not to "submit to the yoke of slavery" (Gal. 5:1) The yoke Paul had in mind was the law of circumcision as the only possible entrance into the community of believers. Today, there is no yoke that compares to patriarchal enslavement and the misery it has brought about, for the family, the church, the nations, and the world.

God knows the inside of this misery not only because God knows our suffering but because we have hanged God on the cross of patriarchy by our exclusively masculine naming and imagining. When we tie God to one-gendered names, titles, and designations, we deny God's own free and dynamic nature. When we deny God the freedom to be who God will be, we also deny ourselves the freedom to be who and what we can be in the gracious, free presence of God.

Glossary

The following definitions are meant to provide the reader with an understanding of the meaning of these words in the usage of the writer. These are not intended as definitive meanings but as working definitions to help in following the discussion.

Bible. The sacred text of Judaism and Christianity is called the Bible. For Judaism, it consists of a collection of books, almost entirely written in Hebrew, approved as authoritative in the Jewish community of the first century C.E. For Christianity, the matter is more complex, since various branches of the Christian family acknowledge different texts as biblical. In general, Protestant Christianity recognizes the collection of texts contained in the Hebrew Bible, traditionally called the Old Testament, together with the writings of the early Church, traditionally called the New Testament, as the Bible. Roman Catholicism, for historical reasons, recognizes additional books as part of Holy Scripture. These are called deuterocanonical books and form a part of the Old Testament. To these belong such books as Ecclesiasticus, Wisdom of Solomon, Judith, and others. They can be found in, for example, the New Oxford Annotated Bible.

Exclusive language. The use of words and phrases that uphold and perpetuate exclusively male concepts and practices. It is also called sexist language, patriarchal language, or androcentric language. Common examples are the use of "man" to indicate "humanity" and the use of the masculine pronoun "he" to indicate both "he" and "she." In religious circles, additional examples are "brothers," "brotherhood," and "men of God." This usage excludes women conceptually from full participation in humanity and thus from full membership in the religious community. Such language supports long-standing practices of exclusion.

Inclusive language. Distinct from exclusive language is the use of words that consciously include women in the naming of themselves and others. In religious language, concern for inclusivity extends to the language for God. This book represents one attempt to seek images and hence language for God that are both inclusive and rooted in biblical traditions.

Feminine and masculine; female and male. Adjectives that indicate biological givens. Feminine and masculine are also used as stereotypes of certain characteristics understood in patriarchal systems to belong to females or males. Many languages structure their nouns into different classes. Hebrew recognizes two classes of nouns, those of what are called feminine and masculine gender. Greek and Latin include a third category, called neuter. I use "masculine" and "feminine" in this book when traditional terminology demands it. Otherwise, I have used "female" and "male," words that are less value-laden.

Feminism. 1. The analysis of the inequality between women and men in structures and concepts. 2. A movement for change. Having analyzed the reality, feminism desires to change this reality. Feminism is not a new phenomenon and has a long history.

Feminist theology. The theology that addresses especially, though not solely, religious concepts and institutions with regard to the issue of inequality between the sexes. It also considers all reality from a theological standpoint. Although there is great variety among feminist theologians and they do not speak in one unanimous voice, in essence all feminist theologians judge *patriarchy* and *sexism* to be sins for which the faith communities need to seek repentance and from which they need transformation into a changed existence. Christian feminists take seriously the saying in Gal. 3:28 that male and female are one in Christ Jesus. Feminist theologians, conscious that the voice of women has not been heard in the theological enterprise of the past, see it as an important task to speak against women's oppression across time and space.

As a feminist, I take my place among those who see patriarchy as a network of oppressive concepts and structures that create conditions of subordination and oppression for large groups of people, including women and children but also men who are not members of the dominating class.[1] As a feminist biblical scholar, my background is Reformed Protestant Christianity, which affords a central place to Scripture in the formulating and ordering of faith and action. I have described the origin and cast of my convictions as a Christian feminist in my work *Reformed and Feminist*. This book may be seen in some ways as a sequel to that endeavor.

Patriarchy. Literally, patriarchy is the organization whereby the male is head of the household, with absolute legal and economic power over other family members, including women and servants. In a broader sense, patriarchy is the social arrangement by which women exercise power legitimately only in the private sphere of home and family. It is the "manifestation and institutionalization of male dominance over women and children in the family and the extension of male dominance over women in society in general. It implies that men hold power in all the important institutions of society and that women are deprived of access to such power."[2] Patriarchy is insidious and pervasive, existing in more or less severe degrees everywhere in the inhabited world. Ultimately, patriarchy is destructive of life. Patriarchy creates a network of oppressive ideologies and behaviors, such as sexism, racism, classism, militarism, and homophobia.

Sexism. The ideology that supports patriarchy. In this ideology, women are judged inferior as a group because of their sex. Men are superior and set the standard. As feminist historian Gerda Lerner points out, "Sexism can exist even in a modified patriarchy, or where patriarchy has been abolished. As long as sexism as an ideology exists, patriarchal relations can easily be re-established, even when legal changes have occurred to outlaw them."[3] Religious sexism is especially devastating because it undermines the value of women in their relation to God as well as to the world.

Note on terminology: Bias shows up in language in many forms, including traditional terminology. "Old Testament," B.C., and spelling out the sacred name of God are practices that are potentially hurtful to communities outside the Christian family. I have replaced "Old Testament" with "Hebrew Bible," when appropriate. This practice was explained more fully in chapter 1. In common with many of my colleagues, I use B.C.E., "before the common era," and C.E., "common era," for B.C., before Christ, and A.D., *anno Domini.* The name of God, YHWH, is either rendered with its four capital letters or as Adonai, with the last two vowels pronounced as "i" in "light." While each of these terms has its shortcomings and problems, it is my intention to act at all times with respect toward the Jewish community, at the same time gaining fresh insight for Christian perspectives.

Notes

Chapter 1. Naming the Holy One

1. "Women-church," a translation of Elisabeth Schüssler Fiorenza's term *ekklesia gynaikon,* was initially used to name a coalition of Roman Catholic women in the United States at their first common conference in 1983. Afterward, it became a self-designation for various ecumenical gatherings and conferences throughout the world. For a discussion of the origin of women-church and its development, see Elisabeth Schüssler Fiorenza, *But She Said—Feminist Practices of Biblical Interpretation* (Boston: Beacon Press, 1992), 126–28.

2. Elizabeth A. Johnson, *She Who Is—The Mystery of God in Feminist Theological Discourse* (New York: Crossroad, 1992).

3. Ibid., 6.

4. Ibid., 9.

5. Steven Greenhouse, "State Department Finds Widespread Abuse of World's Women," *New York Times,* 4 February 1994.

6. As quoted from *Los Angeles Times* and Associated Press dispatches in "Close to Home . . . Two-Thirds of Female Victims of Violence Knew Attacker, Study Finds," Louisville *Courier-Journal,* 31 January 1994.

7. Johanna W. H. van Wijk-Bos, *Reformed and Feminist—A Challenge to the Church* (Louisville: Westminster/John Knox, 1991), 52–55.

8. Ibid., 99–100.

9. "Language about God" (Paper adopted by the 119th General Assembly of the Presbyterian Church in the U.S., 1980), 8.

10. *An Inclusive-Language Lectionary—Readings for Year A,* prepared for experimental and voluntary use in churches by the Inclusive-Language Lectionary Committee appointed by the Division of Education and Ministry, National Council of the Churches of Christ in the U.S.A. (published for the Cooperative Publication Association in Atlanta, New York, and Philadelphia by the John Knox Press, the Pilgrim Press, and the Westminster Press, 1983).

11. See, for example, Sallie McFague, *Metaphorical Theology—Models of God in Religious Language* (Philadelphia: Fortress, 1982) and *Models of God—Theology for an Ecological, Nuclear Age* (Philadelphia: Fortress, 1986); Rosemary Radford Ruether, *Sexism and God-Talk—Toward a Feminist Theology* (London: SCM, 1983); Brian Wren, *What Language Shall I Borrow?— God-Talk in Worship: A Male Response to Feminist Theology* (New York:

Crossroad, 1991); and "The Power of Language among the People of God" (Study paper from the Advisory Council on Discipleship and Worship of The United Presbyterian Church in the U.S.A., 1978). An entire issue of the journal *Reformed Liturgy and Music* was devoted to the subject in the fall of 1983.

12. "Language about God," 2.

13. Johnson, *She Who Is,* 5.

14. Ibid., 57.

15. For a well-argued example, see Daphne Hampson, *Theology and Feminism* (Oxford: Basil Blackwell, 1990). For Hampson, "nothing would seem to indicate better the incompatibility between feminism and Christianity than the difficulty in naming God in a female way within that tradition" (156).

Chapter 2. "To Whom Then Will You Compare Me?"

1. Brian Wren and C. Young, *Bring Many Names* (Carol Stream, Ill.: Hope Publishing Company, 1989).

2. Thus Elizabeth Johnson observes, "This sense of unfathomable depth of mystery, of a vastness of God's glory too great for the human mind to grasp, undergirds the religious significance of speech about God" (*She Who Is—The Mystery of God in Feminist Theological Discourse* [New York: Crossroad, 1992], 105).

3. To arrive at an idea of the dimensions of the destruction wrought on Judah as a result of the Babylonian conquest, note that scholars estimate the population of Judah to have been approximately 250,000 before the exile, half that figure after the deportation of 597 B.C.E., and less than 20,000 after the return of the first exiles during the last quarter of the sixth century B.C.E. See John Bright, *A History of Israel,* 3d ed. (Philadelphia: Westminster, 1981), 344.

4. Translation from *TANAKH—The Holy Scriptures* (Philadelphia, New York, and Jerusalem: The Jewish Publication Society, 1985), 1430.

5. Ibid., 1437.

6. On the basis of the references to King Cyrus in the text, it is possible to date Isaiah 40–55 to 540 B.C.E. or shortly afterward. This dating places the text after Cyrus's major conquests and before his edict that allowed the exiles to return to Judah.

7. Johanna W. H. van Wijk-Bos, *Reformed and Feminist—A Challenge to the Church* (Louisville: Westminster/John Knox, 1991), 43ff. See also James Sanders, *Torah and Canon* (Minneapolis: Augsburg Fortress, 1972).

8. George R. Edwards, "A Biblical View of Gay/Lesbian Liberation" (Speech presented at Louisville Presbyterian Theological Seminary, Louisville, Kentucky, December 1, 1992), 1.

9. Sallie McFague, *Models of God—Theology for an Ecological, Nuclear Age* (Philadelphia: Fortress, 1987), 33–35. See also p. 162.

Chapter 3. Names and the Gender of God

1. For the subsequent material, I acknowledge my debt to Phyllis Trible's interpretation in *God and the Rhetoric of Sexuality* (Philadelphia: Fortress, 1978), 12–30.

2. Ibid., 18.

3. Ibid., 21.

4. M. Weippert, in *Theologisches Handworterbuch zum Alten Testament,* ed. Ernst Jenni and Claus Westermann (Münich: Kaiser Verlag; Zurich: Theologischer Verlag, 1971). See also Leo G. Perdue, "Names of God in the Old Testament," in *Harper's Bible Dictionary,* ed. Paul Achtemeier (San Francisco: Harper & Row, 1985); G. Steins, in *Theologisches Worterbuch zum Alten Testament,* ed. Heinz Joseph Fabry and Helmer Ringgren (Stuttgart, Berlin, and Cologne: W. Kohlhammer, 1993).

5. So *TANAKH—The Holy Scriptures* (Philadelphia, New York, and Jerusalem: The Jewish Publication Society, 1985) throughout.

6. Miriam Therese Winter, *WomanWisdom—A Feminist Lectionary and Psalter,* Part 1: *Women of the Hebrew Scripture* (New York: Crossroad, 1991), 116.

7. So B. W. Anderson, "God, Names of," in *The Interpreter's Dictionary of the Bible,* ed. G. Buttrick (Nashville and New York: Abingdon, 1962), 407–417.

8. The usage of a particular name for God became one of the marks by which different documents were distinguished and traced in the first five books of the Bible. Since the late nineteenth century, it has been commonly hypothesized that four main literary traditions are represented in Genesis through Deuteronomy. Two of these traditions are distinguished by their names for God, one using YHWH, the other Elohim. When the two traditions were combined, the names were combined also.

9. The classical work on this topic is Rudolph Otto, *The Idea of the Holy,* 9th ed., trans. J. Harvey (Oxford: Oxford University Press, 1928). See also James Muilenburg, "Holiness," in *The Interpreter's Dictionary of the Bible,* ed. G. Buttrick (Nashville and New York: Abingdon, 1962), 2: 616–26; John G. Gammie, *Holiness in Israel* (Minneapolis: Fortress, 1989).

10. Commentary by Baruch A. Levine, in *The JPS Torah Commentary—Leviticus* (Philadelphia, New York, and Jerusalem: The Jewish Publication Society, 1989), 256. This volume provides the traditional Hebrew text with the new JPS translation.

11. Gammie, *Holiness in Israel, 195.*

12. Levine, in *JPS Torah Commentary,* 256.

13. Miriam Therese Winter, *Resources for Ritual: Woman Prayer/Woman Song* (New York: Meyer Stone, 1987), 251.

Chapter 4. To Whom Does Scripture Compare God?

1. I have simplified the discussion of speech about God for the sake of clarity. By doing this, I do not mean to do injustice to the complexity of the issue but hope to avoid an entanglement in terminology. For discussion of these issues, see G. B. Caird, *The Language and Imagery of the Bible* (Philadelphia: Westminster, 1980), 144ff. Caird divides comparative language into simile and metaphor and claims that these two "exhaust the possibilities of comparison" (160). Sallie McFague uses the term *metaphor,* while Elizabeth Johnson employs *analogy.* See Sallie McFague, *Metaphorical Theology—Models of God in Religious Language* (Philadelphia: Fortress, 1982); Elizabeth Johnson, *She Who Is—The Mystery of God in Feminist Theological Discourse* (New York: Crossroad, 1992), 113ff.; Brian Wren, *What Language Shall I Bor-*

row?—God-Talk in Worship: A Male Response to Feminist Theology (New York: Crossroad, 1991), 84–110; Janet Martin Soskice, *Metaphor and Religious Language* (Oxford: Clarendon, 1985) and "Can a Feminist Call God Father?" in *Speaking the Christian God—The Holy Trinity and the Challenge of Feminism*, ed. Alvin F. Kimel, Jr. (Grand Rapids: William B. Eerdmans, 1992), 81–94.

Generally, opponents of inclusive imagery and language for God stress the difference between simile and metaphor, claiming that the first only points to a likeness and the second identifies. This argument does not work. The differences between the two are not clear enough, as evidenced by scholarly usage and dictionary definitions of the terms. The very argument creates trouble for the one who uses it, since by its logic God may be identified with a pregnant rock but not with a mother in childbirth (cf. Deut. 32:18 and Isa. 42:14). For an example of this type of argumentation, see Roland M. Frye, "Language for God and Feminist Language: Problems and Principles," in Kimel, ed., *Speaking the Christian God*, 17–43. *Webster's Third International Dictionary* defines *metaphor* as implied comparison and *simile* as explicit comparison. G. B. Caird uses the confusing language of "nonliteral" and "literal" for metaphor and simile. It was nevertheless Caird whose work suggested to me the idea to use the words "comparison" and "comparative language" to embrace all categories.

2. See Johnson, *She Who Is*, 117: "The first expression of unknowability of God is the proliferation of names, images and concepts, each of which provides a different perspective onto divine excellence."

3. The movement that thus takes place in all comparative language for God is described by Caird as a two-part dynamic and more elaborately by Johnson as having three parts: affirmation, negation, and reaffirmation. See Caird, *Language and Imagery*, 177: "No sooner has the metaphor travelled from earth to heaven than it begins the return journey to earth, bearing with it an ideal standard by which the conduct of human judges, kings, fathers, and husbands is to be assessed"; and Johnson, *She Who Is*, 113: "Words about God . . . are analogical, opening through affirmation, negation, and excellence a perspective onto God, directing the mind to God."

4. In the 1970s and 1980s, a number of works appeared that analyzed masculine nouns and pronouns that absorbed the female into the male gender: e.g., Casey Miller and Kate Swift, *Words and Women* (Garden City, N.Y.: Doubleday Anchor Books, 1977); Robin Lakoff, *Language and Women's Place* (New York: Colophon Books, 1975); Mary Daly, *Beyond God the Father—Toward a Philosophy of Women's Liberation* (Boston: Beacon, 1973); Dale Spender, *Man Made Language* (London: Routledge & Kegan Paul, 1980); Alette Olin Hill, *Mother Tongue, Father Time—A Decade of Linguistic Revolt* (Bloomington and Indianapolis: Indiana University Press, 1986); Nancy J. Hardesty, *Inclusive Language* (Atlanta: John Knox, 1984).

5. In Isa. 42:13, however, this image of God is juxtaposed with a woman in labor (vv. 14ff.), which puts the warrior image in an entirely different light. The NRSV renders the expressions used in Exodus 15 and Isaiah 42 as well as another Hebrew term, *gibbor*, as "warrior." *Gibbor* can also be translated as "strong hero" and is not as shocking as the Hebrew *ish milhama* of Exodus 15 and Isaiah 42.

6. For an overview of the titles "king" and "lord" in the entire Bible, see Gerhard Friedrich, ed., *Theological Dictionary of the New Testament*, trans. George W. Bromiley (Grand Rapids: William B. Eerdmans, 1971), 5:2, 3.

7. *Theological Dictionary of the New Testament*, 2:40.

8. See M. Eugene Boring, "Names of God in the New Testament," and Leo G. Perdue, "Names of God in the Old Testament," in *Harper's Bible Dictionary*, ed. Paul Achtemeier (San Francisco: Harper & Row, 1985). Of course, the appellation "father" for the deity is not isolated to the Canaanite and Israelite religions. Zeus and Jupiter were so indicated as well.

9. See Johnson, *She Who Is:* "Critical biblical scholarship points out that, while it is historically most probable that Jesus sometimes addressed God with the Aramaic *Abba*, the paternal metaphor is not necessarily as frequent nor as central as a literal reading of the text might suggest" (80); "Taken as a whole, the gospel tradition demonstrates variety and plurality in Jesus' speech about God rather than the exclusive centrality of speech about God as father" (81).

10. Wren, *What Language Shall I Borrow?* 186.

11. Ibid., 187.

12. Sallie McFague, *Models of God—Theology for an Ecological, Nuclear Age* (Philadelphia: Fortress, 1986), 97.

13. Ibid., 122.

14. Letty M. Russell, "Authority and the Challenge of Feminist Interpretation," in *Feminist Interpretation of the Bible*, ed. Letty M. Russell (Philadelphia: Westminster, 1985), 139

Chapter 5. God—Maker and Mother

1. Mayer I. Gruber, "The Motherhood of God in Second Isaiah," *Revue Biblique* 90 (1983): 359. Gruber observes also that the Isaiah texts "make explicit what is implicit throughout the Hebrew Scriptures, namely that the LORD is neither specifically male nor specifically female. God is above and beyond both sexes. Hence to the very same extent that the God of Israel can be compared to a father the God of Israel can and should be compared also to a mother" (354).

2. Johanna W. H. Bos, "Solidarity with the Stranger," in *A Journey to Justice*, ed. Presbyterian Committee on the Self-Development of People—Report of the Special Task Force, 1993, 45–57.

3. I do not here aim at an exhaustive overview of *all* terms for God that have implicit references to motherhood. Rather, I provide an in-depth scrutiny of a small group of texts.

4. See Gruber, "Motherhood of God," 351–59; Katheryn Pfisterer Darr, "Like Warrior, Like Woman," *Catholic Biblical Quarterly* 49 (1987): 560–71; John J. Schmitt, "The Motherhood of God and Zion as Mother," *Revue Biblique* 92 (1985): 557–69.

5. The Hebrew text uses also *gibbor,* "mighty hero" or "man of might" (see, e.g., Isa. 42:13; Jer. 46:12; and Zeph. 3:17). The NRSV blurs the distinctions by a seemingly arbitrary choice of "warrior" or "soldier" for either *ish milhama* or *gibbor.*

6. The NRSV, for example, makes a clear separation between vv. 13 and 14, whereas the *TANAKH* unites the verses as an introduction to the section of vv. 13–17.

7. For instructive reading on Hebrew poetry, see Robert Alter, *The Art of Biblical Poetry* (New York: Basic Books, 1985).

8. The verbs in connection with the woman in labor are difficult. Gruber translates:

> . . . I will inhale
> and I will exhale simultaneously.

He includes a note that points to the similarity between these expressions and, for example, the contemporary Lamaze technique for breathing during childbirth. ("Motherhood of God," 355). Cf. Katheryn Pfisterer Darr ("Like Warrior, Like Woman," 561):

> Like a travailing woman I will blow;
> I will both gasp and pant.

9. Elizabeth Achtemeier, "Female Language for God: Should the Church Adopt It?" in *The Hermeneutical Quest—Essays in Honor of James Luther Mays*, ed. Donald G. Miller (Allison Park, Pa.: Pickwick Publications, 1986), 108.

10. Walter Brueggemann titles Num. 11:11–15 "Moses' Scolding Tantrum" and observes that this prayer shows that "real piety is speaking with utter candor that takes the covenant partner so seriously that one can and must engage in straight talk" ("Prayer as an Act of Daring Dance," *Reformed Liturgy and Music* 20, 1 [1986]: 35).

11. For an extended discussion of this connection, see Phyllis Trible, *God and the Rhetoric of Sexuality* (Philadelphia: Fortress, 1978), chap. 2.

12. Sallie McFague, *Models of God*, 114.

13. Elizabeth Johnson, *She Who Is—The Mystery of God in Feminist Theological Discourse* (New York: Crossroad, 1992), 177.

Chapter 6. God—Eagle and Spirit

1. Matt. 3:13–17; Mark 1:9–11; Luke 3:21–22; John 1:29–34.

2. Cf. Gen. 1:2 and Deut. 32:11, NRSV.

3. Patrick Johnstone, "God the Mother," *Expository Times* 96 (May 1985): 244.

4. Exodus 19:3–6 is notoriously difficult to assign in terms of the literary traditions of the first five books of the Bible. Most scholars view the passage as a combination of the earliest literary strands, J and E. Such an ascription would place the formation of the text as a literary unit in the ninth or eighth century B.C.E. In my opinion, the origin of the written text of Ex. 19:3–6 may well date to a time before the tenth century.

5. Martin Buber, *Moses—The Revelation and the Covenant* (New York: Harper & Row, 1958), 102.

6. See Johnstone, "God the Mother," 245.

7. In Gerhard Friedrich, ed., *Theological Dictionary of the New Testament*, trans. George W. Bromiley (Grand Rapids: William B. Eerdmans, 1971), 5.6.

8. Hermann Gunkel, "Genesis," in *Handkommentar zum Alten Testament*, ed. D. W. Nowack (Göttingen: Vandenhoeck & Ruprecht, 1902), 91–92.

9. *Ruach* is one of the small number of words in Hebrew that can have either the masculine or the feminine gender. In the case of *ruach*, the feminine predominates.

10. See Elizabeth Johnson, *She Who Is—The Mystery of God in Feminist Theological Discourse* (New York: Crossroad, 1992), 50–54.

11. Genesis 1:1–3 would probably be better translated as one sentence, with the emphasis on the action in verse 3 and treating v. 2 as a series of parenthetical phrases: "When God began to create—the earth being a trackless waste, darkness on the face of the deep, with the Spirit of God hovering on the face of the water—God said, 'Let there be light,' and there was light." It is possible that some further reference to the activity of the Spirit, originally present in the tale, dropped out eventually, as Gunkel suggests ("Genesis," 91–92).

12. This discussion becomes irrelevant if one translates *ruach elohim* with "a wind from God," as the NRSV does, or with "a mighty wind," the option the *TANAKH* chooses. In my opinion, this is not a desirable translation, because in the combination *ruach elohim, ruach* ordinarily points to the Spirit of God (see, e.g., 1 Sam. 10:10; 11:6; Ezek. 11:24).

13. *Midrash Rabbah Genesis* (London and Bournemouth: Soncino, 1951), 18.

14. Gunkel, "Genesis," 91.

Chapter 7. The Paths of Wisdom

1. Elisabeth Schüssler Fiorenza, *In Memory of Her—A Feminist Theological Reconstruction of Christian Origins* (New York: Crossroad, 1983), 130–40.

2. Elizabeth Johnson, *She Who Is—The Mystery of God in Feminist Theological Discourse* (New York: Crossroad, 1992), 91.

3. Helpful resources on the subject are the following: Joan Chamberlain Engelsman, *The Feminine Dimension of the Divine* (Philadelphia: Westminster, 1979); Robert L. Wilken, ed., *Aspects of Wisdom in Judaism and Early Christianity* (London: University of Notre Dame Press, 1975); Claudia V. Camp, "Woman Wisdom as Root Metaphor: A Theological Consideration," in *The Listening Heart—Essays in Wisdom and the Psalms in Honor of Roland E. Murphy, O. Carm.,* ed. K. Hoglund, E. F. Huwiler, J. T. Glass, and R. Lee (Sheffield: JSOT, 1987), and "Wise and Strange: An Interpretation of the Female Imagery in Proverbs in Light of Trickster Mythology," in *Reasoning with the Foxes—Female Wit in a World of Male Power,* ed. Johanna W. H. Bos and J. Cheryl Exum (Semeia 42; Atlanta: Scholars Press, 1988); Carol A. Newsom, "Woman and the Discourse of Patriarchal Wisdom," in *Gender and Difference in Ancient Israel,* ed. Peggy L. Day (Minneapolis: Fortress, 1989); Roland E. Murphy, *The Tree of Life—An Exploration of Biblical Wisdom Literature* (New York: Doubleday, 1990); Athalya Brenner and Fokkelien van Dijk-Hemmes, *On Gendering Texts: Female and Male Voices in the Hebrew Bible* (Leiden: Brill, 1993); Alice Ogden Bellis, *Helpmates, Harlots and Heroes—Women's Stories in the Hebrew Bible* (Louisville: Westminster/John Knox, 1993).

4. These books are included in the biblical canon for only some branches of the Christian community and can be found in a version of the Bible such as *The New Oxford Annotated Bible with the Apocryphal/Deuterocanonical Books* (New York: Oxford University Press, 1991).

5. Susan Cady, Marian Ronan, and Hal Taussig, *Sophia—The Future of Feminist Spirituality* (San Francisco: Harper & Row, 1986), 41.

6. See Gerhard Friedrich, ed., *The Theological Dictionary of the New Testament,* trans. George W. Bromiley (Grand Rapids: William B. Eerdmans, 1971), 5.7, 519.

7. For the discussion on Woman Wisdom, I am indebted to the excellent work of Claudia V. Camp, *Wisdom and the Feminine in the Book of Proverbs,* Bible and Literature, vol. 11 (Sheffield: Almond [JSOT], 1985).

8. See Camp, *Wisdom and the Feminine,* chap. 6.

9. Ibid., 186–208.

10. "One might speculate that, as autonomy and decision-making author-ity flowed back to the collocation of families from the ruined central power structure, the community-wide authority of women in their ongoing role as managers of their households also increased" (Ibid., 261).

11. Claudia Camp's analysis has made clear how these texts fit into their particular postexilic Judahite context, with its concern for land claims and family inheritance. She is not confident that a great deal of borrowing from goddess cults outside of Israel influenced the concept and language of Woman Wisdom. Even if one accepts that a certain amount of borrowing from foreign religions may have occurred, Camp's arguments remain relevant for a proper understanding of both Woman Wisdom and the entire text of Proverbs. See also Schüssler Fiorenza, *In Memory of Her,* chap. 4; Johnson, *She Who Is,* 87ff.

12. Camp, *Wisdom and the Feminine,* 84.

13. Ibid.

14. Johnson, *She Who Is,* 91.

15. See note 4, above.

16. Johnson, *She Who Is,* 155–65.

17. Ibid., 165

18. Murphy, *Tree of Life,* 133.

19. Nelle Morton, *The Journey Is Home* (Boston: Beacon, 1985), 202–10.

20. Cady, Ronan, and Taussig, *Sophia,* 26.

21. Linda A. Mercadante, *Gender, Doctrine and God—The Shakers and Contemporary Theology* (Nashville: Abingdon, 1990), 155.

22. Camp, "Wise and Strange," 29.

Chapter 8. "I Will Be Who I Will Be"

1. Scholars agree in general that Exodus 2–5 belongs among the oldest literary strands of the first five books of the Bible. For an extensive overview of the complexities involved, see, for example, Brevard Childs, *The Book of Exodus—A Critical, Theological Commentary* (Philadelphia: Westminster, 1974), 52ff.

2. This translation was prepared by Greek-speaking Jews in Alexandria, Egypt, between 300 and 100 B.C.E. The translation is called the Septuagint. Because it was adopted by the early church as its sacred text, the Septuagint has exercised a lasting influence on Bible translations up to today. The Sep-tuagint contains what in Protestantism are considered apocryphal or deutero-canonical books. The Protestant Reformation of the sixteenth century returned to the Hebrew canon and the Hebrew language as a primary re-source for knowledge of the biblical text. In spite of this return to Hebrew, the stamp of the Septuagint can be felt today. For a brief discussion of the different collections contained in the biblical canon, see Johanna W. H. van Wijk-Bos, *Reformed and Feminist—A Challenge to the Church* (Louisville: Westminster/John Knox Press, 1991), 34.

3. Martin Buber, *Moses—The Revelation and the Covenant* (New York: Harper & Row, 1958), 52.

4. Ibid.

Conclusion

1. Johnson, *She Who Is,* 155–69.

2. Elisabeth Schüssler Fiorenza, *But She Said—Feminist Practices of Biblical Interpretation* (Boston: Beacon, 1992), 114–18.

Glossary

1. Such a network is described clearly by Elisabeth Schüssler Fiorenza as a "multiplicative pyramid of oppression" in *But She Said—Feminist Practices of Biblical Interpretation* (Boston: Beacon, 1992), 114–18.

2. Gerda Lerner, *The Creation of Patriarchy* (New York: Oxford University Press, 1986). This book contains an excellent list of definitions. See also Johanna W. H. van Wijk-Bos, *Reformed and Feminist—A Challenge to the Church* (Louisville: Westminster/John Knox Press, 1991), 52ff.

3. Lerner, *The Creation of Patriarchy,* 240.

Selected Bibliography

Bellis, Alice Ogden. *Helpmates, Harlots and Heroes—Women's Stories in the Hebrew Bible*. Louisville: Westminster/John Knox, 1993.

Bos, Johanna W. H. van Wijk. *Reformed and Feminist—A Challenge to the Church*. Louisville: Westminster/John Knox, 1991.

———. "Solidarity with the Stranger." In *A Journey to Justice,* edited by the Presbyterian Committee on the Self-Development of People—Report of the Special Task Force, 45–57. 1993.

Bos, Johanna W. H., and J. Cheryl Exum, eds. *Reasoning with the Foxes—Female Wit in a World of Male Power.* Semeia 42. Atlanta: Scholars Press, 1988.

Brenner, Athalya, and Fokkelien van Dijk-Hemmes. *On Gendering Texts: Female and Male Voices in the Hebrew Bible.* Leiden: Brill, 1993.

Buber, Martin. *Moses—The Revelation and the Covenant.* New York: Harper & Row, 1958.

Cady, Susan, Marian Ronan, and Hal Taussig. *Sophia—The Future of Feminist Spirituality.* San Francisco: Harper & Row, 1986.

Caird, G. B. *The Language and Imagery of the Bible.* Philadelphia: Westminster, 1980.

Camp, Claudia V. *Wisdom and the Feminine in the Book of Proverbs.* Sheffield: Almond (JSOT), 1985.

———. "Woman Wisdom as Root Metaphor: A Theological Consideration," In *The Listening Heart—Essays in Wisdom and the Psalms in Honor of Roland E. Murphy, O. Carm.,* edited by K. G. Hoglund, E. F. Huwiler, J. T. Glass, and R. W. Lee, 45–76. Sheffield: JSOT, 1987.

———. "Wise and Strange: An Interpretation of the Female Imagery in Proverbs in Light of Trickster Mythology." In *Reasoning with the Foxes,* edited by J. Cheryl Exum and Johanna W. H. Bos, 14–36.

Chamberlain Engelsman, Joan. *The Feminine Dimension of the Divine*. Philadelphia: Westminster, 1979.

Daly, Mary. *Beyond God the Father—Toward a Philosophy of Women's Liberation*. Boston: Beacon, 1973.

Day, Peggy L., ed. *Gender and Difference in Ancient Israel*. Minneapolis: Fortress, 1989.

Fiorenza, Elisabeth Schüssler. *In Memory of Her—A Feminist Theological Reconstruction of Christian Origins*. New York: Crossroad, 1983.

———. *But She Said—Feminist Practices of Biblical Interpretation*. Boston: Beacon, 1992.

Hampson, Daphne. *Theology and Feminism*. Oxford: Basil Blackwell, 1990.

Hardesty, Nancy. *Inclusive Language*. Atlanta: John Knox, 1984.

Hayes, Mary Cartledge. *To Love Delilah—Claiming the Women of the Bible*. San Diego: LuraMedia, 1990.

Hill, Alette Olin. *Mother Tongue, Father Time—A Decade of Linguistic Revolt*. Bloomington: Indiana University Press, 1986.

Isasi-Díaz, Ada María, and Yolanda Tarango. *Hispanic Women—Prophetic Voice in the Church (Mujer hispana—Voz profetica en la iglesia)* San Francisco: Harper & Row, 1988.

Johnson, Elizabeth A. *She Who Is—The Mystery of God in Feminist Theological Discourse*. New York: Crossroad, 1992.

Kanyoro, Musimbi R. A., and Wendy S. Robins, eds. *The Power We Celebrate—Women's Stories of Faith and Power*. Geneva: WCC Publications, 1992.

Kimer, Alvin F., Jr., ed. *Speaking the Christian God—The Holy Trinity and the Challenge of Feminism*. Grand Rapids: William B. Eerdmans, 1992.

Lakoff, Robin. *Language and Women's Place*. New York: Colophon Books, 1975.

Lerner, Gerda. *The Creation of Patriarchy*. New York: Oxford University Press, 1986.

McFague, Sallie. *Metaphorical Theology—Models of God in Religious Language*. Philadelphia: Fortress, 1982.

———. *Models of God—Theology for an Ecological, Nuclear Age*. Philadelphia: Fortress, 1986.

Mercadante, Linda A. *Gender, Doctrine and God—The Shakers and Contemporary Theology*. Nashville: Abingdon, 1990.

Miller, Casey, and Kate Swift. *Words and Women*. Garden City, N.Y.: Doubleday Anchor Books, 1977.

Mitchell, Rosemary C., and Gail A. Ricciutti. *Birthings and Blessings—Liberating Worship Services for the Inclusive Church*. New York: Crossroad, 1992.

Murphy, Roland E. *The Tree of Life—An Exploration of Biblical Wisdom Literature*. New York: Doubleday, 1990.

Newsom, Carol A. "Woman and the Discourse of Patriarchal Wisdom." In *Gender and Difference in Ancient Israel*, edited by Peggy Day, 141–60. Minneapolis: Fortress, 1989.

Pobee, John S., and Bärbel von Wartenberg-Potter, eds. *New Eyes for Reading—Biblical and Theological Reflections by Women from the Third World*. Oak Park, Ill.: Meyer Stone, 1986.

Ruether, Rosemary Radford. *Sexism and God-Talk—Toward a Feminist Theology*. London: SCM, 1983.

Russell, Letty M. "Authority and the Challenge of Feminist Interpretation," In *Feminist Interpretation of the Bible*, edited by Letty M. Russell, 137–49. Philadelphia: Westminster, 1985.

Spender, Dale. *Man Made Language*. London: Routledge & Kegan Paul, 1980.

Tamez, Elsa, ed. *Through Her Eyes—Women's Theology from Latin America*. New York: Orbis Books, 1989.

Trible, Phyllis. *God and the Rhetoric of Sexuality*. Philadelphia: Fortress, 1978.

Winter, Miriam Therese. *WomanPrayer, WomanSong—Resources for Ritual*. New York: Meyer Stone, 1987.

———. *WomanWisdom—A Feminist Lectionary and Psalter*. Part 1: *Women of the Hebrew Scripture* New York: Crossroad, 1993.

Wren, Brian. *What Language Shall I Borrow?—God-Talk in Worship: A Male Response to Feminist Theology*. New York: Crossroad, 1991.

Scripture Index

Genesis
1–4   26
1:1–2   72–73
1:1–3   111 n.11
1:2   73, 110 n.2
1:26–27   xi, 24–25
2:7   24
14:18–19   26
21:33   26
32:29   23
49:25   27

Exodus
1–2   90, 98
1–15   67
2:23–25   90, 101
3:1–4:17   12, 90
3:1–6   91
3:6   95, 97
3:7–10   92, 101
3:11–14   93–94
3:13   95, 97
3:14   12, 89, 94–98, 100
3:15   30, 95, 97
3:16   95, 97
4:5   95, 97
4:12, 13, 15   93
6:3   27, 30

15   51
15:3   38
15:11   31
16–24   67
19:3–6   xi, 40, 67–69, 110 n.4
19:4   17, 50, 66
19:6   32, 40
22:23   100
23:9   100
24:7   42
33:21, 22   45

Leviticus
19   32
19:2   32
19:18   32, 100
19:24   100
19:34   32

Numbers
11:11–12   58–59
11:16–17   59
11:24–30   59, 72
11:25, 26   75
24:16   27

Deuteronomy
1:16   100
10:17   53

10:18   53, 100
16:11   20
16:19   100
19:19   100
23:17   20
24:17   100
24:17–22   20
26:12   20
27:19   20
28:49   67
32:4   46
32:6   43
32:10–13   xi, 17, 69–70
32:11   72, 110 n.2
32:13   45
32:14   70
32:15   46
32:15–18   70
32:18   46, 59–60
32:20   60

Judges
9:46   26
13:19   45
14:6, 19   74
15:14   74

Ruth
1:22   27

1 Samuel

2:2	45
10:6, 10	72, 74, 75
11:6	74
16:3	74
19:20, 23	75

2 Samuel

1:23	67
7:14	43

1 Kings

22:16	72, 75

1 Chronicles

29:10	43

Nehemiah

9:32	53

Job

28	78
29:6	45

Psalms

17:8	70
18:31	45
19:14	45
22:22	1
31:1–3	45
42:9	45–46
51:11	74
57:1	70
61:4	70
62:2, 6, 7	45
63:7	70
68:6	43
68:14	27
71:3	45
72:2–4, 12–14	39
73:26	45
76:13ff.	31
78:35	45
81:16	45
89:7	31

89:26	43
90:2	58–59
91:1	70
92:15	45
93	39
94:5	39
94:20–21	39
94:22	45
95	39
95:3	39
96	39
97	39
98	39
99	31, 39
103:5	67
104:27	73
104:30	73
111:9	31
121	83
137:5, 6, 8, 9	14–15
139:7	74
144:1ff.	45
145:14	39
145:16	39

Proverbs

1–9	80, 82, 84, 88
1:20, 21	82, 86
1:28	83
1:33	83
2:16–19	87
3:13–18	83–84
3:17	78, 84
3:18, 22	83
4:13	83
5:3–6:5	87
6:24–35	87
7:4	88
7:6–27	87
8:1–3	86
8:15	83
8:22–25	82
8:30b–31	82
8:36	83
9:5–6	83

9:6	83
9:13–18	87
10–30	80
10:4–5	80
10:12	79
14:20	80
14:21	80
22:4	80
24:28	80
25:19	80
26:4–5	80
30:19	67
31	80
31:10–31	80–81

Isaiah

1:17	100
6:3–5	31
40–55	11–22
40:1–2	16
40:8–10	16
40:11	17
40:12–26	16–18
40:27	18
40:28–31	18–19
40:31	67
42:3	33
42:10–12	51
42:13	38, 109 n.5
42:13–14	51–55, 65, 97
42:15–17	51
42:16	52
42:22	51
43:1, 7	50
43:15	39, 50
44:2, 24	50
44:7, 8	17
45:1	56
45:9, 11	50
45:9–13	55–58
45:9–19	17
45:10	59
45:22	56
46:5–11	17
48:12–13	17
49–55	61

49:6	61	*Hosea*		12:9ff.	41		
49:7–13	61	2:14ff.	43, 83	13:54	41		
49:13	61	11:1–2	83	19:16ff.	41		
49:14–17	61–62	11:1–4	17, 44, 60	22:37	41		
49:19–21	62	11:9	32, 35	23:34–39	79		
49:21	62			23:37	71		
51:13	50	*Joel*					
54:5	47, 50	2:28	72	*Mark*			
55	16, 20, 83			1:9–11	119 n.1		
55:1–3	20, 83	*Obadiah*		1:21	41		
55:3	50	4	67	12:31	100		
55:7–9	21						
63:16	43	*Micah*		*Luke*			
64:8	43	2:13	39	1:35	74		
65:2, 12	83			1:52, 53	19		
66:4	83	*Habakkuk*		3:21–22	110 n.1		
66:10–11	63	1:8	67	4:15	41		
66:13	63–64			5:29	19		
				7:31–35	79		
		Zephaniah		10:21–22	79		
Jeremiah		3:15	39	13:34	71		
2:1f	43	3:17	109 n.5	15:1	19		
3:19	43						
4:13	67	*Malachi*		*John*			
7:1–15	100	1:6	43	1:1–3, 14	79		
7:13, 24–27	83			1:29–34	110 n.1		
8:19	39	*Wisdom of*		8:23–24	79		
31:9	43	*Solomon*		12:44–48	79		
46:12	109 n.5	10:17	84	18:20	41		
48:40	67						
49:16, 22	67	*Wisdom of Sirach*		*Acts*			
			84	2:1–4	74		
Lamentations							
1:5	13	*Baruch*		*1 Corinthians*			
1:12	13	4:1	85	1:23–24	78		
2:11, 12	13			1:30	78		
4:9, 10	13	*Matthew*					
4:19	67	3:13–17	110 n.1	*Galatians*			
		4:23	41	3:28	99, 103		
Ezekiel		5:29	19	5:1	101		
1:10	67	9:11	19				
2:2	76	9:35	41	*1 Peter*			
3:14	76	11:1	41	2:9	40		
11:1	76	11:19	19				
11:24	76	11:25–27,	79	*1 John*			
37:1–14	74	28–30		4:8, 16	19		

James Joyce's

A Portrait of the Artist as a Young Man

Text by
Matthew Mitchell
(B.A., Rutgers University)
Department of English
University of Illinois of Urbana-Champaign
Urbana, Illinois

Illustrations by
Thomas E. Cantillon

 Research & Education Association

MAXnotes® for
A PORTRAIT OF THE ARTIST AS A YOUNG MAN

Printed in the United States of America

Library of Congress Catalog Card Number 96-67423

International Standard Book Number 0-87891-041-7

MAXnotes® is a registered trademark of
Research & Education Association, Piscataway, New Jersey 08854

What **MAXnotes**® *Will Do for You*

This book is intended to help you absorb the essential contents and features of James Joyce's *A Portrait of the Artist as a Young Man* and to help you gain a thorough understanding of the work. The book has been designed to do this more quickly and effectively than any other study guide.

For best results, this **MAXnotes** book should be used as a companion to the actual work, not instead of it. The interaction between the two will greatly benefit you.

To help you in your studies, this book presents the most up-to-date interpretations of every section of the actual work, followed by questions and fully explained answers that will enable you to analyze the material critically. The questions also will help you to test your understanding of the work and will prepare you for discussions and exams.

Meaningful illustrations are included to further enhance your understanding and enjoyment of the literary work. The illustrations are designed to place you into the mood and spirit of the work's settings.

The **MAXnotes** also include summaries, character lists, explanations of plot, and section-by-section analyses. A biography of the author and discussion of the work's historical context will help you put this literary piece into the proper perspective of what is taking place.

The use of this study guide will save you the hours of preparation time that would ordinarily be required to arrive at a complete grasp of this work of literature. You will be well prepared for classroom discussions, homework, and exams. The guidelines that are included for writing papers and reports on various topics will prepare you for any added work which may be assigned.

The **MAXnotes** will take your grades "to the max."

Dr. Max Fogiel
Program Director

Contents

Section One: *Introduction* 1

    The Life and Work of James Joyce 1

    Historical Background 5

    Master List of Characters 7

    Summary of the Novel 11

    Estimated Reading Time 13

**Each Chapter includes List of Characters,
Summary, Analysis, Study Questions and
Answers, and Suggested Essay Topics.**

Section Two: *Chapter 1* 14

Section Three: *Chapter 2* 30

Section Four: *Chapter 3* 49

Section Five: *Chapter 4* 68

Section Six: *Chapter 5* 89

Section Seven: *Sample Analytical Paper Topics*.... 119

Section Eight: *Bibliography* 123

Introduction

The Life and Work of James Joyce

James Joyce was born in Dublin, Ireland, on February 2, 1882. He was the oldest of ten children, and was born into a comfortable and, by some standards, wealthy home. However, while Joyce was growing up, his family's economic situation became progressively worse.

He was able to attend Clongowes Wood College, an exclusive Jesuit boarding school, from age six to nine, but was forced to leave in 1891 when his father, John Stanislaus Joyce, lost his position as collector of rates in Dublin and could no longer afford to send James to school. After a brief stint at the Christian Brothers' School, James was allowed to attend the Jesuit Belvedere College, thanks to a special arrangement by a former rector at Clongowes, Father John Conmee. Father Conmee had become prefect of studies at Belvedere and, remembering James' ability as a student, arranged for him and his brothers to attend Belvedere without fees.

Joyce was a distinguished student at Belvedere, winning several exhibitions (cash prizes for scholarship in national competitions), and being elected, two years in a row, to the office of prefect of the Sodality of the Blessed Virgin Mary, the highest honor at Belvedere. He became interested in poetry, drama, philosophy and languages, and upon graduation in 1898, entered University College, Dublin at age 16.

Joyce gained a reputation as a radical thinker by reading a paper entitled "Drama and Life" before the Literary and Historical Society. He published an essay in the *Fortnightly Review* entitled "Ibsen's New Drama," defending the controversial playwright. In these and other essays and reviews he wrote during this period, Joyce defended a realistic representation of life on stage, as opposed to what he took to be a sentimental and moralistic nationalism. The trouble he faced getting permission from the president of the university to read "Drama and Life" was the first of many struggles with censorship in Joyce's career. He graduated in 1902, with a degree in modern languages, having studied Italian, French, German, and literary Norwegian as well as Latin.

The Joyce family during this time had been getting both larger and poorer—they had to move around frequently, setting up temporary residences, and were forced to sell many of their possessions to keep creditors at bay. Anxious to escape what he saw as a confining and restrictive environment in Dublin, Joyce left in 1902 to live in self-imposed "exile" in Paris. He had to return, however, in April 1903, as his mother was dying. Mary Jane Joyce died in August of that year, and James Joyce remained in Dublin for over a year, during which time he wrote and published poetry, worked on short stories (some of which were eventually published in the *Dubliners* collection), and began the initial draft of *A Portrait of the Artist as a Young Man*, then entitled *Stephen Hero*.

He left Dublin again in October 1904, with Nora Barnacle. Joyce never returned to Dublin, except for a few brief visits (the last of which was in 1912), though his home city and country continued to dominate his imagination. He lived and taught in Trieste and Rome until World War I, then moved with Nora, their son Giorgio and daughter Lucia to neutral Zurich, where they stayed until 1920. The Joyces then moved to Paris, where they lived until 1940. James and Nora then returned to Zurich, where James Joyce died on January 13, 1941.

A Portrait of the Artist as a Young Man was published in 1916, but the story of its composition covers a ten-year span in Joyce's life. At the end of the novel, we see the words "Dublin 1904—Trieste 1914." This does not mean, as we might expect, that Joyce spent these ten years working on the text as we have it. In 1904, he wrote a combination short story and autobiographical essay entitled "A Portrait of the Artist." When he could not get it published, he began to rewrite it as a novel with the working title *Stephen Hero*. Joyce worked on *Stephen Hero* intermittently for four years, but became ultimately dissatisfied with his lengthy and cumbersome method.

He decided to rewrite the unfinished *Stephen Hero* in five long chapters, selecting and condensing only the most significant episodes in Stephen Dedalus' development. This novel, *A Portrait of the Artist as a Young Man*, was finished in 1914, published serially in *The Egoist* during 1914 and 1915, and finally published by B. W. Huebsch in New York in 1916. As with his other work, Joyce had considerable trouble getting *Portrait* published, both because of the obscenity laws and because of his unconventional literary form.

James Joyce's literary reputation is remarkable when we consider his relatively scant output. Aside from his play, *Exiles*, and a few books of poetry, which have not earned much attention, Joyce's canon consists of a collection of stories, *Dubliners* (1914), and three novels—besides *Portrait*, the mammoth *Ulysses* (1922) and the even more mammoth *Finnegans Wake* (1939). Each of these represents a cornerstone of modernist fiction, and in each work Joyce extends his innovative and experimental style to further limits, leaving a permanent mark on the development of twentieth-century literature. His reputation and influence are as strong today as ever—from high school classrooms to graduate seminars and international professional conferences, Joyce's work continues to generate a staggering degree of critical interest. As Richard Ellmann wrote, "We are still learning to be James Joyce's contemporaries."

Perhaps the first thing that will strike a first-time reader of *A Portrait of the Artist as a Young Man* is the initial strangeness of the language. Joyce's technique is to have the language of the narration try to mirror the linguistic and intellectual development of Stephen Dedalus—therefore, in the first chapter, the vocabulary and sentence structure are more simplistic, limited, and childlike. The narrative is closely aligned with Stephen's consciousness and perspective—therefore, the narrative style could be said to mature along with young Stephen. As the novel progresses, and Stephen becomes better acclimatized to his world, the language expands and develops accordingly.

Whereas in the *Stephen Hero* stage of the novel's composition Joyce was trying to cram every detail about Stephen's life into the narrative, in *A Portrait of the Artist as a Young Man* he exercises much more selectivity. The novel presents only the most important events in Stephen's life, without as much attention to chronological and temporal sequence as we would find in a traditional novel. The subject of the novel is Stephen's internal intellectual and artistic development, so the conflicts and climaxes which would motivate a traditionally plotted novel are in this case a matter of internal relations. A conflict is important because it is so for Stephen; a climax is such because of its importance in Stephen's ultimate spiritual development Each scene or episode in the novel, then, will be loaded with significance on a number of levels.

Fundamental to the technique and structure of this novel is Joyce's conception of *epiphany.* An epiphany, as Joyce conceives it, is a moment of intense perception, or a feeling of total understanding; one's life is punctuated by such moments. In *Stephen Hero*, Joyce defines his (and Stephen's) conception of epiphany thus:

> By an epiphany he meant a sudden spiritual manifestation, whether in the vulgarity of speech or of gesture or in a memorable phase of the mind itself. He believed that it was for the man of letters to record these epiphanies with extreme care, seeing that they themselves are the most delicate and evanescent of moments.   -

The epiphany is a moment of extreme significance for the subject, or the beholder, and for the object which he or she observes— the epiphany reveals something essential about the person or thing that is observed. Stephen and Joyce understand that the purpose of the artist is to record and present these moments of privileged spiritual insight. The religious source of Joyce's conception (the feast day celebrating the revelation of the infant Christ to the Magi) indicates that this is a spiritual, non-rational conception of knowledge.

A Portrait of the Artist as a Young Man represents the growth and development of Stephen's soul, and the novel is structured around the epiphanies Stephen experiences while growing up. Thus, the narrator is less concerned with dates, ages, time, and a clear chronological sequence. Joyce's conception of epiphany allows us to view time in the novel as a coalescence of past, present, and future. This means, then, for our reading and interpretation of the novel, that each scene will be dense with significance, shedding light on past events in the narrative as well as looking forward to future developments. Joyce is extremely selective—there are many gaps in the story of Stephen's life we must fill in while reading. But this means that we must pay extra attention to the episodes we are given, and the language in which they are told.

Historical Background

A Portrait of the Artist as a Young Man is an autobiographical novel—Stephen Dedalus is Joyce's fictional figure for himself in the early years of his life, and the events in the novel closely parallel those of Joyce's own life. We should be careful not to push this identification of Stephen with young Joyce too far, for the author of a novel is certainly free to take creative liberties that the author of a strict biography would not take. The novel should and does stand as an autonomous artifact in its own right. It is clear, however, that the historical and cultural context of Dublin in the 1890s is as crucial toward our understanding of Stephen Dedalus and his world as it is toward our understanding of Joyce and his world.

Though the novel is ambiguous when it comes to precise dates, the events in *A Portrait of the Artist as a Young Man* cover the period from roughly 1890 through the end of the century. Ireland was then, as it indeed is now, a country torn apart by politics and religion. The Republic of Ireland had not yet won its independence from the British crown, though the liberation movement was fervent. Battle lines were drawn between Protestants and Catholics. Institutionalized religious discrimination had long been used by the Protestant British government as a means of division and control of the Irish-Catholic population, and this naturally trickled down into day-to-day hostility and resentment between Protestant and Catholic people in Ireland. The lines were not always quite this clear, however; there were many among the liberationists who criticized the Catholic church for hindering the anti-British cause.

This anti-Catholic sentiment—which we hear voiced in the novel by Stephen's father and Mr. Casey at Christmas dinner in Chapter 1—is due in large degree to the downfall of Charles Stewart Parnell. Parnell was a liberation leader who was extremely popular, powerful and influential; he was seen by many as the savior of Ireland. However, a scandal erupted in 1889 and 1890, when Captain William Henry O'Shea filed for divorce from his wife, Kitty, on grounds of her adultery with Parnell. The controversy surrounding this affair led directly to the dissolution of Parnell's party, and he died within a year. Parnell's devotees then saw him as a kind of tragic hero, and criticized the Catholic church for their role in condemning the Irish Nationalist leader. They would argue that Parnell's "sin" was a personal matter that should not have jeopardized what they saw as their greatest hope for independence. Joyce, in particular, saw Parnell's case as an apt illustration of what was wrong with Ireland: he was persecuted and discredited, on moralistic grounds, by the same people he had spent his life trying to liberate.

As the largest and most cosmopolitan city in Ireland, Dublin was a hotbed of political and religious conflict in the 1890s. In the arts, too, there was fierce debate as to what direction Ireland should take. The poet and playwright William Butler Yeats was instrumental in working toward an Irish literature, in English, that could become a recognized and appreciated part of European culture. At the same time, however, a more conservative nationalist element called for, along with a renewed interest in Irish folklore and a Gaelic language, positive or "pure" representations of Irish culture in the arts. Therefore, much of the groundbreaking dramatic work of Yeats and J. M. Synge was condemned loudly by many critics, reviewers, and audiences. Joyce associated this kind of attitude with a puritanical orthodoxy which he dislikes intensely. His personal literary development tended to move apart from the Irish literary revival.

It stands to reason, then, that Joyce would feel a need to "escape" from Ireland. He was more interested in studying Italian or German than Gaelic, and was more interested in reading European literature than Irish folktales. However, it is equally clear that the end of the nineteenth century in Dublin, and the political and cultural conflicts which dominated the world into which Joyce grew, continued to have a profound grip on his imagination. Dublin is the setting for all of his literary work, even though he was living in Europe while most of it was written. These formative years, which are detailed in *A Portrait of the Artist as a Young Man*, are the only time Joyce really lived in Ireland. His self-imposed "exile," however, should not be seen as a total rejection of Ireland. He retained a profoundly ambivalent attitude toward his home city for the rest of his life; he despised aspects of it, but remained fascinated by it.

The publication of Joyce's work caused something of a scandal in Dublin. His portrayal of the city is not always flattering, and he frequently incorporates real people from the city into his work. It is obvious why a nationalistic reader, who thinks that Irish literature should be primarily concerned with representing Ireland in a positive light, would think Joyce something of a national embarrassment. Initial reviews a *A Portrait of the Artist as a Young Man*, both in Ireland and abroad, often alternated between recognition and praise of the artistic skill of the novel, while balking at some of the offensive and crude realism in the novel.

For a first novel, Joyce's *Portrait* got a substantial critical response, gaining the attention of contemporary literary figures such as Ezra Pound, W. B. Yeats, H. G. Wells, and Wyndham Lewis. He did not gain his full reputation as an avant-garde innovator in the art of prose, however, until the publication of *Ulysses*, which is more radical in its formal departures from literary conventions.

A Portrait of the Artist as a Young Man will obviously have a strong appeal to young adults with a Catholic upbringing or an artistic disposition. Such students will surely identify specifically with much of Stephen's experience. However, the more general theme of a young person coming of age, and the complex interplay of rebellion and conformity which this involves—growing away from the world of parents and the church as well as growing within it—has had and will continue to have a more universal appeal to younger readers from various backgrounds.

Master List of Characters

Simon Dedalus—*Stephen's father, originally from the city of Cork, a friendly and humorous man, a strong and vocal supporter of Parnell; his wealth declines throughout the novel.*

Mary Dedalus—*Stephen's mother, a quiet, religious woman, who wants Stephen to observe his Easter duties at the end of the novel.*

Stephen Dedalus—*The protagonist and focal character of the narrative; it is essentially "his" story we are reading, following him from about age six until age eighteen, as he grows through and past the Catholic church, deciding finally to leave Dublin for Europe to become an artist.*

Uncle Charles—*Simon's uncle, Stephen's granduncle, who lives with the Dedalus family in the early stage of the novel; trying to preserve calm with Mrs. Dedalus, he remains noncommittal through the Christmas dinner argument.*

Dante—*Stephen's governess, a nickname for "aunt." A well-read and intelligent woman who teaches Stephen geography. She is vehement in her devotion to the Catholic church, and joins it in condemning Parnell despite her desire for liberation.*

Brigid—*The Dedalus' maid; she only appears in the first chapter, and stands as an indication of their relative wealth as the novel begins.*

Mr. Casey—*A close friend of the Dedalus family, who attends Christmas dinner, and is instrumental in provoking the argument with Dante. Mr. Casey, like Mr. Dedalus, is a devout supporter of Parnell.*

Rody Kickham—*A student at Clongowes, a good football player and, according to young Stephen, a "descent fellow."*

Nasty Roche—*A student at Clongowes, whose father is a magistrate. He questions Stephen about his own father, and teases him about his unusual name. Stephen considers him a "stink."*

Wells—*The student at Clongowes who pushes Stephen into the square ditch (the drainage for the outhouse). He teases and intimidates Stephen, but when it is clear that he has made Stephen ill by pushing him into the ditch, Wells begs him not to tell the rector.*

Jack Lawton—*Classmate of Stephen's at Clongowes; he is Stephen's "rival" in academic classroom competitions.*

Simon Moonan and Tusker Boyle—*Students at Clongowes, in Stephen's class, who were allegedly caught "smugging" (a mild form of homosexual petting) with three older students. Stephen and the others discuss how Moonan and Boyle will be flogged.*

Father Arnall—*Stephen's math and Latin teacher at Clongowes; he excuses Stephen from his lesson since he broke his glasses. He reappears in Chapter Three, and leads the retreat of St. Francis Xavier.*

Fleming—*A student at Clongowes, who is friendly and sympathetic to Stephen. He asks if Stephen is okay when he wakes up ill, then urges him to stay in bed.*

Father Dolan—*The prefect of studies and disciplinarian at Clongowes, who comes in and interrupts Latin class.*

Brother Michael—*The medical attendant at the infirmary when Stephen is ill.*

Athy—*The older student (in the third of grammar) who Stephen meets in the infirmary. He is friendly and tells Stephen riddles.*

Eileen—*A friend of Stephen's at home. She is a Protestant, and Stephen associates her white hands with the tower of Ivory.*

Cecil Thunder—*A classmate of Stephen's at Clongowes.*

Corrigan—*One of the older students involved in the smuggling incident with Moonan and Boyle; given the choice between expulsion and flogging, Athy claims that Corrigan opted for flogging by Mr. Gleeson.*

Mr. Harford—*Stephen's writing teacher at Clongowes.*

Father Conmee—*The rector at Clongowes; Stephen goes to speak to him about Father Dolan; Father Conmee is sympathetic and promises to speak to the prefect.*

Mike Flynn—*An old friend of Simon Dedalus, who is Stephen's running trainer.*

Aubrey Mills—*Stephen's childhood friend at home after Stephen leaves Clongowes; the two boys play adventure games together.*

Maurice—*Stephen's younger brother, who is sent with Stephen to Belvedere College.*

Vincent Heron—*Stephen's friend, antagonist, and "rival" at Belvedere; he delights in Stephen's acts of "heresy," yet condemns Byron, Stephen's favorite poet, as a heretic.*

Wallis—*Heron's sidekick; Stephen sees them together smoking outside of the play, and they, jokingly, make him recite the* Confiteor.

Mr. Tate—*Stephen's English teacher at Belvedere, who accuses Stephen of heresy in an essay.*

Boland and Nash—*Heron's two friends; the "dunce" and "idler" of the class, respectively. They try to argue with Stephen about poetry, mostly aping Heron's opinion that Tennyson is the "best poet." They condemn Stephen's favorite, Byron, as a heretic.*

Doyle—*The director of the play Stephen is in at Belvedere.*

Johnny Cashman—*An old man to whom Stephen and his father speak while visiting Cork; Johnny claims to know many of Stephen's ancestors.*

E--- C--- / Emma—*The girl to whom Stephen addresses his poems; she doesn't actually appear in the novel, except through Stephen's memories (the "her" throughout Chapter 5).*

Ennis—*A classmate of Stephen's at Belvedere.*

Old Woman—*Stephen meets her in the street. She directs him to the Church Street chapel.*

Priest—*The priest at the Church Street chapel to whom Stephen confesses, rather than the priest at the retreat.*

The Director—*At Belvedere College, he asks Stephen if he has considered joining the priesthood.*

Dan Crosby—*A tutor; goes with Simon Dedalus to find out about the university for Stephen.*

Dwyer, Towser, Shuley, Ennis, Connolly—*Acquaintances of Stephen; he sees them swimming as he walks along the strand. They seem to him grotesque and immature.*

Katey, Boody, Maggie—*Stephen's younger sisters.*

Cranly—*Stephen's friend and confidant at the university; Stephen speaks to him about his plans to leave Ireland, and Cranly urges Stephen to appease him mother and observe his Easter duties.*

Davin—*A friend of Stephen's at the university; he is from a rural area of Ireland, a "peasant student," the other students tend to romanticize his accent and his "simple" ways.*

Dean of Studies—*An Englishman who talks with Stephen about his developing theory of aesthetics.*

Moynihan—*A fellow university student who tells ribald jokes during lecture.*

Professor of Physics—*Stephen attends his lecture, but is not engaged.*

MacAlister—*A fellow student from the north of Ireland whom Stephen dislikes intensely.*

MacCann—*A student at the university, a socialist and political activist who engages Stephen in a brief public debate outside of the physics lecture.*

Temple—*A student at the university, a gypsy and a socialist, he admires Stephen immensely, much to the chagrin of Cranly, who finds Temple repulsive.*

Lynch—*A student at the university, to whom Stephen talks about his theory of aesthetics and morality.*

Donovan—*A student who Stephen and Lynch encounter during their walk; Stephen dislikes him.*

Father Moran—*A priest with whom Stephen thinks Emma has been flirting.*

Dixon—*The medical student at the library with Cranly.*

The Captain—*A dwarfish old man who Stephen, Dixon, and Cranly see at the library.*

O'Keefe—*A student who riles Temple outside the library.*

Goggins—*A stout student, part of the crowd outside the library.*

Glynn—*A young man at the library.*

Summary of the Novel

A Portrait of the Artist as a Young Man covers the childhood and adolescence of Stephen Dedalus. We see him, over the course of the novel, grow from a little boy to a young man of eighteen who has decided to leave his country for Europe, in order to be an artist.

At the start of the novel, Stephen is a young boy, probably about five-years-old. He is one of the younger students at Clongowes Wood College for boys (a Jesuit elementary school, not a "college" in the American sense). He had been pushed into an outhouse drainage ditch by a student named Wells a few days earlier, and he wakes up ill. While in the infirmary, Stephen dreams of going home for the Christmas holidays. We then see the Dedalus family at Christmas dinner, and a heated argument erupts between Stephen's father and Dante, Stephen's governess, about Parnell and the Catholic church. Back at school, Stephen has broken his glasses and has been excused from classwork by his teacher, Father Arnall. The prefect of studies, Father Dolan, comes into class to discipline the students, and singles out Stephen as a "lazy idle little loafer." Stephen is pandied (his knuckles beaten with a bat) in front of the class, and feels the injustice of his punishment deeply. The other students urge him to speak to the rector of the college. He gets up the courage to do so, and the rector promises to speak to Father Dolan. Stephen is cheered by the other students.

In the second chapter, Stephen is a few years older. He is no longer at Clongowes but at Belvedere College. He has started to become interested in literature, and tends to romanticize his life based on what he reads. He tries to write a poem to the girl he loves, but cannot. He is in a play at Belvedere, and outside of the theater he sees two other students, Heron and Wallis, who tease him about the play, and jokingly make him recite the *Confiteor.* Stephen, while doing so, remembers a recent incident when his English teacher suspected him of heresy. Stephen takes a trip to Cork with his father, and his father shows him the town where he was born and raised, and the school he attended when he was Stephen's age. Back in Dublin, Stephen wins a sum of money for an essay competition, and, for a brief time, treats himself and his family to a "season of pleasure." When the money runs out, we can see him wandering the red light districts of Dublin, fantasizing about the prostitutes. As the chapter ends, Stephen has his first experience with a prostitute.

In Chapter Three, it is apparent that Stephen has made a habit of soliciting prostitutes. He goes through the motions in school and at church, and is not bothered by the duplicity of his life. He goes on a religious retreat with his class, and the priest's sermon about sin and damnation affects Stephen deeply. He repents, goes to confession at the chapel across town, and takes communion.

Stephen has now dedicated his life to God. He prays constantly, and goes about mortifying his senses. He has completely renounced his sinful relations with the prostitutes, and the director at Belvedere speaks to him about becoming a priest. The idea first seems to appeal to Stephen, but he ultimately decides that he could not become a priest.

His father is making plans for Stephen, now 16, to enter the university. Walking along the seashore one afternoon, thinking about poetry, Stephen sees a young woman bathing. They stare at each other, but do not speak. Stephen takes this as a spiritual sign, and he excitedly decides to dedicate his life to art.

In the final chapter, Stephen is at the university. He is lazy about his classes but vehement about his developing theory of aesthetics. He refuses to sign a political petition, trying to set himself apart from the concerns of his country's politics or religion. Talking to his close friend, Cranly, Stephen announces that he has decided to leave Ireland for Europe to pursue his artistic vocation. The novel closes with a few pages out of Stephen's diary, as he makes plans to leave for the continent.

Estimated Reading Time

A Portrait of the Artist as a Young Man is broken up into five chapters—the first four are about equal in length; the fifth is about twice as long as the others. Each chapter should take about an hour to read, though the language and unconventional narration style may take some getting used to. Spending two separate hour-long sittings on the fifth chapter, a student should be able to read the novel in six one-hour sittings.

Chapter 1

New Characters:

Mr. Dedalus: *Stephen's father*

Mrs. Dedalus: *Stephen's mother*

Stephen Dedalus: *the protagonist and focal character of the narrative*

Uncle Charles: *Stephen's granduncle*

Dante: *Stephen's governess*

Brigid: *the Dedalus' maid*

Rody Kickham: *student at Clongowes*

Nasty Roche: *student at Clongowes*

Wells: *student at Clongowes who pushed Stephen into the ditch*

Simon Moonan: *student at Clongowes, caught "smugging"*

Tusker Boyle: *student at Clongowes, caught "smugging" with Simon*

Jack Lawton: *Stephen's competitor in class*

Father Arnall: *Stephen's math and Latin teacher*

Fleming: *student at Clongowes; Stephen's friend*

Father Dolan: *prefect of studies at Clongowes*

Brother Michael: *medical attendant in the infirmary*

Athy: *student at Clongowes*

Mr. Casey: *friend of the Dedalus family*

Eileen: *Stephen's friend, a Protestant*

Cecil Thunder: *student at Clongowes*

Corrigan: *older student at Clongowes*

Mr. Gleeson: *teacher at Clongowes, will flog Corrigan*

Mr. Harford: *Stephen's writing teacher at Clongowes*

Father Conmee: *the rector at Clongowes*

Summary

In the first brief section of the chapter, Stephen is very young. He remembers a story his father told him, and a song he likes to sing. He thinks about Dante, and her brushes (maroon for Michael Davitt, green for Parnell—both Irish nationalist leaders), and about their neighbors, the Vances.

Next, Stephen is at Clongowes Wood College. Stephen is playing football (soccer) with the others, but stays outside of the action because he is younger, smaller, and weaker. He remembers another student, Nasty Roche, questioning him about his name and his father. He remembers being left at school by his mother and father, his mother crying, and his father telling him to write if he wanted anything, and "never to peach on a fellow." He remembers being pushed into a drainage ditch by a student named Wells. Stephen is cold and obviously homesick, and is counting the days until Christmas break.

The boys go inside, into a math class. The teacher, Father Arnall, has a game where the students are divided into teams, York and Lancaster (after the English War of the Roses), and Stephen is struggling with the difficult math. He and another student, Jack Lawton, are constantly competing for first place in these classroom games.

At dinner, Stephen is not hungry and only drinks tea. He feels ill, and thinks about being home. Later, in the playroom, he is teased by Wells about whether or not he kisses his mother before going to bed. In study hall, he changes the number on his desk from 27 to 26 days until the Christmas holiday. He tries to study geography but cannot concentrate. His mind wanders, and he thinks about his father, Dante, and Mr. Casey arguing about politics—Stephen does not understand politics, but wishes he did.

They go to chapel for night prayers, and then go to be. In bed, Stephen fantasizes about traveling home for the holidays. When he wakes up, he feels even more ill, and his friend Fleming tells him to stay in bed. Wells, worried that he has made Stephen ill by pushing him into the ditch, begs Stephen not to tell on him. The prefect comes, and, convinced that Stephen is really ill, tells him to go to the infirmary. In the infirmary, Stephen meets Brother Michael, and thinks once again of home and his parents. He is afraid he might die before he sees them again. He talks to an older boy, Athy, who tells him riddles. In the infirmary, Stephen thinks about his father and his grandfather, and about the death of Parnell.

In the next section, Stephen is home for Christmas dinner. His family, Dante, and Mr. Casey are there. The meal is lavish, prepared and served by servants. An argument erupts at the table between Mr. Dedalus, Mr. Casey, and Dante about the Catholic church and its role in political matters. Stephen's mother and Uncle Charles try to end it, not taking sides and pleading that they not discuss politics at Christmas. The discussion continues, and moves to the more specific and recent issue of Parnell and the role of the church in his downfall. Despite the urgings of Mrs. Dedalus and Uncle Charles, the conflict continues on a subtler level, as Mr. Casey tells an "instructive" anecdote aimed to provoke Dante, about spitting in the eye of a woman who was taunting him about Parnell. This brings the conflict to a boil, and the section ends with Mr. Casey and Dante shouting at each other across the table, Mr. Casey saying "no God for Ireland," and Dante calling him a blasphemer. As Dante storms out of the room, Stephen notices that Mr. Casey and his father are crying for Parnell.

In the next section, Stephen is back at Clongowes. He and the other students are talking about some boys who were in trouble at the school—some say they stole cash, others that they drank the altar wine, and Athy says they are all wrong, that the boys were caught "smugging," a mild form of homosexual petting. The conversation then moves to the question of what punishment the boys will receive. The younger of the five, Simon Moonan and Tusker Boyle, will be flogged, while the three older boys can choose between expulsion and flogging.

They are called in from the playground, and in writing class Stephen has trouble because he has broken his glasses on the

cinderpath. In Latin class, Father Arnall has exempted Stephen from work. The prefect of studies comes in to intimidate and discipline the students. First, he punishes Fleming, who Father Arnall had made kneel in the aisle for writing a bad theme and missing a question in grammar. He then singles out Stephen, and punishes him for not working, thinking that Stephen has tricked Father Arnall. When he is gone, Father Arnall lets them return to their seats, and Stephen is bewildered and upset at his unfair punishment.

Outside of the class, the other boys sympathize with Stephen, and urge him to go tell the rector. At lunch, Stephen decides that he will go and speak to the rector, though he remains hesitant and unsure until the last minute. As he leaves the refectory, he gets up the courage to turn and climb the stairs to the rector's office.

After Stephen explains his case, the rector says that he is sure that Father Dolan made a mistake, and that he will speak to him. Stephen hurries out to the other students, who loudly cheer his success, lifting him onto their shoulders. The crowd dissipates, and at the end of the chapter Stephen is standing alone as the other students play cricket.

Analysis

The novel begins with a cliched storytelling device: "Once upon a time…," be we soon learn that this is not a conventional narrative. The initially confusing and opaque first paragraph represents a story Mr. Dedalus had told Stephen, who is very young in this first short section of the novel. Stephen is identified with the subject of the story ("He was baby tuckoo"), and it quickly becomes clear that the narrative is closely aligned with his perspective. The narrative is thus purposely limited by his immature vocabulary. For example, when we read, "his father looked at him through a glass: he had a hair face," we are to understand that Stephen does not yet know the word "beard." Stephen remembers a song he likes to sing, "O, the wild rose blossoms / On the little green place," but the narrator shows us that he is not yet old enough to pronounce it correctly: "O, the green wothe botheth." These first two pages are fragmentary and scattered, in order to represent the associative and impression-istic mind of a young child. Even in these seemingly random and

incoherent fragments of his consciousness, the greater themes of the novel and the motivating forces of Stephen's world are represented in microcosm. The political world is represented by Dante's two brushes. The world of his family is shown to us. Sexuality is hinted at: ("when he was grown up he was going to marry Eileen"). Art is represented through his father's story and Stephen's song.

In these early pages of the novel, we are being introduced to the world of the protagonist, Stephen Dedalus, as well as being shown Joyce's original and unusual narrative style. Although it is not a first-person narrative, the narrator is intimately engaged with Stephen's consciousness throughout. This method has been called "free indirect discourse," a third-person narrator, with many first-person characteristics. The narrator does not have a voice that is clearly distinct from Stephen's, and he does not comment explicitly on the action. It is not a detached or conventionally omniscient storyteller, but is rather closely aligned with Stephen's consciousness, mirroring his intellectual and linguistic development. It is not clear that the narrator knows more than Stephen does. Can the narrator, then, like the young man, be mistaken or deluded? Throughout the novel, there is the persistent possibility that we should not take the narrator's words at face value, and that Stephen is being treated by the author with a subtle irony.

Throughout the first chapter, Joyce is trying to recreate the impressionistic world of a young child. After the first brief section, Stephen is older—probably about five or six years old. The novel is not always clear about dates, ages, and chronological time. Months and years will pass without mention, and we must infer Stephen's age and maturity from various clues in the narration. A person's life, as Joyce conceives it, is not significant because of its events or the order and circumstances in which they occur. Rather, memories are always colored by the present moment and expectations for the future; likewise, the present is always colored by memories and past experiences. Joyce's narrative tries to capture this more fluid conception of the protagonist's life, and is thus not concerned with establishing clear dates and times.

The narrative in the first chapter is highly impressionistic. Stephen's senses are active—sight, smell, sound, and touch are all emphasized throughout. He is sensitive to color, and especially to hot and cold. His experience of being at school at Clongowes is

characteristically cold and damp; his memories of home are characteristically warm and dry. This betrays both a childlike sensitivity to simple sense perception, as well as suggesting the early stages of Stephen's developing artistic disposition. Stephen's young imagination is especially vivid, and his sense perceptions are often, in this chapter, closely associated with an imaginative flight (such as when he dreams of going home).

Stephen's reactions to his world are colored heavily by the influence of others—Dante, his father, and the older students. When Wells is questioning Stephen about whether or not he kisses his mother before going to bed, and then teases him when he says yes and when he says no, Stephen despairs: "What was the right answer to the question? He had given two and still Wells laughed." It is not that Stephen is concerned with the true answer, but with the *right* one, the one that will allow him to fit into the social situation at hand. Stephen is, throughout the first chapter, trying to acclimatize himself to the existing social, political, and familial structures of his world. He is younger and smaller than the other students, and not at all self-confident.

Another aspect of the older students' influence on young Stephen is his tendency to use their slang to explain things. When Stephen encounters some strange and ambiguous graffiti in the square, he confidently asserts, "Some fellows had drawn it there for a cod." He is using his classmates' slang, but it is not clear that he is at home with their language, that he either understands the joke itself, or even what a "cod" is at all. The words seem somewhat uncomfortable to him, as if he is quoting someone else. He will use this, throughout the chapter, as a way of "understanding" what is going on around him, but it is as if we don't quite believe that he does in fact understand.

It is important to recognize that Stephen's way of making sense involves a particular specific concern with language, here in the first chapter as throughout the novel. He is fascinated by words as names—his own name, as well as others:

> God was God's name just as his name was Stephen. *Dieu* was the French for God and that was God's name too; and when anyone prayed to God and said *Dieu* then God knew at once that it was a French person that was praying.

This passage represents an interesting and illustrative combination of Stephen's early capacity for abstract, complex, metaphysical thought, as well as the comically childlike simplicity of his understanding of language and religion. Stephen is fascinated by language, by the very fact that a word can represent a person, or even God.

Stephen is also intrigued by meaning, especially cases of double meaning: "He kept his hands in the sidepockets of his belted grey suit. That was a belt round his pocket. And belt was also to give a fellow a belt." Note the confident simplicity of Stephen's tone. Recognizing a new aspect of language is, for Stephen, to have gained a new level of understanding.

Stephen's life at Clongowes is presented as alternating between a hostile and unpleasant present and a more desirable alternative. The strength of his young imagination contributes greatly to this—he is constantly imagining, in vivid detail, his impending journey home for the holidays. While his impression of Clongowes is constantly couched in terms of coldness and wetness, unfriendliness and unfamiliarity, he imagines his home as warm, dry, familiar, and friendly. So it is appropriate that the next section, as Stephen is home at Christmas, begins with this description:

> A great fire, banked high and red, flamed in the grate and under the ivytwined branches of the chandelier the Christmas table was spread.

The narrator, assuming Stephen's level of associations, sets up the scene at home using language of warmth, comfort, and tranquility. Stephen is more at ease there, though he is still an outsider. This is the first year he is old enough to sit with the adults, so he feels a distance and alienation from them similar to what he felt at Clongowes. He is a total stranger to the world of politics that dominates their discussion, and once again we see him sit silently, observing and reacting rather than acting and speaking himself.

Stephen's understanding of politics, as described in the earlier section, is typical in its binary construction:

> He wondered if they were arguing at home about that. That was called politics. There were two sides in it: Dante was on

one side and his father and Mr. Casey were on the other side but his mother and Uncle Charles were on no side. Every day there was something in the paper about it. It pained him that he did not know well what politics meant...

The world which Stephen is growing into is highly politically charged—he is aware of this, but also aware that he does not understand it and must remain, for the time being, outside of this dynamic.

The argument at Christmas dinner both confirms and alters the conception of politics Stephen had. The "two sides," at his house anyway, are clear. Mr. Casey and his father are devout supporters of Parnell, and spare no words in their criticism and even condemnation of the Catholic church. Dante, though also a supporter of Irish liberation, is foremost a Catholic, and condemns Parnell for his adulterous affair. We hear Stephen remember her ripping the green velvet back from the Parnell brush when the scandal broke.

Stephen is, of course, silent during the argument, though Uncle Charles and Dante periodically refer to his presence, scolding Mr. Dedalus for his language in front of the child. Although he is silent and passive, we are aware that his mind, as ever, is active. As he tries to understand the conflict he has witnessed, he must complicate some of the categories and binaries he has constructed:

> Stephen looked with affection at Mr. Casey's face which stared across the table over his joined hands.... But why was he against the priests? Because Dante must be right then. But he had heard his father say that she was a spoiled nun and that she had come out of the convent in the Alleghanies when her brother had got the money from the savages for the trinkets and the chainies. Perhaps that made her severe against Parnell.

Stephen clearly does not understand the terms of the conflict, and in a sense the specifics are not what are important here. This is a significant, perhaps epiphanous, moment in Stephen's life—not because of what he learned about Irish politics at the dinner table, but because he is forced to consider his sources of authority. He likes his father, Dante and Mr. Casey equally, and must come to terms with their radical disagreement. This memory becomes significant for Stephen because of its more general implications for his understanding of national and religious politics, which he eventually seeks to escape altogether. The stable world of Stephen's binaries—right, wrong; good, bad—seems threatened here.

Mr. Dedalus' vocal and quite crass questioning of Catholic authority shocks Stephen, but influences him profoundly. His father's criticism of the church prefigures his own questioning of Jesuit authority at the end of this chapter, and ultimately his rejection of the church as a young adult.

If we understand Stephen as a figure for the young artist, then we can see Clongowes and the Jesuit authority as representing many of the forces active in Ireland that, in Joyce's conception, repressed the artist. First, the incident with Wells pushing him into the ditch places Stephen in the role of the righteous innocent victim, which the other boys seem to support by agreeing that "it was a mean thing to do." He comes to embrace this image as the novel progresses. His alienation from the other students and his existence along the margins of the social scene at the school prefigure his sense of the necessity of "exile" from his home country.

When Stephen, at the start of the final section of this chapter, hears the other students discussing Simon Moonan and Tusker Boyle, he is primarily trying to figure out what they did wrong; he does not think to question that they did wrong. It would never occur to him to question the school authorities here. It is clear that Stephen is convinced that the students must have been doing something wrong for them to be punished so severely.

When he is punished unjustly by Father Dolan, he seems immediately certain that the authority, in this case, has made a mistake. Stephen never wavers in his moral indignation—he is certain that the punishment was indeed "cruel and unfair." The pain of his punishment is moral rather than physical—his ego and his integrity are hurt more than his hand. Likewise, his hesitation when it comes to informing the rector is practical, not moral—he thinks the rector might not believe him, in which case the other students will laugh at him. That might just mean more pandying at the hands of Father Dolan. However, for the first time in the novel, Stephen decides to act of his own accord, and his certainty is rewarded. His "success" in going to speak to the rector is one of many "climaxes" in the novel. It represents an important moment in the development of Stephen's soul; this questioning of authority prefigures his later rebellions.

At the end of the chapter, the tone is triumphant. Stephen is cheered by his classmates, and carried on their shoulders—symbolically centralized among them, rather than marginalized. However, the crowd soon dissipates and Stephen is alone once again. He observes rather than participates in the cricket match, but this time his isolation and distance seem different. Rather than feeling uncomfortably alienated, he feels good to be alone—"He was happy and free." This kind of "happy exile," or willful alienation, will come to characterize Stephen's relationship with the politics and religion of his country as he gets older. He is still outside of the game as the chapter ends, but he has achieved an apparently significant moral victory for himself.

Study Questions

1. Through which characters' consciousness is the narrative focused?

2. Who is "baby tuckoo"?

3. What is the significance of Dante's maroon and green brushes?

4. What advice does Stephen's father give him as they leave him off at Clongowes?

5. Why did Wells push Stephen into the ditch?

6. How does Mrs. Dedalus respond to the argument at the Christmas dinner table?

7. What is the story Mr. Casey tells at dinner?

8. According to Athy, why are Simon Moonan and Tusker Boyle in trouble?

9. Why was Stephen exempt from classwork by Father Arnall?

10. What do Stephen's classmates encourage him to do after Father Conmee pandies him?

Answers

1. The narrative is focused, in the style of "free indirect dis-course," through Stephen Dedalus' consciousness.

2. "Baby Tuckoo" is the "nicens little boy" in the story Stephen's father tells him when he is very young. It is a figure for Stephen himself.

3. The maroon brush stands for Michael Davitt, and the green brush stands for Parnell, the famous Irish nationalist leaders.

4. He tells him to write home if he wanted anything, and "whatever he did, never to peach on a fellow."

5. Wells pushed Stephen into the ditch because Stephen refused to swap his snuffbox for Wells' "seasoned hacking chestnut."

6. Mrs. Dedalus does not take sides in the debate. She wants them to refrain from discussing politics, if only on this one day of the year, Christmas.

7. Mr. Casey tells a story, designed to provoke Dante, about being harassed by a woman who was condemning Parnell's affair with Kitty O'Shea. He says that he heard her call Kitty O'Shea a name that he won't repeat, and so he spit his mouthful of tobacco juice in her face.

8. He says that they were caught in the square with three older students "smugging." Since homosexual activity is against the rules at Clongowes, they are to be flogged.

9. Stephen was exempted from classwork until his new glasses arrive; he accidentally broke them when he fell on the cinderpath, and cannot see well enough without them to participate.

10. Stephen's classmates urge him to go speak to the rector, since his punishment was cruel and unfair.

Suggested Essay Topics

1. Discuss Stephen's relationship with language in his chapter. Why is his interest in language significant at this early age? Does this make him more or less engaged with the other students his age? Are there any political implications, in light of the Irish nationalist movement, to his identification of English as "his" language?

2. At various points in this chapter, Stephen proposes a theory of language based upon onomatopoeia—the idea that a word's sound has a kind of concordance to its meaning. Examples of onamatopoeia would be "splat, bam, pow." In what ways does Joyce's narration in this chapter use the *sound* of language to achieve its effects? How would you characterize the tone of the narrator at the start of the chapter? At the end? Is there a thematic connection?

3. Stephen's senses are very acute, and throughout the first chapter Joyce makes us aware of the color, smell, temperature, and sound of Stephen's surroundings. Trace the language of the senses in this chapter. How does Joyce use repeating sense-images to characterize Clongowes or Stephen's home in Dublin?

Chapter 2

New Characters:

Mike Flynn: *Stephen's running coach*

Aubrey Mills: *Stephen's friend in Blackrock*

Maurice: *Stephen's younger brother*

Vincent Heron: *Stephen's friend and "rival" at Belvedere*

Wallis: *Heron's friend*

Mr. Tate: *Stephen's English teacher at Belvedere*

Boland and Nash: *Heron's two friends*

Doyle: *the director of the play Stephen is in at Belvedere*

Johnny Cashman: *an old friend of Simon Dedalus in Cork*

E--- C--- / Emma: *the girl Stephen secretly admires*

Summary

In the first section, the narrator says that Uncle Charles smokes his morning pipe in the outhouse, because Stephen's father finds the tobacco smell unbearable. The Dedalus family has now moved to Blackrock, a suburb of Dublin, and it is summer. Stephen is spending a lot of time with Uncle Charles, going around town doing errands, and practicing track running in the park with Mike Flynn, a friend of Stephen's father. After practice, they often go to chapel, where Charles prays piously, while Stephen sits respectfully. He would go on long walks every Sunday with his father and Uncle Charles, during which he would listen to them talk about politics

and family history. At night, he would read a translation of *The Count of Monte Cristo*. The hero of this book, Edmond Dantes, appeals to Stephen, and he imagines his own life to be heroic and romantic. He has become friends with a boy named Aubrey Mills. They have formed a gang, and play adventure games together, in which Stephen, rather than dressing in a costume, makes a point of imitating Napoleon's plain style of dress.

In September, Stephen does not go back to Clongowes because his father cannot afford to send him. Mike Flynn is in the hospital, and Aubrey is at school, so Stephen starts driving around with the milkman on his route. His family's wealth is declining, and Stephen begins to imagine a female figure, such as Mercedes in *The Count of Monte Cristo*, who will transfigure and save him from the plainness of his life.

In the next section, the family has moved from Blackrock back to the city, and most of their furniture has just been reposessed by Mr. Dedalus' creditors. Stephen understands that his father is in trouble, but does not know the details. Uncle Charles has gotten too old to go outside, so Stephen explores Dublin on his own. He visits relatives with his mother, but continues to feel bitter and aloof. After a children's party, he takes the last tram home with the girl he admires. They stand near each other and, though they remain silent, Stephen feels a kind of connection with her. He thinks that she wants him to hold and kiss her, but he hesitates. The next day, he tries to write a poem to her. In the poem, he alters some of the details from the previous night—they are under trees rather than on a tram, and at the "moment of farewell," this time, they kiss.

One night, Stephen learns that his father has arranged for him and his brother, Maurice, to attend Belvedere College, another Jesuit school. His father then recounts, at dinner, how Father Conmee told him about Stephen going to speak to him about Father Dolan. Mr. Dedalus imitates Father Conmee saying they had a "hearty laugh together over it."

In the next section, Stephen is near the end of his second year at Belvedere. It is the night of the school play, and Stephen has the leading role in the second section, playing a comical teacher. Stephen, impatient with the first act, goes out of the chapel where

the play is being staged. He encounters two of his classmates—Heron and Wallis—smoking outside. Heron urges Stephen to imitate the rector of Belvedere in the play. Heron says that he saw Stephen's father going in, and teases him because Emma was with him. Their jesting makes Stephen angry and uncomfortable, but this mood soon passes. As they jokingly implore him to "admit" that he is "no saint," Stephen plays along, reciting the *Confiteor.*

While doing so, Stephen's mind wanders to a time, about a year back, when his writing teacher had found a mild example of heresy in one of his essays. Stephen does not argue, but corrects his error. A few days later, however, Heron and two others stop him and tease him about it, asking him who the "greatest writer" and "best poet" are. When Stephen says that Byron is the best poet, Heron mocks him, calling Byron a heretic. They hold Stephen and hit him with a cane and cabbage stump, telling him to "admit that Byron was no good."

Remembering the incident now, he is not angry. He is thinking of the fact that Emma will be in the audience, and he tries to remember what she looks like. A younger student comes up and tells Stephen he'd better hurry back and dress for the play.

He goes back in and gets his face painted for the part. He is not nervous, though he is humiliated by the silliness of the part he has to play. The play goes well, and Stephen leaves in a hurry as soon as it is over. Seeing his family outside, and noting that Emma is not with them, he leaves ahead of them—angry, frustrated, and restless.

In the next section, Stephen is on a train to Cork with his father. Cork is the city where Simon Dedalus grew up. They are traveling now because the Dedalus' properties are going to be sold. His father tells stories about his youth in Cork, but Stephen listens without sympathy or pity. In Cork, Mr. Dedalus asks just about everyone they meet about local news, and people he used to know, which makes Stephen restless and impatient. While visiting the Queen's College, Stephen becomes depressed looking at the carvings on the desks, imagining the lives of the students. His father finds his own initials, carved years ago, which only depresses Stephen further.

Hearing his father tell more stories, Stephen thinks of his own position at Belvedere. His father gives him advice, to "always mix with gentlemen," and reminisces about his own father. Stephen is

ashamed of his father, and thinks that the people they meet are condescending and patronizing. He feels distant from the world of his father, and the section ends with Stephen repeating to himself lines from Shelley's poem, "To The Moon."

In the final section, Stephen has won 33 pounds in an essay competition. He takes his parents to dinner, telling his mother not to worry about the cost. He orders fruits and groceries, takes people to the theater, gives gifts, and spends his money generously, if unwisely. His "season of pleasure," however, doesn't last long, and soon life returns to normal. He is dismayed that he was unable to stop the family's decline, which causes him so much shame.

He begins to wander the seedy parts of Dublin, this time searching for a woman to sin with, rather than for the Mercedes-figure from the start of the chapter. At the close of the chapter, he has his first encounter with a prostitute. She seduces him, and Stephen's reaction is passive and submissive.

Analysis

After the dramatic ending of the first chapter, which closes with Stephen winning the approval of his classmates, the beginning of this chapter might be something of a let-down. Rather than immediately continuing Stephen's story, the narrative spends the first page or so describing seemingly banal, incidental, and trivial details about how Uncle Charles goes out to the outhouse to smoke his tobacco, because Stephen's father can't stand the smell. The tone of this chapter, as it begins, suggests routinization, habit—rather than presenting singular events, the narrator describes what Uncle Charles would do "every morning," or what he and Stephen would do "on week days." The long and ultimately circular walks Stephen takes, every Sunday, with his father and Uncle Charles, suggest how much his life has become a progression of routines, and how much his freedom is limited by the adult world once again, Though he is no longer at Clongowes, he is still, to some degree, at the disposal of adult authority. His literal, physical freedom is limited, and his means of escape, throughout this chapter, becomes imaginative.

This juxtaposition of a dramatic moment at the end of one chapter, and a tone of routinization which tends to deflate that climax at the start of the next chapter, initiates a pattern that will

continue throughout the novel. Each chapter will characteristically end with an energetic climax, a moment of enlightenment for Stephen, while the next chapter, as it begins, will seem to show that this moment may not have been as significant as we had thought. This might suggest that the narrator, despite his close engagement with Stephen's perspective, has a tendency to ironize or parody aspects of his youthful triumphs. It may be that we feel that we can see or know more than Stephen, as Stephen is so young that he does not know all he thinks he does. This is the case throughout the novel, though it is perhaps less obvious as he gets older. The narrator always asks us to consider Stephen in a critical light, even when the language of the narration seems to be wholeheartedly affirming him.

This point is made especially specific in the second chapter, as we (and Stephen) hear Mr. Dedalus recount, over dinner, an encounter with Father Conmee, the rector at Clongowes. He retells the story, which had seemed like such an unambiguous triumph for young Stephen at the end of the previous chapter, in a patronizing, almost ridiculing tone:

> …we were chatting away quite friendly and he asked me did our friend here wear glasses still and then he told me the whole story.
> —And was he annoyed, Simon?
> —Annoyed! Note he! *Manly little chap!* he said. Mr Dedalus imitated the mincing nasal tone of the provincial.
> —Father Dolan and I, when I told them all at dinner about it, Father Dolan and I had a great laugh over it. You *better mind yourself, Father Dolan,* said I, or *young Dedalus will send you up for twice nine.* We had a famous laugh together over it. Ha! Ha! Ha!

Stephen's great act of self-assertion, heroism and confidence is reduced here to a comic anecdote; the champion of justice and the Roman people and senate is here reduced to a "manly little chap." While this passage is on the one hand, evidence of his father's insensitivity to his son—we will tend to sympathize with Stephen here—it will also cause us to reconsider the dramatic ending of the previous chapter in a different light.

One important effect of this moment for Stephen, we imagine, is upon his trust in authority. The confidence which he thought he shared with Father Conmee has been betrayed. Rather than reprimanding Father Dolan for his unfair treatment, the two joked about Stephen together. Throughout the second chapter, Stephen becomes more suspicious of authority figures. He has matured in many ways from the naive young boy of the first chapter. He is older now, and living in a different place—Blackrock, a suburb of Dublin. The spatial and temporal distance from Clongowes mirrors the other ways in which he has grown apart from his earlier life.

A telling example of this change in Stephen's attitude occurs early in the chapter, as he is training with Mike Flynn, an old friend of his father:

> Though he had heard his father say that Mike Flynn had put some of the best runners of modern times through his hands Stephen often glanced with mistrust at his trainer's flabby stubblecovered face, as it bent over the long stained fingers through which he rolled his cigarette, and with pity at the mild lusterless blue eyes which would look up suddenly from the task and gaze vaguely into the blue distance....

Contrast this mistrustful and suspicious attitude toward his father's recommended running trainer with the way Stephen asserts throughout the first chapter what "father said," or "Dante said," or "Uncle Charles said." There is a subtle sense of arrogance in the way Stephen looks "with pity" upon the man who is his trainer, his elder, and a close friend of his father. However, we must remember that, despite these changes in Stephen's attitude, he is still at the disposal of adult authority—there is no indication that Stephen is enrolled in track training because he wants to be. Although Mike Flynn's style of running—"his head high lifted, his knees well lifted and his hands held straight down by his sides"—seems antiquated and absurd to Stephen, he complies nonetheless.

Stephen's attitude toward religion, which is of course closely related to his attitude toward adult authority in general, is also changing as he gets older. This too is evident early on in the chapter, as Stephen visits the chapel with Uncle Charles. While Charles prays habitually and piously, Stephen is respectful, "though he did not share [Charles'] piety":

> He often wondered what his granduncle prayed for so
> seriously. Perhaps he prayed for the souls of purgatory or for
> the grace of a happy death or perhaps he prayed that God
> might send him back a part of the big fortune he squandered
> in Cork.

Stephen not only does not understand his uncle's religious belief,
the familiar questioning tone which we recognize from the first
chapter has now a sharper, subtly sarcastic edge. By suggesting that
Charles might be praying for God to "send him back" the fortune
he "squandered," Stephen is not only making a critique of Charles'
religious faith (equating the selfless prayers with the selfish), but
expressing his dissatisfaction with the family's declining economic
status. This suggests the extent to which he is beginning to blame
his father and Charles for being careless.

Stephen's faith in authority has weakened. He assumes a highly
critical, almost arrogant, attitude toward those in a position of
authority. His father is in serious economic trouble. Father Conmee
has betrayed his confidence. Stephen is at once betrayed by and
disappointed in various figures of authority in his life, while at the
same time he begins to assume such roles himself. He is the leader
of the boys' gang in their adventure games, fashioning himself after
Napoleon. He is the leader of his class. He has been elected
secretary of the gymnasium. He even assumes the paternal role of
economic provider when he distributes the prize money from the
essay contest.

Stephen is quick to set himself apart from his peers and to
assume responsibility himself. As the day-to-day circumstances of
his life become more dreary, and as the family is continually forced
to move and to sell its property, Stephen's hopes become pinned
to some kind of deliverance. His attitude throughout the chapter
is a kind of restless expectation, an impatience with his prosaic
surroundings, and a reliance upon his increasingly poetic
imagination. More than once we are told of his sense of destiny,
how he feels greater things are in store for him, and that his
hardship is only temporary. While he listens to his father and Uncle
Charles talk about Irish politics, history, and folktales, Stephen is
silent, but intrigued.

The life that has seemed so incomprehensible to him in the first chapter now seems like a world of not-too-distant potential. However, it soon becomes clear that this is not a matter of following in his father's and Charles' footsteps; Stephen's sense of uniqueness and potential moves him away from his family's plight, and into the "intangible fantasies" of his own mind.

Stephen's increasingly critical attitude toward authority does not lead to a spirit of conflict. Rather, he assumes a pose of detachment. As when Uncle Charles was praying, and Stephen has an air of what we could call "respectful" silence, he feels a disengaged dissatisfaction with his family's declining wealth. When he feels that his father expects his support, that he "was being enlisted for the fight" his family was going to have with its creditors, Stephen's reaction is to remain as detached as possible, to think again of the future.

The change in the family's situation has clearly changed Stephen's perception of the world: "For some time he had felt the slight changes in his house; and those changes in what he had deemed unchangeable were so many slight shocks to his boyish conception of the world." This shaking of his faith in his father's stability results, in part, in a suspicion of his father, and in a sense that he must try to become more independent. He begins to consciously assume and accept the role of the exile or pariah that he was uncomfortable with in the first chapter.

Stephen's pose of detachment, then, does not lead to any direct rebellion at this point. Unlike Heron, his classroom rival who delights in bullying younger students and disrespecting the teachers (at least behind their backs), Stephen does not sway from his "quiet obedience." Amidst all the worldly voices surrounding him at school and at home, Stephen pins his hopes on his imagination. He begins to look at his present surroundings as temporary—he is trapped by circumstance, but feels that he will be able to be free soon. His longings are of course heavily colored by the literature he reads. Literature, for Stephen, provides a means of escape from the reality of his surroundings. While reading *The Count of Monte Cristo,* he fancies himself the dark romantic hero, proud in his exile. He imagines his wanderings through the city as a "quest" for a figure like Mercedes, who would have the power to "transfigure" him, at which time "weakness and timidity and inexperience would fall from him."

This idealized Mercedes—which of course doesn't connect with anything in Stephen's experience—forms his attitude toward Emma, and women more generally, throughout the novel. Emma or "E---C---," is rarely mentioned by name in the novel. She is most often referred to as "her" or "she," which is significant because it shows how Stephen reduces her to a symbolic, and highly literary, "woman-figure" rather than perceiving her as a thinking and feeling person in her own right. She functions for Stephen, throughout the novel, more as an idea than as an actual person. As he imagines her waiting in the audience at the play, and is anxious and apparently in love, it is telling that he cannot even recall what she looks like: "He tried to recall her appearance but could not. He could only remember that she had worn a shawl about her head like a cowl and that her dark eyes had invited and unnerved him." It is telling that, as Stephen tries to recall something about her appearance, his mind reverts immediately to the effect she had on him.

Our perspective, as with everywhere else in the novel, is limited to Stephen, and in the case of Emma we sense this acutely. How different, we imagine, would Emma's account of their ride on the tram be? Whenever Stephen is obsessing over her, we cannot but suspect that here, as elsewhere, his imagination is largely responsible. It is significant that Emma is hard to distinguish from other female figures in the novel, such as Eileen, his childhood friend, and Mercedes, for whom he searches the city. Stephen treats women as symbolic and abstract figures in his life, and not as actualities. Therefore, this "image" will always be in conflict with the actuality of her behavior. In the second chapter and throughout the novel, we suspect that Emma would be surprised by Stephen's descriptions and fantasies. We wonder, with him, whether he is present in her mind at all. However, we hesitate to assign to her any "unfaithfulness" for this as he does. Given the scarcity of their actual contact, it is quite reasonable that she doesn't think of him.

This situation is illustrated nowhere better than in the poem Stephen composes for her. This is our first glimpse at an attempt of artistic creation on Stephen's part. The narrator mentions an attempt, after the Christmas dinner in the first chapter, when Stephen tried to write a poem about Parnell, but couldn't because "his brain had then refused to grapple with the theme." This time,

Stephen succeeds in composing a poem, though we do not get to see it. This suggests, given the selectivity of this narrative, that the circumstances surrounding the act of creation are more important than the product of its labors. He is inspired by the incident on the late night tram with Emma, and his poem is supposedly written for her.

Stephen's composition is highly formal—he seems more enamored of the idea of writing a poem than of the poem itself. He entitles it before he starts writing, and is sure to draw an "ornamental line" underneath the title. His paper is headed with the Jesuit motto, "A.M.D.G." *("Ad Majerum Dei Gloriam"),* and at the foot of the page he writes another motto, "L.D.S." *("Laus Deo Semper").* His title shows how much he sees himself as working within a tradition of English poetry. He titles it "To E--- C---," asserting that "He knew it was right to begin so for he had seen similar titles in the collected poems of Lord Byron." The influence of Byron, however, is as superficial as the Jesuit mottoes, which he includes "from force of habit." It is as if all these extraneous, decorative surroundings—the title, the ornamental line, the Jesuit mottoes, the new bottle of ink, new pen, and new notebook—all get in the way of his creation.

It is no surprise, then, that once he is able to compose his poem (after a brief daydream), that it is as removed as possible from the scene the night before which inspired it. Stephen uses his art to transform and obscure reality, while improving on it. If he hesitates to kiss her in life, he doesn't in the poem. Just as his way of dealing with his family's financial trouble is to detach himself, his way of escaping the "squalor" of his life is to engage in imaginative fantasy. His poem serves just this purpose. Just as his interest in Emma is more in the idea of a female-figure in his life, his interest in poetry, at this point, is more in the idea of being a poet. It is personal and private—he hides the book, and as far as we know doesn't show anyone. Art for Stephen, at this point, is another means of escape and detachment from reality.

Language, throughout this chapter, continues to be fascination for Stephen, and a key aspect of the way his mind works (and, consequently, of the way this narrative works). Consider how, when Heron and Wallis are harassing him, it is the word "Admit!" which sets his mind off on the long digression about the time his English teacher accused him of heresy. This memory is spurred by this "familiar word of admonition"—he recalls how that time, too, Heron had tried to force him to "admit" that Byron is a heretic. The logic of this narrative is associative, and such transitions and digressions are justified by the associations in Stephen's mind. As we noted in the previous chapter, these are frequently linguistic.

This capacity for a word to spawn a virtual mental flood for Stephen is not simply limited to cases of memory, however. While visiting Queen's College in Cork with his father, he sees the word *Foetus* carved into a desk. Its effect on Stephen is instantaneous:

> The sudden legend startled his blood: he seemed to feel the absent students of the college about him and to shrink from their company. A vision of their life, which his father's words had been powerless to evoke, sprang up before him out of the word cut in the desk.

Words in their active application do not have this kind of force for Stephen—his father's constant descriptions and anecdotes about his school days had bored and annoyed Stephen. But this word, carved into a desk and removed from any active or purposeful use, brings the scene immediately to life. It is as if this potential resides somewhere in the word itself.

As we soon learn, the force of this experience is greater because this word and its associations—which for Stephen are primarily sexual—resonate with his own life. Stephen experiences normal, adolescent, sexual awakening as a profoundly singular, abnormal, "brutish and individual malady." We learn that the reason that the word *Foetus* has such an effect on him is because it shocks him that other boys would think about the same "monstrous" things as he does. Again, Stephen tends to see his own experience as unique—he shies from any deep connection with others, and thus assumes that he is the only one who feels as he does. We could also read Stephen's hyperbolic reaction as a critique of Catholic teaching on adolescent sexuality—despite his pose of singularity and uniqueness, we know that Stephen did not get the idea that this is "monstrous" on his own.

Stephen's somewhat excessive reaction here is typical, especially in this chapter. As we have noted, he tends to romanticize his life, and has begun to relish the role of the sensitive and misunderstood exile. If at times Stephen seems to overdramatize himself, the narrator certainly has a role in this. As we saw earlier, this narrator is trying to mirror, through language, aspects of Stephen's personality as it develops. Throughout Chapter Two, his language is often somewhat excessive and melodramatic, to mirror Stephen's tendencies to view himself in this light. The narrative participates, with a seemingly straight face, in Stephen's posturings, presenting them as it were at face value. But do we take Stephen seriously throughout this chapter? Or might the narrator, by choosing such extreme language, be subtly parodying him?

When the narrator describes Stephen as answering Heron "urbanely," "Might I ask what you are talking about?," are we to understand that 16-year-old Stephen was "really" more urbane and sophisticated than his rude classmate, or that he was *acting* this way, putting on airs? His pretentious, elevated style of speech is not lost on Heron, anyway, who responds, "Indeed you might." Throughout this chapter, it seems that the narrator will participate in Stephen's posturings, using excessive or melodramatic language to describe his stance or tone of voice, while subtly undercutting him, or inviting us to be critical of him.

Like Stephen's poem, the narrator's language, by "participating" in Stephen's state of mind to this degree, often renders it difficult to distinguish exactly what is happening. For example, near the end of the chapter, after Stephen had squandered his money and has taken to wandering the seedy areas of Dublin at night, the narrator tells of his "shameful" and "secret riots." Only after a very close reading does it become clear that these are only in his mind, and that his encounter with the prostitute at the close of the chapter is his first. The narrator distorts the actuality in a similar way as Stephen himself does—we are to understand, after the *Foetus* episode, that he experiences his sexuality and fantasies in this extreme manner. The narrator is attempting to replicate and reflect the state of Stephen's mind; by doing so, he often participates in the same kind of distortions as Stephen.

Throughout this chapter, Stephen sets himself as far apart as possible from his surroundings. His family and his city are a source of shame, and the binary between fantasy and reality is operative throughout the chapter. Stephen begins to assume the role of the exile, modeling himself after Lord Byron and Edmond Dantes from *The Count of Monte Cristo*. He has a vague sense of a "calling," some "special purpose" for his life, though it is not yet clear what this will be. He sets himself apart from the other students at the school, and from the members of his family; he is convinced that he is unique. However, in many ways the narrative seems to suggest that Stephen might not be as different as he thinks. The fact that other boys his age have and have always had sexual fantasies comes as an absolute shock to him. He characterizes his sexuality in extreme, abnormal terms but the narrator seems to suggest that it is not as strange as he might think. And, although he criticizes his father and Uncle Charles for their irresponsibility with money, Stephen's excess and carelessness with his prize money shows us that he might not be as far from his father's world as he would like to think. He assumes the role of paternal provider, to try "to build a breakwater of order and elegance against the sordid tide of life," but realizes, of course, that he cannot sustain it. Alongside all of Stephen's assertions that he is a unique figure, the narrative continues to suggest ways he is not.

Study Questions

1. Where is the Dedalus family living at the start of the chapter?

2. What does Stephen read alone in his room at night?

3. Why does Stephen not return to Clongowes in September?

4. When the family has moved back to Dublin, why does Stephen spend so much time alone?

5. Why does Stephen feel it is appropriate to entitle his poem, "To E--- C---"?

6. Where does Stephen go to school after Clongowes?

7. Why does Heron mock Byron, who Stephen says is "the best poet"?

8. What word does Stephen see carved on a desk at Queen's College in Cork?

9. Where does Stephen get the money for his "season of pleasure"?

10. How does Stephen react to the prostitute at the end of the chapter?

Answers

1. The family has moved to Blackrock, a suburb on the coast southeast of Dublin.

2. Stephen reads a translation of *The Count of Monte Cristo* by Alexandre Dumas.

3. Stephen is unable to return to Clongowes because his father can no longer afford to send him.

4. Stephen spends so much time alone in Dublin because he has few friends, and his Uncle Charles has gotten too old to go outside.

5. Stephen imitates the titles of some poems he has seen in the collected works of Lord Byron, the English Romantic poet.

6. Stephen is sent to Belvedere College by special arrangement by Father Conmee, Stephen's former rector at Clongowes. Conmee is now at Belvedere, and arranges for Stephen and his brother Maurice to attend the Jesuit academy.

7. Heron says that Byron was a heretic.

8. Stephen sees the word *"Foetus"* carved in the desk in the lecture hall at Queen's College.

9. Stephen wins 33 pounds in an essay competition, which he spends lavishly and generously, if quickly and irresponsibly.

10. Stephen's reaction to the prostitute is passive and submissive.

Suggested Essay Topics

1. Stephen's attitude toward authority and authority figures undergoes some important changes in Chapter Two. Discuss some ways in which Stephen's behavior in this chapter contrasts with his behavior in the first chapter. Examine specific scenes and passages where this contrast is evident.

2. Throughout Chapter Two, we learn much about Stephen's attitude toward women. From the Mercedes-figure in the early pages to the prostitute at the end, we see his idea and ideal of women develop. Compare and contrast the female-figures in the novel (Mercedes, Emma, the prostitutes) and the place they hold in Stephen's imaginative life.

3. In what ways does this narrator seem to undercut Stephen's sense of uniqueness and singularity? Examine some scenes where it seems that the narrator takes an ironic view toward Stephen.

SECTION FOUR

Chapter 3

New Characters:

Ennis: *a classmate of Stephen's at Belvedere*

Old Woman: *in the street, who directs Stephen to the chapel*

Priest: *at the Church Street chapel where Stephen confesses*

Summary

Stephen has now made a habit of visiting brothels. In school, he is bored and uninspired, and the narrative details the wanderings of his mind while he sits in class. He is not plagued by guilt for his sins, but rather feels a "cold lucid indifference." He feels that he is beyond salvation, and can do nothing to control his lust. He has begun to despise his fellow students, in part because of what he sees as an empty and hypocritical piety on their part. He serves as prefect of the sodality of the Blessed Virgin Mary—a highly esteemed religious organization at Belvedere—but feels no guilt at the "falsehood of his position." He sometimes considers confessing to the members of the sodality, but feels such contempt for them that he does not.

After the math class is over, the other students urge Stephen to try and stall the teacher of the next class by asking difficult questions about the catechism. Before the religion class, Stephen enjoys contemplating the theological dilemmas. When the rector comes in, he announces that a religious retreat in honor of St. Francis Xavier will begin on Wednesday afternoon. He tells the class about Francis Xavier's life—he was one of the first followers of

Ignatius, the Founder of the Jesuit order. He spends his career converting pagans in the Indies, Africa and Asia, and is known for the great number of converts he amassed. Stephen anticipates the coming retreat with anxiety and fear.

In the next section, Stephen is at the retreat. Father Arnall is giving an introductory sermon, which causes Stephen to remember his days at Clongowes. Father Arnall welcomes the boys, and speaks of the tradition of this retreat. He talks of the boys who have done it in years past, and wonders where they are now. He explains the significance and importance of a periodic retreat from ordinary life, and says that during the retreat they will be taught about the "four last things": death, judgment, hell, and heaven. He encourages them to clear their minds of worldly thoughts, and to attend to their souls. Father Arnall claims that this retreat will have a profound impact on their lives.

After dinner, it is clear that the promise of the next four days has already had an effect on Stephen—he perceives himself as a "beast," and begins to feel fear.

This fear becomes "a terror of spirit" as the sermon makes Stephen think of his own death and judgment in morbid detail. This leads him to consider Doomsday, the final judgment. The sermon affects Stephen deeply and personally, and he feels how his "soul was festering in sin."

Walking home, he hears a girl laughing, which causes him intense shame. He thinks of Emma, and is ashamed as he imagines how she would react to his lifestyle. He imagines repenting, and her forgiving him, and he imagines the Virgin Mary simultaneously marrying and forgiving the both of them. It is raining, and Stephen thinks of the biblical flood.

Next, we hear a sermon which solidifies Stephen's conviction that he must repent. Beginning with Creation and Original Sin, the sermon reaches the story of Jesus and the importance of repentance and God's forgiveness. Then follows a lengthy and detailed description of the torments of hell and damnation—it is a physical and geographical account of hell, and a graphic depiction of the bodily and psychological torments hell inflicts on the damned.

As he leaves the chapel, Stephen is greatly upset by the sermon. He fears hell and death, and decides that there is still time to

change his life. In class, Stephen's thoughts are saturated with the language of the sermon. When confessions are being heard, Stephen feels that he must confess, but wonders if he can. He decides that he cannot confess in the college chapel, but must go elsewhere.

That night, the sermon focuses upon the spiritual torments of hell. It details how the damned have a full awareness of what they have lost, and that their conscience will continue to plague them with guilt. He reminds the boys of the eternity of hell, and describes how the awareness of this would torment the damned. He describes sin as a personal affront to Jesus, and the sermon ends with a prayer of repentance, which Stephen takes to heart.

After dinner, Stephen goes up to his room to pray, still feeling the effects of the sermon. He thinks about his sins, and feels surprised that God has allowed him to live this long. With his eyes closed, he has a vision of hell—Stephen's hell is a land of dry thistle and weed, solid excrement, dim light, and goat-like, half-human creatures who mumble and circle around him. His vision of hell sickens and frightens him. He almost faints, then vomits, and, weakened, he prays.

In the evening, he leaves the house, looking to confess his sins, but is scared that he won't be able to. Seeing some poor girls sitting on the side of the street, Stephen is ashamed at the thought that their souls are dearer to God than his. He asks an old woman where the nearest chapel is, and she directs him.

Inside the Church St. Chapel, he kneels at the last bench. Once the priest arrives and the other people in the chapel begin going in for confession, Stephen has second thoughts. When his turn comes, however, he goes in almost automatically. Inside the confessional, he recites the *Confiteor,* and tells the priest that it has been eight months since his last confession. First he confesses more minor sins—masses he missed, prayers not said—then gradually reaches his "sins of impurity." He tells the priest all the details. When the priest asks how old he is, Stephen answers, "sixteen." The priest implores Stephen to repent and to change his lifestyle, suggesting that he pray to the Virgin Mary when he is tempted. The priest blesses him, and Stephen prays fervently.

On his way home, Stephen is ecstatic, feeling an inner peace in his life. In the morning, he takes communion with his classmates.

The ritual affects Stephen deeply, and he feels that a new life has begun for him.

Analysis

Once again, the chapter begins with a sense of dull routine. The excitement of his transgression, which had ended Chapter Two is here deflated—there is no indication of any sense of thrill or danger in Stephen's now frequent visits to the brothels. Instead, they have become as dull and ordinary for him as the rest of the Dublin society from which he seeks to distance himself. Stephen's attempts to set himself apart from his surroundings seem frustrated—the narrator is showing us, at the start of this chapter, that perhaps Stephen's experience with the prostitute was not the significant transformative experience that he had thought.

The verb tense throughout the opening paragraphs, as Stephen is in class thinking of the night to come, suggests just how much of a habit this has become for him:

> It would be a gloomy secret night. After early nightfall the yellow lamps would light up, here and there, the squalid quarter of the brothels. He would follow a devious course up and down the streets....

Clearly, this "gloomy secret night" will not differ greatly from any other night of the week for Stephen. Visiting the brothels seems to have become as much a part of his daily routine as school.

However, the fact that this habit has lost its charge of excitement for Stephen is made clear by the narrator's use of light imagery, which characterizes Stephen's present life as dull, dusky, and dim:

> The swift December dusk had come tumbling clownishly after its dull day and, as he started through the dull square window of the schoolroom, he felt his belly crave for its food.

The repetition of "dull" and "dusk" throughout the opening pages of the chapter suggests both habit and stasis, while the metaphorical language of dusk and dullness suggests just how plain and unappealing Stephen's lifestyle has become for him.

In a sense, this first paragraph represents Stephen's moral state at the start of this chapter. Chapter Three is thematically concerned

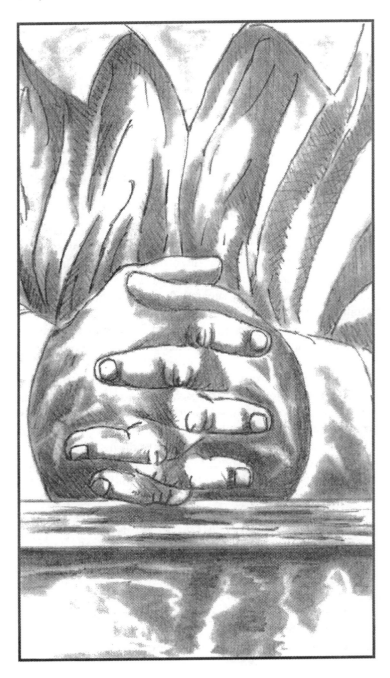

with Stephen's moral and religious state, which undergoes a major transformation over the course of the five days covered by the chapter. As the chapter opens, he is in class daydreaming about dinner:

> He hoped there would be stew for dinner, turnips and carrots and bruised potatoes and fat mutton pieces to be ladled out in thick peppered flourfattened sauce. Stuff it into you, his belly counselled him.

His intellect, or spirit, is subsumed in favor of his bodily appetites, a clear echo of the lustful nature of his sin. That this sin has become dull and unappealing in itself is suggested by the quality of food Stephen expects: bruised, fat, thick, and flourfattened. He does not indicate that there is something about the food itself which appeals to him. Rather, its chief quality that is that it will satisfy a bodily need, evidenced by the crudity of the phrase, "stuff it into you." Stephen is now motivated by the physical and worldly—his "belly" is personified as an entity separate from and dominant over his mind. His lust for food is clearly associated with his sexual lust, as his mind seems to progress naturally from thinking about dinner to thinking about wandering the brothel district. Both cravings are equally devoid of feeling.

As the novel's central chapter, Chapter Three is the most temporally and thematically focused and concentrated. Whereas the other chapters in the novel cover anywhere from a few months to a few years in Stephen's life, Chapter Three intensely focuses on five crucial days. Even within these five days, the narrative excludes everything except what specifically concerns Stephen's spiritual and religious status. We have the impression that this retreat consists only of Stephen hearing sermons, then cowering in his room, and eventually walking across town for confession. While he surely did many other things during these days, this narrator is interested only in presenting the details essential to the development of Stephen's soul. Therefore, the focus of the narrative in this chapter is intensely concentrated.

John Blades describes it as a "chapter of excesses." Father Arnall's sermons are excessive in their scope, and in their morbid and explicit attention to detail. The narrative is excessive in its unrelenting and comprehensive presentation of these sermons.

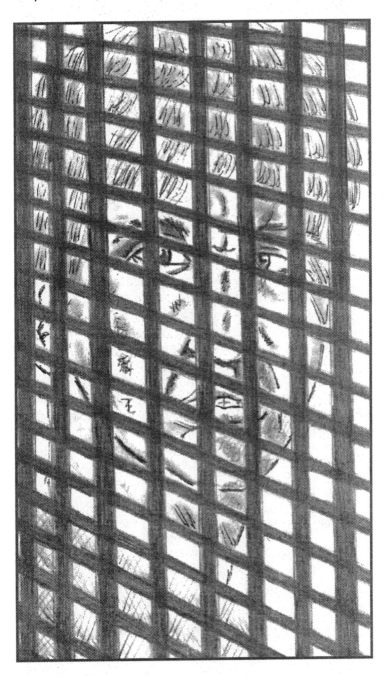

It shifts from direct quotation of the priest to the style of paraphrase that seems to present Stephen's reactions to the sermon at the same time, but our overall impression of this section of the chapter is like sitting through these entire sermons. There is very little narrative presence interrupting the relentless flow of the priest's words. Stephen's response is also somewhat excessive, feeling that "every word was for him," and fearing an immediate death at the hand of God on his way back to his room.

One important change in Stephen's character in this chapter is in his attitude toward his peers. What we recognize in Chapter Two as a pose of detachment has now become a more explicit "contempt" for his peers. He perceives their acts of piety and religious devotion as hypocritical, easy and shallow, and feels no shame about his "double life" around them. The pose of exile and detachment here takes on a distinctly sinful quality—pride. This is an extreme manifestation of his feelings of uniqueness and exile in Chapter Two, and one which suggests the sinful state of his soul. The restlessness and impatience with the world of his family and his classmates, and the pervasive hope that some great calling awaits him, has now become a "cold lucid indifference" toward his own soul, and toward the extent to which he continues to live in sin.

While Stephen tries to convince himself that he is indifferent to his sin, and feels no regret or discomfort with "the falsehood of his position" as prefect of the sodality of the Blessed Virgin Mary, it is clear that he has been not able to escape the influence of the Catholic church. First of all, his sinful lifestyle does to constitute a rejection of or loss of belief in God:

> What did it avail to pray when he knew that his soul lusted after its own destruction? A certain pride, a certain awe, withheld him from offering to God even one prayer at night though he knew it was in God's power to take away his life while he slept and hurl his soul hellward ere he could beg for mercy.

Stephen seems to fashion himself here after Milton's Satan; we can sense a romantic pleasure in his defiance of God's power. For Stephen never expresses disbelief of or lack of faith in God, and he is still intimately familiar with the tenents of the Catholic faith (evidenced by his role as resident expert in his class on obscure questions about the catechism). Stephen seems to take both pride and morbid and masochistic pleasure in his deep theological knowledge:

> It was strange too that he found an arid pleasure in following up to the end of rigid lines of the doctrines of the church and penetrating into obscure silences only to hear and feel the more deeply his own condemnation.

His interest in the details of Catholic doctrine has a certain detached quality—as if religion were a series of puzzling intellectual questions and obscure knowledge. At the same time, however, Stephen seems to find a certain thrill in applying the consequences of these doctrines to his own sinful life. He is deeply aware of the "letter of the law," but this awareness never translates into a reaction to the "spirit of the law" until after the retreat. His interest in theological questions bears a very limited connection to his daily life. Up to this point, Stephen's relationship to the church is both an idle intellectual game, and a useful romantic trope for his imaginative construction of his own life.

Though he manages to remain detached to this degree, he is never outside of the structures of the church. He always refers to his "sin" and to his "condemnation," terms that have no application outside of the framework of religious doctrine and belief. By identifying his behavior as a "sin," and by dwelling on it to this degree, we can see how much the language and beliefs of the Catholic church continue to have a hold on him. We can see, from the start of the chapter, just how ripe Stephen is to be swayed by the sermon.

The centerpiece of this chapter is the pair of sermons Father Arnall gives concerning hell and damnation. He quite literally puts "the fear of God" into Stephen, who, at the end of the chapter, repents, confesses, and begins a new life in the service of God. The narrator, as a recognizable presence, all but drops out of the picture in this section. Stephen speaks very little in this chapter, but listens and reacts internally to the sermon. The narrator is able to illustrate this by recreating Stephen's experience for the reader—we are made to listen to the sermon almost word-for-word, which recreates

Stephen's experience in the congregation, continuing to align us exclusively with his perspective.

Although the narrative starts by quoting large portions of the sermon, we soon are able to recognize many characteristics of Father Arnall's language in the narrator's "own" narration, paraphrasing to the extent that the narrator's voice sounds like the priest's:

> At the last moment of consciousness the whole earthly life passed before the vision of the soul and, ere it had time to reflect, the body had died and the soul stood terrified before the judgement seat. God, who had long been merciful, would then be just....

Eventually, the narration starts to present the sermon directly, but without quoting, and without the marks of paraphrase in its syntax. The two voices seem to have merged completely:

> And this day will come, shall come, must come; the day of death and the day of judgment. It is appointed unto man to die and after death the judgment. Death is certain. The time and manner are uncertain...

The narrator no longer seems to be telling us what the priest said, so much as saying it directly. Our close alignment with Stephen's perspective allows us to "experience" this sermon more or less from his position as an audience member in the congregation.

The priest's rhetoric becomes the "action" of this chapter. Since Stephen is convinced that "every word was for him," when we read the narrator's paraphrase of the sermon, we are able to gauge Stephen's reaction at the same time. Father Arnall, who presumably gives the sermon (since he is running the retreat), is named initially before being reduced to "the priest." He eventually recedes as a direct presence in the narrative altogether. His language becomes, then, much less personalized, underscoring just how much Stephen is tending to take this as God's direct word, and as an unadulterated voice of absolute authority.

Stephen's reaction to the sermon, then, represents a kind of regression. Throughout Chapter Two, as we recognized, Stephen was becoming increasingly suspicious of authority figures. In the early section of Chapter Three, as his classmates are encouraging him to stall the teacher with a series of obscure and difficult theological questions, we are reminded of his lack of deep regard for authority. However, throughout Chapter Three, he becomes less critical and more accepting of the authority of the clergy, represented by Father Arnall at the retreat, and the old priest at the chapel to whom Stephen confesses. His relationship to religion here is more emotional and simplistic. He does not question the authorities on the finer points of Catholic doctrine, but fears and respects them, and takes their words and their power directly to heart.

This is one of several ways in which Stephen's repentance represents a return to innocence. The reappearance of Father Arnall in the novel, whom we last saw in Chapter One, at Clongowes, recalls us to the time when Stephen was younger:

> The figure of his old master, so strangely rearisen, brought back to Stephen's mind his life at Clongowes: the wide playgrounds, swarming with boys, the square ditch, the little cemetery off the main avenue of limes where he had dreamed of being buried, the firelight on the wall of the infirmary where he lay sick, the sorrowful face of Brother Michael. His soul, as these memories came back to him, became again a child's soul.

Whereas in Chapter Two, Stephen was eager to distance himself from those days, when "the memory of his childhood [was] dim" and he could not "call forth...vivid moments" but "only names," seeing Father Arnall calls up vivid and detailed memories for Stephen. In a sense, these are "memories" for the reader, too, as they cause us to recall how Stephen was then. The very appearance of Father Arnall symbolizes how this retreat will be a return to a state of innocence for Stephen, who assumes a childlike openness as he listens to the sermon. The narrator's language at the end of the chapter, after Stephen has repented and confessed, recalls the more childlike rhythms of Chapter One:

> He had confessed and God had pardoned him. His soul was made fair and holy once more, holy and happy. It would be beautiful to die if God so willed. It was beautiful to live if God so willed, to live in grace a life of peace and virtue and forbearance with others.

The convention of the priest calling him "my child" takes on special significance, as Stephen's confession represents a revision to his more childlike submission to voices of authority.

If the effect of Stephen's repentance is a seeming return to a state of lost innocence, then the priest's sermon certainly contributes to this. Stephen's repentance and change of heart are motivated by fear more than anything else. The sermon focuses solely on the threat of the tortures of hell; the method is to intimidate the young boys into behaving according to the law of God. His reason for living a pious life never move beyond intimidation. He spends a large portion of his sermon describing hell's geographical and physical characteristics with quasi-scientific exactness, comparing hell's heat and fire to heat and fire on earth, trying to impress upon the boys in earthly terms the inconceivable and unearthly extremity and eternity of hell's torments. The priest never offers a positive reason to believe in and follow God, but rests his argument solely on the consequences of a sinful life.

His very poetic and imaginative reconstruction of hell appeals to Stephen's artistic sensibility rather than to his intellect. Stephen's remorse, then, is not moral or intellectual in character—it is motivated primarily by fear of hell, God's wrath, and eternal damnation. Like the omnipresent threat of pandying or flogging at Clongowes, hell functions as an intimidation tactic, divorced from any moral choice. In Chapter Three, Joyce seems to be making his most explicit critique of the Catholic church. Although the church functions throughout the novel as one of the primary fetters which Stephen Dedalus tries to free himself from, in this chapter its mechanisms are portrayed most explicitly as coercive, simplistic, and reductive.

Stephen's repentance and spiritual rebirth has an immediate effect on his attitude toward his peers. Walking home from confession, he is pleased "to live in grace a life of peace and virtue and forbearance with others." At communion the next day, he partakes humbly of the communal spirit of the ritual:

> The boys were all there, kneeling in their places. He knelt among them, happy and shy....
> He knelt before the altar with his classmates, holding the altar cloth with them over a living rail of hands.

Stephen seems to feel a connection with his peers for the first time in the novel. His alienation and insecurity, which he felt as a child, and his proud exile, which developed as an adolescent, all seem to be abandoned in favor of this feeling of brotherhood and connectedness.

Before his confession, however, Stephen's sense of detachment and singularity is still present. His reaction to the sermon is intensely personal—he interprets it as a personal message from God, and the narrator illustrates how Stephen's extreme reaction is unique among his classmates. After the first sermon, while Stephen is vividly imagining his own death and damnation, the other students' voices serve to undercut and deflate his personal drama:

> His flesh shrank together as it felt the approach of the ravenous tongues of flames, dried up as it felt about it the swirl of stifling air. He had died. Yes. He was judged. A wave of fire swept through his body: the first. Again a wave. His brain began to glow. Another. His brain was simmering and bubbling within the cracking tenement of the skull. Flames burst forth from his skull like a corolla, shrieking like voices:
>
> —Hell! Hell! Hell! Hell! Hell!
> Voices spoke near him:
> —On hell.
> —I suppose he rubbed it into you well.
> —You bet he did. He put us all into a blue funk.
> —That's what you fellows want: and plenty of it to make you work.

The sound, *like* voices, in Stephen's imagination is juxtaposed with the actual voices of Mr. Tate and Vincent Heron. The colloquial chattiness of their reaction—"he rubbed it into you," "you bet he did"—presents a plainer reality next to Stephen's imaginative life, suggesting that Stephen's egotism results in an overreaction on his part. Mr. Tate jokingly reduces the voice of God which has quaked Stephen's soul to a mere scare tactic to keep the students working. The narrator presents Stephen's experience of these things literally, physically, which furthers this sense of two separate realities here. Stephen's skull is melting, flames are shooting from his head, while Mr. Tate and Heron joke about the students being put into a "blue funk."

We might sense a tone of elitism or superiority in Stephen's reaction, if we keep in mind his attitude of contempt toward the other students' shows of piety earlier. It is easy to see how his reaction would seem, to him, as the "real" or "righteous" one, while theirs is shallow and trivial. The same kind of operative distinction between Stephen's imaginative reality and ordinary life, which characterized Chapter Two, is at work here. We can see, in this scene, Stephen's poetic and dramatic imagination coloring his experience as unique and incommunicable, participating in and contributing to his feeling of alienation.

His feelings of contempt and disdain for his peers might still be somewhat active as he decides that he must confess his sins, "but not there among his school companions." Ostensibly, his motive here is "shame" and "abjection of spirit"—he feels he is not worthy to confess in the college chapel among their "boyish hearts." Implicit in this humility, however, is the same kind of feeling of exile, detachment, and superiority which motivated his "contempt" for them earlier in the chapter. Stephen does not feel that he is a part of this community. Before, he had seen their "boyishness" as a limiting and infuriating immaturity. Now, however, he sees it as an innocence which he has lost.

As he is wandering the streets looking for a chapel, he sees "frowsy girls" along the side of the road. His "humiliation" that their souls may be dearer to God than his has its root in an implicit feeling of superiority or egotism. The implication, we suppose, is that he feels his soul should be dearer to God. Stephen's confession and repentance is motivated, in part, by a desire to change all this—while waiting his turn in the chapel, he is inspired by thinking about Jesus, and his love for the "poor and simple people." Before confession, Stephen's motivation is expressed thus:

> He would be at one with others and with God. He would love his neighbor. He would love God Who had made and loved him. He would kneel and pray with others and be happy. God would look down on him and on them and would love them all.

This communally oriented spirit is uncharacteristic of the Stephen we know. He seeks to identify himself with the group, to have his individual identity—which until now has been most important to him—subsumed under a group identity, and under God.

This represents another important reversion of the tendencies we recognized in Chapter Two. Stephen is trying to relinquish the role of exile he began to assume then. His confession and repentance is motivated by and seems to result in a feeling of brotherhood and communion with humanity. His religious rebirth "sets back the clock" in various ways. It represents a return to a state of innocence, reconciling his sins with God; it represents a new, less critical attitude toward authority, and a less hostile attitude toward his peers. Up to this point, Stephen's individual identity was most important, and he sought only to find some means of escape from ordinary Dublin life, but he now seems reconciled to his peers and to his environment. The image of Stephen wandering the dark streets to find a chapel near the end of Chapter Three is a clear echo of the end of Chapter Two, when he wanders the streets looking for a woman. Do we understand this as a kind of revision of this earlier scene, an attempt at starting over, this time on the "right foot"? Or do we hear an ironic echo of the earlier Stephen even here, suggesting that perhaps his change of heart is neither permanent nor desirable? He seems to have changed profoundly as Chapter Three closes—he seems happy to be a part of a "living rail of hands," to have conformed to the authority of God and the church. However, we should be suspicious, by now, of this novel's climaxes, and wonder, as we begin Chapter Four, whether this transformation is really for the better.

Study Questions

1. What is Stephen's attitude toward his sinful lifestyle as Chapter Three opens?

2. What religious office does Stephen hold at Belvedere?

3. What is important about St. Francis Xavier, according to the rector?

4. What are the "four last things" the sermons will cover during the retreat?

5. What effect does seeing Father Arnall have upon Stephen?

6. Why does Stephen feel he cannot confess at the college chapel?

7. Describe Stephen's vision of hell.

8. What effect does seeing the "frowsy girls" on the side of the road have on Stephen?

9. How old is Stephen in Chapter Three?

10. What does the priest tell Stephen after confession?

Answers

1. Stephen claims to be indifferent; he does not feel shame or guilt around his classmates, and is too proud to pray to God and repent.

2. Stephen is prefect of the sodality of the Blessed Virgin Mary.

3. The rector tells the boys that St. Francis Xavier was one of the original Jesuits, one of the first followers of Ignatius. He was known for converting people in the Indies, Africa, and Asia. According to the rector, he once converted 10,000 in one month.

4. The "four last things" are death, judgment, hell, and heaven. The topic of the sermons never reach heaven, as promised.

5. Seeing Father Arnall recalls Stephen to his Clongowes days, making his soul "become again a child's soul," symbolizing how this retreat signifies a return to innocence for him.

6. Stephen does not want to confess along with his classmates out of shame for the extent of his sins.

7. Stephen imagines hell as peopled with goat-like, half-human creatures who encircle him, mumbling incoherently. It is a land of dry thistle and weeds, solid excrement, and dim light.

8. When Stephen sees the poor girls, he is ashamed and humiliated at the thought that their souls are dearer to God than his.

9. Stephen tells the priest during confession that he is 16 years old.

10. The priest tells Stephen to resist the Devil's temptation, to repent, and to give up his life of sin. He tells Stephen to pray to the Virgin Mary when he is tempted.

Suggested Essay Topics

1. In many ways, Chapter Three represents a reversal of some of the tendencies Stephen developed in Chapter Two. Discuss the changes in his attitude toward authority figures, his peers, and his identity as an individual. In what ways does Stephen seem to have changed as the chapter closes?

2. Stephen interprets Father Arnall's sermons as a personal message, sensing that "every word" of it was intended "for him." Reread the sermons carefully. What can you identify about the language and rhetorical strategy of the sermons that would appeal so strongly to Stephen? Some things to look for in the descriptions of hell might include: the descriptions of hell's torments, the language of exile used here; the poetic and metaphorical language; and the language of the senses and the body.

3. What is the effect of the narrator aligning us with Stephen Dedalus' perspective during the sermons? How does this color our perspective toward the sermons, which seem otherwise to be presented word-for-word? How would the chapter read differently if it were aligned with the perspective of Vincent Heron, for example? Does our awareness of Stephen's idiosyncratic character affect our understanding of the communion scene at the end?

Chapter 4

New Characters:

The Director: *at Belvedere College, asks Stephen to consider joining the priesthood*

Dan Crosby: *a tutor, who goes with Stephen's father to find out about the university for Stephen*

Dwyer, Towser, Shuley, Ennis, Connolly: *acquaintances of Stephen's; he sees them swimming near the strand*

Summary

Stephen has now dedicated his life to the service of God—each day is structured around prayer, ritual, and religious devotions. He attends mass each morning, and offers ejaculations and prayers each day for the souls in purgatory. He sees his daily life now in terms of eternity, and senses an immediate connection between his acts on earth and their repercussions in heaven. Each of his three daily chaplets is dedicated to one of the "three theological virtues," Father, Son and Holy Ghost; each day of the week is devoted toward gaining one of the seven gifts of the Holy Ghost, and toward driving out each of the seven deadly sins.

Stephen views every aspect of his life as a gift from God; the world now exists for him "as a theorem of divine power and love and universality." He tries to mortify and discipline each of his senses. He keeps his eyes to the ground, doesn't try to avoid loud or unpleasant noises, intentionally subjects himself to unpleasant smells, and is strict about his diet, making sure he does not enjoy his food. He goes to great efforts to remain physically uncomfortable, both while sleeping and awake.

He is discouraged that, despite his efforts, he continues to get angry or impatient with others for trivial reasons. However, he takes great pleasure in being able to avoid temptation, though he periodically doubts how completely he has changed his life. In confession, he sometimes has to repeat an earlier sin because he sins so infrequently now. Stephen is frustrated, because it seems that he will never be able to fully escape the sins which he had struggled to confess at the end of Chapter Three.

In the next section, Stephen is speaking with the director of Belvedere College. He has been summoned to the director's office, and, while making friendly and respectful small-talk, Stephen wonders why he has really been sent there. They begin talking about the Dominican and Franciscan orders, and of their respective styles of dress.

Stephen begins to think about his experiences with the Jesuits at school. He continues to hold them in high regard, although they sometimes seem "a little childish" in their judgments.

The director soon comes to the point, however, asking if Stephen has ever felt a vocation to join the priesthood. Stephen starts to answer "yes," but remains silent. He tells the priest that he has "sometimes thought of it." The priest tells him that only one or two boys from the college will be the sort who will be called by God, and suggests that Stephen, with his intelligence, devotion, and leadership qualities, might be one. The priest begins to talk of the power and authority a priest has, which reminds Stephen of "his own proud musings" on the subject, when he had imagined himself as a priest. The idea seems to appeal to him—he is attracted to the secret knowledge and power the priesthood could give him.

The priest tells him that his mass the next morning will be specially dedicated so that God may reveal His will to Stephen. He cautions Stephen to be certain of his decision, because it is a final one, on which the salvation of his soul may depend.

As he leaves the director's office, Stephen and the director shake hands. Stephen notes the gravity of the expression on the priest's face. Walking home, he tries to imagine himself as a priest. Remembering the "troubling odour" of Clongowes, he begins to

feel restless and confused. He begins to imagine how restless and unhappy he would be, and quickly decides that he could not become a priest, that "he would fall," and that "his destiny was to be elusive of social or religious orders."

Stephen arrives at home, where his brothers and sisters are having tea. He learns that his parents have gone to look at another home. The family is moving again, under pressure from the landlord. The children start to sing, and soon Stephen joins them. It pains him to hear the "overture of weariness" in their young voices, and he thinks sadly of the "weariness and pain" of all generations of children.

In the next section, Stephen is pacing anxiously as his father and Dan Crosby, his tutor, have gone to find out about the university for him. After an hour of waiting, he leaves for the Bull, a sandy island near the mouth of the Liffey.

While walking, he thinks of the university. He knows his mother is hostile to the idea, which Stephen takes as an indication of how their lives are drifting apart. He still feels that he has been born for some special purpose, and he senses that the university will lead to new adventures.

As he crosses the bridge on the way to the Bull, he passes a squad of Christian Brothers, walking two by two. He has a moment of shame or regret for refusing to join the priesthood, but reassures himself that their life is not for him.

He thinks of a phrase he has read, "A day of dappled seaborne clouds," and marvels at how the words seem to capture the moment so perfectly. He muses about what it is that fascinates him about words.

Having crossed the bridge, he heads toward the sea. Looking at the clouds coming in from the sea, he thinks of Europe, where they have come from. His reverie is interrupted, however, by a group of his classmates who are bathing in the sea. They call to him, and he stops briefly to chat, impatient with their immaturity, and repulsed by their adolescent nakedness. They call his name in Latinate and Greek forms, "Stephenos Dedalos" and "Stephanoumenos," which makes him think of his name as a prophecy. He understands Daedalus, the mythical artificer, as a "symbol of the artist forging anew in his workshop out of the

sluggish matter of the earth a new soaring impalpable imperishable being," and wonders if this is an indication of his calling in life. He feels excited, and knows he must dedicate his life and soul to art.

He walks away from the boys, heading down the strand, along the sea. He sees a girl alone, wading in the sea, with her skirts pinned up around her waist. She seems to him like a bird, and he takes her as a sign of his newly chosen destiny. Their eyes meet, but they do not speak. Stephen wanders off, delirious with excitement. He has lost track of time and, realizing it is late and he has wandered far out of his way, he runs back toward the land. He lays down before long, and sleeps. When he awakes, it is evening, and the new moon has risen.

Analysis

In this crucial, climactic chapter, Stephen's awareness of his artistic vision begins to crystallize. Over the course of the chapter, he frees himself from the "nets" of the church, and from his family, embracing the role of the exile figure more explicitly than before. As the chapter ends, Stephen is alone on the seashore, facing away from Ireland, toward Europe. He has literally left his father behind, who had gone to see about the university for him. And he has left the church behind, as he decides he cannot become a priest, and must instead discover his destiny on his own, apart from the trappings of religion, family, or nation. Just as, over the course of Chapter Three, Stephen had undergone an almost total religious transformation, over the course of this chapter his outlook changes greatly. There is a progression in Chapter Four from the rigid order of Stephen's religious devotion and the promise of an even more rigid order in the priesthood, to uncertainty and loss of faith, disorder and confusion, and back to a certainty in a different kind of calling, that of creative art.

Stephen's religious devotion, at the start of this chapter, has none of the passion of his conversion. Stephen's piety is rigidly structured, almost monkish—the narrator's language in this first section is prosaic, dry and businesslike, cataloging Stephen's tight and orderly schedule of religious devotion. Again, we see how what had seemed a passionate and climactic epiphany—Stephen's repentance and

religious awakening at the end of Chapter Three—seems to become, at the start of the next chapter, a dull and habitual routine.

Stephen's religious devotion has a particularly mathematical and economical character, which tends to undercut our sense of his seriousness. The weeks and even the days of his life are broken down into numbered segments. His prayers for the souls in purgatory are described as a kind of transaction with God; Stephen is anxious that he "could never know how much temporal punishment he had remitted by way of suffrage for the agonizing souls." He constantly frets that he has not been able to amass enough to make an appreciable difference. The economic metaphors are made more explicit further on, as Stephen imagines the immediate repercussions in heaven of his acts of devotion on earth:

> At times his sense of such immediate repercussion was so lively that he seemed to feel his soul in devotion pressing like fingers the keyboard of a great cash register and to see the amount of his purchase start forth immediately in heaven.

Though Stephen is certainly adamant in his dedication to the religious life, the narrator seems to be subtly parodying his piety in passages like this. When Stephen views his prayers in terms of "the amount of his purchase," imagining a "great cash register" in heaven, his religious dedication seems simplistic and reductive.

While on the one hand this portrayal of Stephen's faith seems rather ridiculous and simplistic, on the other hand, it represents a vividly imaginative kind of belief. In a manner which is typical of Stephen, his religious life colors his daily life in every aspect—he now understands his life in terms of eternity, and imagines heaven's response to his every action. His imagination is typically poetic and metaphorical in character. For example, when he recites the rosary prayers while walking down the street, he imagines the beads "transformed...into coronals of flowers of such vague unearthly texture that they seemed to him as hueless and odorless as they were nameless." His daily rituals, although certainly routine and habitualized to an extreme degree, represent for Stephen an active and vivid imaginative life.

Religion, for Stephen, serves to keep him detached from ordinary Dublin life—its effect on his imagination can be accurately compared to the effect of the *Count of Monte Cristo in* Chapter Two. Although it is imaginative, however, his devotion becomes less and less passionate. He can comprehend minute theological details, but cannot conceive of the notion of God's eternal love:

> The imagery through which the nature and kinship of the Three Persons of the Trinity were darkly shadowed forth in the books of devotion which he read...were easier of acceptance by his mind by reason of their august incomprehensibility that was the simple fact that God had loved his soul from all eternity, for ages before he had been born into the world, for ages before the world itself had existed.

It is not just God's love which Stephen finds difficult to understand or to feel:

> He had heard the names of the passions of love and hate pronounced solemnly on the stage and in the pulpit, had found them set forth solemnly in books, and had wondered why his soul was unable to harbour them for any time or to force his lips to utter their names with conviction.

Books do not connect to life for Stephen, and his faith is more intellectual than emotional. Once the lust from which he suffered has been effectively banished, his mind is left "lucid and indifferent." The same kind of indifference that had characterized Stephen's spiritual life before his conversion is used to characterize him now—the narrator suggests that in some sense maybe Stephen's life has not charged as completely as it may seem.

He is still cut off from other people, for example. There is a detached, intellectual quality to his religious faith. He looks at the world as evidence of divine power, but in a way that does not necessarily reveal any appreciation or love for the beauty in the world:

> The world for all its solid substance and complexity no longer existed for his soul save as a theorem of divine power and love and universality.

Stephen is certainly "otherworldly" in his religious devotion. It is as if his life is only a brief preparation for eternity, part of some "divine purpose" that he "dared not question." It is difficult for him to "understand why it was in any way necessary that he should continue to live."

The absurdities of his efforts to mortify his senses illustrate how his religious faith is cutting him off from the world around him. This contrasts strongly with the extremely physical language which characterized Stephen at the start of Chapter Three, and represents one way that he has changed in Chapter Four. One way he has not changed, however, is how detached he is from life around him. In Chapter Three, it was as a result of this physicality, and the nature of his sin, that he felt no sense of community with those around him. In this chapter, after the communion scene with Stephen kneeling among his classmates, we might assume that he is now on some common ground with them, and is a part of their community. Instead, however, he finds that "To merge his life in the common tide of other lives was harder for him than any fasting or prayer." Despite his efforts, he is still isolated from his peers. Religion for Stephen is an intensely private, almost solipsistic experience, and becomes only one more way that he feels alienated from those around him.

In some ways, we might suspect that Stephen's religious transformation is incomplete. But his dedication is so extreme that when the director of Belvedere asks him if he has considered joining the priesthood, we may very well assume that he will accept the offer. His devotion is already very priestlike in its rigid self-discipline, and in its effect of keeping him cut off from the flow of ordinary life. He indeed seems, as the priest suggests, an ideal candidate.

At the same time, however, many aspects of the language used to describe this scene prefigure Stephen's rejection of the offer, and ultimately of the church and religious life altogether. The priest himself is described in the language of death and stagnation:

> The priest's face was in total shadow but the waning daylight from behind him touched the deeply grooved temples and the curves of the skull.

His face, which we would associate with a living individual, is not visible in the dim light. Only his skull, which we associate with anonymity and death, can be perceived. His voice is described more than once as "grave and cordial," and the double meaning of "grave" resonates strongly. The hour of dusk suggests a fading and waning life.

When they begin talking about the styles of dress of different orders of the priesthood, and how they are often impractical and ridiculous, the extent to which a priest must remain detached from normal life is emphasized. This, of course, should appeal to Stephen, as he has seen himself as detached from normal life for some time now. But the wandering of Stephen's mind as the priest is slowly leading up to his point suggests that perhaps he is not ready for this kind of commitment:

> The names of articles of dress worn by women or of certain soft and delicate stuffs used in their making brought always to his mind a delicate and sinful perfume.... It had shocked him too when he had felt for the first time beneath his tremulous fingers the brittle texture of a woman's stocking....

It is not an encouraging sign that Stephen is thinking, with no sign of guilt or regret, of his experiences with the prostitutes while the priest is building up toward asking him to consider joining the priesthood.

Stephen's attitude toward the priest is similarly suggestive of his eventual refusal. He is respectful, but also somewhat impatient and indulgent as he waits for the priest to stop beating around the bush. This reflects his overall attitude toward the Jesuits these days. He is respectful of the order, and all they have done for him, but he is also subtly dissatisfied with them. He thinks fondly and without resentment of the way they ran the schools he has attended—he has even forgiven the pandying incident from Chapter One. However, he associates the Jesuits with a younger phase of his life, and it does not seem that he will continue among them:

> Lately some of their judgments had sounded a little childish in his ears and had made him feel a regret and pity as though he were slowly passing out of an accustomed world and were hearing its language for the last time.

He remembers an incident where a priest was condemning Victor Hugo for turning against the church, which incites an "unresting doubt" in Stephen's mind. He associates Jesuit authority with his childhood, and it is apparent that he has matured since then, and is beginning to feel superior to them in some ways.

Despite these numerous suggestions to the contrary, the idea of the priesthood does appeal to Stephen initially. He has indeed thought of it before this, and the priest speaks directly to the aspects of the priesthood that appeal most to Stephen: the privilege, power, and prestige of the office. His initial response is positive:

> A flame began to flutter again on Stephen's cheek as he heard in this proud address an echo of his own proud musings. How often he had seen himself as a priest wielding calmly and humbly the awful power of which angels and saints stood in reverence! His soul loved to muse in secret on this desire. He had seen himself, a young and silent mannered priest, entering a confession swiftly, incensing, genuflecting, accomplishing the vague acts of the priesthood which pleased him by reason of their semblance of reality and of their distance from it.

Both the priest's description and Stephen's response recall one of his earlier vices: pride. The appeal of the priesthood for Stephen involves power, secrecy, and access to privileged knowledge. He pictures himself a priest, in a highly dramatic and literary fashion. It represents for him a "secret desire," a fantasy. There is an unhealthy degree of sexual voyeurism and self-satisfied pride in his hope to "know the sins, the sinful longings and sinful thoughts and sinful acts, of others, hearing them murmured into his ears in the confessional under the shame of a darkened chapel by the lips of women and girls."

Stephen imagines taking pleasure in hearing other people's sins, and in the pride he would feel at being above and beyond such a sinful existence: "no touch of sin would linger upon the hands with which he would elevate and break the host." It is almost as if the priesthood would afford an opportunity to vent the desires he apparently is not free from, but in a "safe," sinless environment.

His reasons for being attracted to the priesthood are all self-indulgent and proud. He has no thoughts of helping others, of the benefits of his works on the world around him. The priest's description of the power and privilege, and Stephen's fantasies, all glorify the priesthood for the wrong reasons. This suggests again that Stephen is perhaps not as changed as it would seem.

Stephen's picture of a priestly life is one of isolation, which is consistent with the role of exile which has appealed to him in different forms throughout the novel. As he comes out of the director's office, this isolation from his peers is emphasized:

> Towards Findlater's church a quartet of young men were striding along with linked arms, swaying their heads and stepping to the agile melody of their leader's concertina.

Stephen stands apart, alone; we could never picture him strolling across campus in this manner. The students' "linked arms" recall the "living rail of hands" of which Stephen is a part in the communion scene at the end of Chapter Three. His aspiration to become a part of his community has been abandoned, and indeed his imaginative visualization of himself as a priest emphasizes his singularity and detachment.

In fact, it is the thought of the community of the priesthood which changes his mind. He realizes that life as a priest would cost him the individuality he has cultivated for so long:

> The chill and order of the life repelled him. He saw himself rising in the cold of the morning and filing down with the others to early mass and trying vainly to struggle with his prayers against the fainting sickness of his stomach. He saw himself sitting at dinner with the community of a college. What, then, had become of that deeprooted shyness of his which had made him loth to eat or drink under a strange roof? What had come of the pride of his spirit which had always made him conceive of himself as a being apart in every order?

Again, he imagines himself, pictures himself a priest, but this time in a more negative light. The idea of being part of a community of priests, one among many, does not appeal to Stephen's sense of pride or individuality. He remembers that his sense of a special purpose for his life had always been rooted in the keen sense that he is special, that he is unlike other people, a "being apart in every order":

> He would never swing the thurible before the tabernacle as a priest. His destiny was to be elusive of social or religious orders.... He was destined to learn his own wisdom apart from others or to learn the wisdom of others himself wandering among the snares of the world.

The commitment involved in joining the community of the priesthood threatens to stifle Stephen's individual ego. When he rejects the priesthood, he affirms the "snares of the world," and accepts the idea that to fulfill his destiny, he may have to sin in the eyes of the church:

> The snares of the world were its ways of sin. He would fall. He had not yet fallen but he would fall silently, in an instant. Not to fall was too hard, too hard....

Stephen accepts the idea that to sin is human, and that the rigid constraints of his religious faith will continue to threaten his freedom to develop.

As he returns, the disorder of the Dedalus household symbolically contrasts with the "order" of the priesthood. While earlier in the novel, the declining status of the family's wealth had caused Stephen despair and shame, he now embraces it. This represents his new perspective on his life: Stephen affirms disorder, fluidity and change over the rigidity and commitment of the priesthood. As he joins his younger brothers and sisters in song— probably the most notable example of familial love in the novel— he seems to feel more at home with them than he would ever feel in the company of priests. As this section ends, Stephen is thinking of the privileges he has had, which his younger siblings will not have. "All that had been denied them had been freely given to him, the eldest: but the quiet glow of evening showed him in their faces no sign of rancour." In a rare selfless moment, Stephen seems to appreciate the opportunities he had despite his family's decline.

In the final section of the chapter, we have what is considered by most readers to be the major climax of the novel. Stephen has gone off alone, along the seashore. Seeing a girl bathing alone, he has an intense vision of his life as an artist. However, the narrative leaves open the possibility that this climax may be somewhat ironic, and that Stephen might be under a delusion. After all, Chapter Three had ended with a spiritual climax of comparable energy— by now we are perhaps more suspicious.

Stephen's artistic awakening is spawned initially by a poetic phrase, "A day of dappled seaborne clouds," which came to mind as he walked alone. Stephen has been fascinated by language since he was a young boy, only here his enthusiasm is given a more complete expression, and more directly affects his conception of his life. He turns this phrase over and over in his mind, fascinated by the sound and rhythm of the words themselves.

His reverie is interrupted, however, as he comes across a group of his classmates bathing. Once again, Stephen's imaginative "voices," in this case the European voices "from beyond the world" of Dublin, are interrupted by literal, earthbound voices, those of the boys calling his name. This is similar to the moment when, in his religious trance, Stephen heard the voices of hell and the narrator juxtaposed those against the voices of Mr. Tate and Vincent Heron speaking in ordinary, casual voices. Here, the narrator creates a stark contrast between the world of Stephen's imagination and the reality that surrounds him. He is repulsed by the sight and sound of these boys, and sets himself apart from them:

> He stood still in deference to their calls and parried their banter with easy words. How characterless they looked: Shuley without his deep unbuttoned collar, Ennis without his scarlet belt with the snaky clasp, and Connolly without his Norfolk coat with the flapless sidepockets! It was a pain to see them and a swordlike pain to see the signs of adolescence that made repellent their pitiable nakedness.... But he, apart from them and in silence, remembered in what dread he stood of the mystery of his own body.

There is an interesting combination of identification and distance in this passage. Stephen is still clearly trying to separate himself from the other boys his age—he stands apart, silent, and only engages with them in a superficial and detached manner. He is pained by what he has in common with them, but in this pain he recognizes a kind of common bond with his peers, a limit to his pose of detachment. The narrator shows us both how distinct Stephen is from others his age, while at the same time suggesting that his dreams and fantasies are primarily imaginative. He is perhaps not as different from other boys as he thinks.

When Stephen sees the girl bathing in the sea, he interprets every aspect of their wordless encounter in symbolic terms—she seems to him like a bird, representing Ireland, sexuality, femininity and creation all at once. The image of a bird suggests Stephen's new desire for flight from Ireland, to be free of the "nets" of religion, nation, and family. He interprets this encounter as an otherworldly visitation, a profound spiritual experience that validates and christens his new conception of himself as an artist.

When he encounters the girl, we already know that Stephen is especially ripe to interpret things symbolically. This new capacity is one manifestation of his artistic and poetic awakening, and stems directly from his meditation on language and its mysterious appeal. When the boys interrupt his thoughts about language and poetry, they call his name in pseudo-Greek and Latinate constructions. Stephen then recognizes an aspect of his name that he had not considered before—he thinks of the mythological figure of Daedalus, the great artificer, and Icarus his son, who escaped from Crete using wings which Daedalus created out of feathers and beeswax. He takes this as a kind of "prophecy," a sign that the role of creator is the special purpose he has sensed since childhood. The figure of Daedalus also suggests the escape Stephen imagines his art will be able to provide—an escape both from dull, ordinary life, and from Dublin and Ireland:

> Now, at the name of the fabulous artificer, he seemed to hear the noise of dim waves and to see a winged form flying above the waves and slowly climbing the air. What did it mean? Was it a quaint device opening a page of some medieval book of prophecies and symbols, a hawklike man flying sunward above the sea, a prophecy of the end he had been born to serve and had been following through the mists of childhood and boyhood, a symbol of the artist forging anew in his workshop out of the sluggish matter of the earth a new soaring impalpable imperishable being?

The reference to a "hawklike man flying sunward" suggests Icarus rather than Daedalus, who disregarded his father's advice and flew too close to the sun, fatally melting his wings. This suggests the amount of risk involved in Stephen's imaginative bid for freedom, and how the pride that has been his vice in the past might ultimately lead to his destruction.

Thinking about his name and the vision it inspires, Stephen immediately asks himself, "what did it mean?" He now assumes that things around him can have symbolic import, and so when he encounters the girl in the water, his immediate perception reveals a complex process of interpretation:

> A girl stood before him in midstream, alone and still, gazing out to sea. She seemed like one whom magic had changed into the likeness of a strange and beautiful seabird. Her long slender bare legs were delicate as a crane's and pure save where an emerald trail of seaweed had fashioned itself as a sign upon the flesh.

This scene, like any in the novel, is mediated by Stephen's consciousness. We observe him interpreting her as a symbol, rather than reading her as one ourselves. Stephen is transforming everything about her as he perceives it, and we are always aware that this is only a representation of how she "seemed" to him. And his interpretive process is complex and multi-leveled: she is as a seabird, and both the sea and the potential for flight suggest Stephen's turn of attention away from Ireland and toward Europe. The "emerald" trail of seaweed clearly suggests Ireland (the "emerald isle), and he interprets this immediately and without hesitation "as a sign."

This scene is richly suggestive in its symbolism in its own right, and can indeed inform and influence our interpretation of the novel and Stephen's artistic awakening. This double-leveled structure, by which we are experiencing the symbol at a remove, seeing him make a symbol out of her, allows us a distinct distance from the scene. We might feel that this is not "really" a symbol at all, but merely an example of the narrator showing us the temper of Stephen's mind at the time, which causes him to see his life in a symbolic light. We might feel that the narrator is creating another "false climax," as he has in every chapter so far, and that Stephen is really deluded in his enthusiasm and certainty. By now we are certainly suspicious of Stephen's revelations; we might not be as sure as Stephen that his name is a "prophecy."

The narrative artfully leaves all its options alive. The tone of these closing pages is genuinely triumphant, and these symbols, which Stephen recognizes, are indeed richly suggestive and multivalent in their own right, and really do offer some useful interpretive perspectives on the meaning of the novel as a whole. At the same time, the pace of this narrative has fostered in us a suspicious and subtly ironic attitude toward Stephen. We are not easily convinced, by this point in the novel, that Stephen's epiphanies are genuine. Our experience of this profound moment of significance in Stephen's life remains contingent on the developments of the next chapter. Either Stephen has had a spiritual awakening and will dedicate his life to artistic creation, and will continue to distance himself from his religion and nation in an effort to serve this end, or, like his religious awaking, this will prove to be another instructive delusion.

Study Questions

1. Describe Stephen's daily life at the start of Chapter Four.

2. Why does Stephen have trouble mortifying his sense of smell?

3. What is Stephen's opinion of the Jesuits now?

4. How does Stephen reply when the director of Belvedere asks him if he feels he may have a vocation for the priesthood?

5. What appeals to Stephen about the priesthood?

6. What repels Stephen about the priesthood?

7. Why aren't Stephen's parents at home when he gets in?

8. What phrase comes to Stephen's mind as he crosses the bridge to the Bull?

9. What symbolic import does Stephen recognize in his name?

10. How does Stephen interpret his encounter with the bathing girl along the strand?

Answers

1. Stephen's day is structured around religious devotions—he attends morning Mass each day, carries his rosary in his pocket, and prays systematically throughout the day. He says three chaplets a day for the three theological virtues, while dedicating each day toward gaining one of the seven gifts of the Holy Ghost, and toward driving out each of the seven deadly sins.

2. Stephen has trouble mortifying his sense of smell because he finds that he has little natural repugnance to odor, and it is difficult for him to find a smell unpleasant enough to disturb him. He ultimately finds that the smell of "long-standing urine" does the trick.

3. Stephen still respects the Jesuits, and is grateful for all they have done for him, but he admits that their judgments and opinions now seem "a little childish" to him. It is clear that Stephen feels that he is outgrowing a phase of his life that the Jesuits represent.

4. Stephen replies that he has "sometimes thought of it," but he remains noncommittal.

5. Stephen is attracted to the power, privilege, and secret knowledge that the priesthood would offer. He is eager to learn the theological secrets, and to hear people's secret confessions.

6. Stephen realizes that to become a priest would be to sacrifice an important degree of his individuality. The idea of being an anonymous member of a community of priests ultimately causes Stephen to reject the director's offer.

7. His younger sister tells him that they have gone to look at another house. Apparently, the family will have to move again, under pressure from the landlord.

8. Stephen thinks of the phrase "A day of dappled seaborne clouds," and is fascinated by the way it seems to capture the moment perfectly. Stephen is fascinated by the sound and rhythm of the words as much as their sense.

9. Stephen reads his name, Dedalus, as a "prophecy." Daedalus was the mythical artificer who escaped from Crete with his son Icarus, using wings built from wax and feathers. Stephen sees Daedalus as a symbol of both art and flight.

10. Stephen interprets her as a symbol, an affirmative sign of his new understanding of his destiny as an artist. She seems to him like a seabird, who represents art, sexuality, femininity, and Ireland.

Suggested Essay Topics

1. Consider the narrator's description of Stephen's daily religious devotions. What does the language used suggest about the nature of Stephen's piety? Does it foreshadow in any way his ultimate rejection of religious life?

2. Compare Stephen's artistic awakening in Chapter Four to his religious awakening in Chapter Three. How are they similar in their effects on Stephen's life, and in the language in which they are presented? In what ways are they different? What do these similarities and differences suggest about the larger themes of the novel?

3. At the end of Chapter Four, Stephen begins to read his name symbolically, as a "prophecy." Then, as he sees the girl bathing on the strand, he interprets this, too, as a "sign." Reread these scenes carefully. What do the symbolic meanings suggested here tell us about the novel as a whole? How do they add to our understanding of Stephen's character?

Chapter 5

New Characters:

Temple: *a gypsy socialist student, he is the instigator of the debate*

Lynch: *student at the university, to whom Stephen sounds off about his theory of aesthetics*

Donovan: *student whom Stephen dislikes; Stephen and Lynch see him on their walk*

Father Moran: *priest with whom Stephen thinks Emma flirts*

Dixon: *medical student at the library with Cranly*

The Captain: *a dwarfish old man, whom Stephen sees at the library*

O'Keefe: *student who riles Temple outside the library*

Goggins: *stout student outside the library*

Glynn: *young man at the library*

Summary

At the start of the final chapter, Stephen is sitting at breakfast in his parents' house. Pawn tickets for clothing are on the table next to him, indicating that the family had to sell more possessions. He asks his mother how fast the clock is, and she tells him he had better hurry. His sisters are asked to clear a spot for Stephen to wash at the sink, and his mother scrubs his neck and ears for him, remarking how dirty he is. His father shouts down to ask if Stephen has left yet, and his sister answers "yes." Stephen makes a sarcastic remark and leaves out the back.

As he is walking, he hears a mad nun yelling in the madhouse, "Jesus! O Jesus! Jesus!," which disturbs and angers Stephen. He is trying to forget about the "voices" of his parents, and religion. Walking alone, he thinks of plays and poems, and the aesthetic theories of Aristotle and Aquinas. He passes a clock that tells him it is eleven o'clock. He tries to remember the day of the week, thinks of the lectures he is scheduled to attend, and realizes that he is late for English. He thinks of that class, and begins to think about his close friend, Cranly. He composes nonsense verse idly in his head, and thinks of the etymology of the word "ivory." He thinks of his Latin studies and Roman history. He sees Trinity, which depresses him, and he looks at the statue of Thomas Moore, the national poet of Ireland. He thinks with affection of his friend Davin, the peasant student, and of Davin's nationalistic sympathies for Ireland. Stephen remembers a story Davin told him once, about encountering a woman alone at night while he was walking on the road, and being invited to her house to spend the night.

His reverie is interrupted by a flower seller, whom Stephen tells he has no money. He walks on and, when he arrives, he realizes it is too late for his French class, too. He goes in early to physics, instead. The physics hall is empty, except for the Dean of Studies, who is lighting a fire. The dean tells Stephen to pay attention, and learn the art of firestarting, one of the "useful arts." Stephen watches silently. They begin comparing different conceptions of art and beauty. Stephen quotes Aquinas, and defines beauty as "that which, when seen, pleases us." The priest asks Stephen when he plans to write his aesthetic theory, and Stephen humbly says he hopes to work up some ideas from Aristotle and Aquinas. Stephen begins to feel uncomfortable around the dean, and perceives the dean's partial attention to what he is saying. They begin to casually debate the usage of the world "funnel," which Stephen does not recognize because in Ireland it is called a "tundish." The priest is English, and Stephen thinks his interest in the new word is feigned. Stephen tries to return to his original subject, and thinks with some distress that the language they are speaking is the dean's national language, not his. Stephen becomes disheartened with their conversation, and the class begins to fill with students. The priest gives Stephen some conventional advice,

and hurries away. Stephen stands at a distance and watches him greet the students.

When the professor comes in, the students respond with "Kentish fire"—a stomping of the feet which could represent either applause or impatience. The professor calls roll, and Stephen's friend Cranly is not in class. A student named Moynihan sarcastically suggests that Cranly is at Leopardstown, a horse racing track. Stephen borrows a piece of notepaper from Moynihan, and idly begins to take notes. Moynihan whispers a ribald joke about "ellipsoidal balls," which causes Stephen to imagine the faculty of the university playing and laughing like animals. A northern Irish student, MacAlister, asks a question, and Stephen thinks about how much he hates this student.

After class, as the students file into the hall, they encounter a student named MacCann who is gathering signatures for a political petition. Cranly, who is waiting outside for Stephen, says, in Latin, that he has signed the petition "for universal peace," in support of Czar Nicholas II. He asks if Stephen is in a bad mood, and Stephen answers, "no." When Moynihan walks by, makes a sarcastic comment about MacCann, and then proceeds to sign the petition, Cranly expresses his disgust. MacCann then sees and greets Stephen, gently teasing him for being late. Students begin to gather, anticipating a "war of wits." MacCann asks Stephen to sign, and a "gipsy student" named Temple begins to talk about socialism and universal brotherhood. Stephen finally responds that he is not interested, and MacCann insults him by calling him a "minor poet." Stephen tells then "keep your icon," referring to the picture of the Czar, and begins to walk away with Temple following him. Cranly leads Temple and Stephen away.

As they talk, it is clear that Temple is annoying Cranly, who attacks him periodically, and pleads with Stephen to ignore Temple. They stop with Davin to watch handball, and Cranly becomes increasingly impatient with Temple. Though Temple appears undaunted by Cranly's insults, he soon leaves. Stephen and Cranly then see their friend Lynch, and Cranly and Lynch begin to wrestle. Stephen asks Davin if he has signed the petition, and Davin nods yes. When Stephen says he hasn't signed, Davin calls him a "born sneerer." When Davin asks why he does not study Irish, Stephen

implies that it is because Emma flirts with the teacher of the Irish course. They begin to discuss Stephen's attitude toward Irish nationalism and culture. Stephen claims to want to "fly by" the "nets" of nationality, language, and religion.

Davin walks off to join Cranly and the handball players, and Stephen and Lynch walk away. They share a cigarette, and Stephen begins to explain his aesthetic theory to Lynch, who pretends to resist, claiming to be hung-over. Stephen defines "pity" and "terror" as they relate to tragedy, defining the "dramatic" and "esthetic" emotions as "static," or arrested, "raised above desire and loathing." Stephen feels that art should not excite "kinetic emotions" like desire, but should serve a more "detached" function, calling forth an "ideal pity" or "ideal desire."

Lynch continues to listen to Stephen, although reluctantly, claiming that he doesn't care about it. Stephen continues to define beauty, using Aquinas' definition, as he did while speaking to the dean earlier. He then discusses the relation between beauty and truth, according to Plato and Aristotle. His discourse is interrupted first by a drag full of iron, then by another student, Donovan, who tells them about exam results, and the field club. As he leaves, Stephen continues to detail his concept of universal beauty, and its relation to perception, and artistic structure, with Lynch now egging him on. Stephen is concerned with what he calls the three basic forms of art: lyrical, epical and dramatic, and the inter-relationship between them. Stephen's picture of artistic creation is of the artist as a kind of God, indifferent to his creation, "paring his fingernails."

As it starts to rain, they head to the library. Lynch tells Stephen that his "beloved" (presumably Emma) is there. He stands with the group silently, glancing at her from time to time. She ignores him, and soon leaves with her friends. Stephen is first bitter and resentful, but then wonders if he has judged her harshly.

As the next section begins, Stephen is waking up at dawn. He feels a seemingly divine inspiration, and begins almost spontaneously to compose lines of verse in his head. Fearing he may lose his inspiration, he gropes around and finds a pencil and cigarette pack, and writes down the first two stanzas of a villanelle. It is clear that he is thinking of Emma as he writes, and he begins to imagine himself singing songs to her. He recalls a brief exchange with her at a dance, and imagines himself as a heretical monk. He thinks of her flirting with a priest, and tells himself that he scorns her, though he admits that this is also a "form of homage."

Having composed an entire villanelle, Stephen recalls writing a poem for her ten years before (in Chapter Two), after they rode the last tram home together. He imagines sending her the poem, and thinks of her family reading and mocking it over breakfast. He then corrects himself, and says that she is "innocent," though still a "temptress." The section ends with Stephen's villanelle:

> Are you not weary of ardent ways,
> Lure of the fallen seraphim?
> Tell no more of enchanted days.
>
> Your eyes have set man's heart ablaze
> And you have had your will of him.
> Are you not weary of ardent ways?
>
> Above the flame the smoke of praise
> Goes up from ocean rim to rim.
> Tell no more of enchanted days.
>
> Our broken cries and mournful lays
> Rise in one eucharistic hymn.
> Are you not weary of ardent ways?
>
> While sacrificing hands upraise
> The chalice flowing to the brim,
> Tell no more of enchanted days.
>
> And still you hold our longing gaze
> With languorous look and lavish limb!
> Are you not weary of ardent ways?
> Tell no more of enchanted days.

In the next section, Stephen is standing on the library steps, watching birds in the sky. He is thinking about his mother, and his plans to leave the country. He thinks of a line from Yeats' play *The Countess Cathleen*, and delights in the pleasurable sound of the words. He thinks with disgust of the opening night of the national theater, where the Dublin audience booed Yeats' play.

Stephen goes inside and meets his friend Cranly, who is talking with a medical student named Dixon. A priest has gone to complain about their chatter, so they decide to leave. They encounter an old man they call "the captain," who is known for his fondness for reading Sir Walter Scott. They encounter a group of students, with Temple at the center. They are joking around, for the most part, teasing Temple. Temple tries to engage Stephen into the discussion, asking if he believes in the law of heredity, while Cranly expresses his disgust. Temple says that he admits that he is a "ballocks," but that Cranly is too, and won't admit it. Emma walks past them, and greets Cranly casually. Stephen thinks of his friend Cranly, and wanders about, on the outskirts of the group thinking to himself. His reverie is interrupted as he picks a louse off his collar—his thoughts then revert to his despair about his impoverished state.

Stephen walks back to the group just as a student named Glynn has come out. They engage in further discussion, this time around the biblical phrase "suffer little children to come unto me." Temple tries to engage the group in a theological debate, but they disregard him. He pursues this, until Cranly chases him away. Stephen tells Cranly he wants to speak with him, and they walk away together.

Cranly stops to say some parting words to the other students, and Stephen goes on ahead to wait. While waiting, he looks in the window of a hotel drawing room and thinks angrily of the "patricians" of Ireland. Stephen wonders how, with his art, he could "hit their conscience" or "cast his shadow over the imaginations of their daughters."

He is soon joined by Cranly, and as they walk off arm in arm Cranly makes an angry remark about Temple. Stephen tells Cranly that he had an "unpleasant quarrel" with his mother over religion earlier that night. Mrs. Dedalus wants Stephen to observe his Easter duty, but he refuses to. Cranly calls Stephen an "excitable man" and warns him to "go easy." Cranly ask Stephen if he believes in the Eucharist, and Stephen answers that he neither believes nor disbelieves, and does not wish to overcome his doubts. Cranly remarks that Stephen's mind is "supersaturated" with the religion he professes to disbelieve.

When Cranly asks if Stephen was "happier" when he believed, Stephen responds by saying that he was "someone else" then.

Cranly asks Stephen if he loves his mother, and Stephen says he does not understand the question. He says that he tried to love God, but is not sure if he succeeded. Cranly asks if Stephen's mother has had a "happy life," and Stephen responds, "how do I know?" Cranly asks about the Dedalus family's economic history, and learns that they were once much wealthier than now. Cranly then supposes that Mrs. Dedalus has suffered much, and encourages Stephen to try to "save her from suffering more." Cranly says that a mother's love is the one sure thing in this world, and tells Stephen that this is more important than this "ideas and ambitions."

Stephen counters by naming prominent intellectuals who placed their "ideas" before their mother's love, and Cranly calls them all pigs. Stephen suggests that Jesus too treated his mother with "scant attention in public," and Cranly replies that perhaps Jesus was "not who he pretended to be," and that he was "a conscious hypocrite." When Cranly asks if it shocked Stephen to hear him say this, Stephen admits that it did. Cranly asks him why a blasphemy would shock someone who professed not to believe, and Stephen replies that he is "not at all sure" that the Catholic religion is false. Stephen admits that part of the reason he will not take communion is because he fears that God might be real. Stephen then checks himself, saying that it is not the power of the Roman Catholic version of God that he fears, but the danger to his soul of committing false homage. When Cranly asks if he will now become a Protestant, Stephen replies dryly that he has not lost his self-respect.

They pass a servant singing in a kitchen as she sharpens knives, and they stop to listen. As they move on, Cranly asks Stephen if he considers the song she sang, "Rosie O' Grady," to be "poetry," and Stephen replies that he would have to see Rosie before he could say. He then announces his plans to go away from Ireland. Cranly suggests that the church is not driving Stephen away, and that if he leaves he leaves of his own accord. He questions Stephen on some moral issues, and Stephen responds by saying that he will not serve any church or country, but will seek the freedom to express himself apart from these bonds. He says that he is not afraid to live alone, or to have made a "great," eternal "mistake." The section ends as Cranly asks Stephen how he could live with no

friends at all. Stephen suspects that Cranly is thinking of himself, but when he asks Cranly does not answer.

The novel ends with excerpts from Stephen's journal, beginning with an entry for the night following his conversation with Cranly. He writes about following women with Lynch, discussing religion with his mother (who claims he has a "queer mind" and that he reads too much), arguing about heresy with other students, and wondering what Emma is doing and thinking. He writes of his plans to leave, and he writes about a final encounter with Emma when he told her he was leaving. They shook hands, and Stephen concludes that it was "friendly." He tells himself, however, that he is over his obsession. The journal ends as Stephen is about to depart—as he vows "to encounter for the millionth time the reality of experience and to forge in the smithy of [his] soul the uncreated conscience of [his] race."

Analysis

If the novel had ended with Chapter Four, it would have been an unambiguous climax, an affirmation of Stephen's artistic vision. Such an ending would, however, have left many important questions unanswered. How would Stephen reconcile his new vision for his life with the reality of his surroundings? After all, we might say, deciding to become an artist does not make you an artist. By including Chapter Five, Joyce makes Stephen's vision more realistic. By showing the day-to-day reality the artist will still have to face, we are given a sense of how Stephen's newly understood role will play out in his life—we can see how he attempts to live up to his new ideal. Though the tone of this chapter is harder to gauge perhaps than the ending of Chapter Four—there are many instances where we suspect that Stephen is being treated somewhat ironically by the narrator—Chapter Five represents the culmination of the main themes of the novel. In this chapter we read about Stephen's developing aesthetic or artistic theory, we see the first example of his own artistic composition, and we hear of his preparation to leave Ireland for Europe.

In Chapter Five, Stephen fully articulates and defends his conception of what it takes to be an artist, and we see him progress further toward assuming and embracing the role of solitary exile which we have seen him tending toward all along. Though this chapter consists of a good deal of dialogue—Stephen speaks with others more than in any other chapter of the novel—these conversations serve to gradually set him further and further apart from his surroundings. In them, Stephen articulates his need to be alone, free of the "nets" of family, religion, and nation. As the chapter, and the novel, ends, we have Stephen's voice all alone, addressing himself in the form of a journal, unmediated by any narrative presence. Over the course of this chapter Stephen moves closer to the solitude he deems necessary for artistic creation.

As with other chapters previously, the opening pages of Chapter Five serve as an abrupt anticlimax after the triumphant and inspired tone in which Chapter Four ended. We have already recognized that of all the potential climaxes of the novel, Stephen's artistic awakening in Chapter Four seems least prone to the narrator's irony. In Joyce's novel, the ideal of a "climax" is not the same as in more conventional fiction, where the climax is defined by the progression and culmination of a plot. In *A Portrait of the Artist as a Young Man*, all the significant "action" is internal, and therefore the climax of the novel will be in the form of a significant moment for the protagonist—a moment of "epiphany." The moment where Stephen decides he must reject his country and his religion in the name of art, when he begins to perceive his life in symbolic terms and therefore to "understand" the significance of his name, is clearly a pivotal and climactic moment in the novel—one on which our ultimate understanding of Stephen's character rests. However, this tone of triumph is sobered dramatically as Chapter Five begins.

The language with which the narrator describes Stephen at breakfast is dismal and depersonalized:

> He drained his third cup of watery tea to the dregs and set to chewing the crusts of fried bread that were scattered near him, staring into the dark pool of the jar. The yellow dripping had been scooped out like a boghole....

The way his eating is described makes it seem mechanical and numb—he "drains" the cup of tea, and "sets to chewing" the crusts of bread. The sense of images in this opening paragraph are all rather unpleasant—the "dark pool," "yellow drippings," and "boghole" are all distinctly unappetizing. We are reminded that the family is in dire economic shape by the pawning tickets on the table—Mr. Dedalus has made some of them out under false names, presumably out of shame. These first pages represent a marked drop in intensity from the previous chapter.

There is some suggestion in these opening pages that Stephen has perhaps not grown past the trappings of his surroundings at all, and that indeed he has regressed. In the first paragraph, we are told that the contents of the jar remind him of "the dark turfcoloured water of the bath in Clongowes, and we recall Stephen's younger days in the first chapter. By pulling our attention backwards in this way, after the forward-looking ending of the previous chapter, the narrator reminds us of Stephen's past, and how illusory some other "awakenings" have proven. This is further emphasized as Stephen's mother must remind him of the time, chastise him for being late for class, and even wash his face and neck for him.

His lackadaisical attitude toward his classes might seem at odds with the "new adventures" the university represented to him in the previous chapter. While Stephen's idleness and casualness at the start of the chapter might on the one hand seem like laziness or lack of energy, it also suggests a kind of patience, an attitude of inner peace and calm in the midst of his chaotic surroundings. For it is apparent that the *effects* of the previous chapter's climax are still active in Stephen's mind. There is a distinct sense, which Stephen shares, that his surroundings are holding him back, and this is the reason for the anticlimax in this chapter. It is not the case, as before, that we feel that Stephen is somehow deluded. When we saw how his religious fervor deteriorated into a dry and lifeless routine, our sense was that Stephen did not recognize this, and that the narrator was, through his choice of language, showing us that Stephen was deluded. The difference in Chapter Five is that Stephen understands that his surroundings are profoundly at odds with his conception of himself as an artist. The major substance of this chapter consists of Stephen attempting to change the squalid circumstances of his life by leaving. His daily existence then becomes a kind of challenge to his will, a test of his convictions.

That the ideals of his artistic awakening are still fully present in Stephen's mind is made clear as he leaves his house. He hears a mad nun wailing in an insane asylum, and his reaction symbolically leaves religion and family behind:

—Jesus! O Jesus! Jesus!
He shook the sound out of his ears by an angry toss of his head and hurried on, stumbling though the mouldering offal, his heart already bitten by an ache of loathing and bitterness. His father's whistle, his mother's mutterings, the screech of an unseen maniac were to him now so many voices offending and threatening to humble the pride of his youth. He drove their echoes even out of his heart with an execration....

He can now reduce the effects of the "voices" of family and church to simple personal threats—threats to his freedom, which he attempts to shake away with an "angry toss of the head." This chapter represents Stephen's articulation and defense of his motives and methods for seeking to distance himself from all such obligations. The calmness and quite priestlike seriousness with which he conducts himself around his friends should not be understood as a lazy kind of idleness, but rather as an attitude of patience in preparation for his life's calling. Stephen attempts to assume such a detached and disengaged posture because this is how he conceives of the proper attitude of artists in relation to their surroundings.

Stephen's artistic conversion, as he understands it, means that he must try and set himself apart form national, political, religious, and familial concerns. We have such a clear understanding of Stephen's conviction on this point because a large portion of this chapter consists of Stephen engaged in a series of significant conversations in which he defines and defends his understanding of art and its purpose, his attitude toward his country and toward political concerns, and his attitude toward his family and religion. Whereas he had been a silent observer for the greater part of the novel up to this point, now Stephen is portrayed as a relentless talker, sounding off about his developing theory of aesthetics to anyone who will listen. Four such significant conversations are the structuring principle of this chapter. We understand crucial aspects of Stephen's point of view, as well as some serious objections to it, through the conversations he has with the dean of studies, Davin, Lynch, and, most importantly, Cranly.

Stephen's conversation with the dean of studies reveals a marked change in his attitude toward authority figures once again. Priests have occupied a role of religious and practical authority for Stephen throughout the novel, though, as we observed in the last chapter, his attitude toward them had been changing of late. The subtle dissatisfaction he had felt with the Jesuits in general is now manifest in an almost condescending attitude toward the dean, who is for Stephen supposed to be a figure of academic as well as religious authority. As the dean promises to teach Stephen the art of lighting a fire, Stephen reflects to himself that the dean seems fawning and servile:

> Kneeling thus on the flagstone to kindle the fire and busied with the disposition of the wisps of paper and candelbutts he seemed more than ever a humble server making ready the place of sacrifice in an empty temple, a levite of the Lord. …His very body had waxed old in lowly service of the Lord…and yet had remained ungraced by aught of saintly or of prelatic beauty.

Stephen now sees no value in such servitude—indeed, the theme of this chapter for him is an attempt to separate himself from all sorts of service to others. His disdain for the priest's air of servitude recalls his reaction to the "droll statue" of the national poet of Ireland on his way to class, in which he detects "sloth of the body and of the soul," and a "servile head…humbly conscious of its indignity." Stephen is now eager both to judge, and to set himself apart from, figures of authority both in the artistic and religious realms.

Stephen's attitude toward the dean during their brief discussion is one of polite impatience, almost condescension. While he sets the dean up in his mind as an example of all that is wrong with the priesthood, there is much about this man's manner in particular which irritates Stephen. When the dean invites him to learn one of the "useful" arts, this sets up Stephen's discourse about aesthetics perfectly, since his conception, as we will see, is that "usefulness" is not one of the proper purposes for art. The priest asks Stephen how he would define the "beautiful," and Stephen quotes Aquinas—"beauty is that which, when seen, pleases us." The dean encourages Stephen to pursue these questions, and to write something on them, but his responses to Stephen indicate that he is not especially interested. He is noncommittal and unconvincing in his remarks. When the dean says, "Quite so, you have certainly hit the nail on the head," or, "I see. I quite see your point," we are not at all convinced that he either understands or is interested. We can perhaps read his words of encouragement more as a somewhat perfunctory exercise of his duties as dean of the university. Stephen seems to perceive this, and eventually loses interest in the conversation. The dean does not function for Stephen here as an intellectual peer to engage and interact with in a discussion of ideas. Rather, Stephen takes this opportunity to speak about himself and his interests (an opportunity, as we will see, that he rarely passes up), and we can tell by his private responses to the dean that he is never seriously considering the dean's remarks, but rather using him as an example of the priesthood in general.

Part of Stephen's feeling of distance from the dean seems to come from the fact that the dean is English. When the dean uses the word "funnel," Stephen says that he has not heard this word before. Stephen calls this a "tundish," a word the priest claims not to have heard before. The priest concludes that "tundish" must be the Irish word for the English "funnel," and he offers a halfhearted interest in the question, claiming, "That is a most interesting word. I must look that word up. Upon my word I must." This marks a turning point in Stephen's attitude toward the priest, as he becomes less patient, and effectively stops the conversation. This apparently is a nationalistic issue for Stephen, as he reflects to himself:

—The language in which we are speaking is his before it is mine. How different are the words *home, Christ, ale, master,* on his lips and on mine! I cannot speak or write these words without unrest of spirit. His language, so familiar and so foreign, will always be for me an acquired speech. I have not made or accepted its words. My voice holds them at bay. My soul frets in the shadow of his language.

Stephen seems to be voicing his anxiety over the fact that the Irish people, as a whole, no longer speak the Irish language. The priest then would be a representative of the conquering country, England.

These quasi-nationalistic sentiments certainly seem uncharacteristic of Stephen. English, we might say, has not seemed "uncomfortable" for him before—it was the English language in fact which he found so beautiful and rhythmic at the end of Chapter Four. Rather than take this passage at face value, as representative of Stephen's true feelings toward the language question, it is more likely that he is finding reasons to dislike the priest. The funnel/tundish debate seems to bring the issue of nationality to the foreground, but Stephen had been getting impatient with the priest's noncommittal politeness before this. The issue stays on his mind, however, as we learn in his journal that he has looked up "tundish," and found it to be an English word after all. Stephen's resentment toward the priest as it is expressed in the journal seems more personally than nationally motivated: "Damn the dean of studies and his funnel! What did he come here for to teach us his own language or to learn it from us? Damn him one way or the other."

On the same day as this conflict with the dean, we see Stephen discussing this very question with his friend Davin. Davin comes from the country, in the west of Ireland, and represents Irish nationalism in the novel—he seeks both political and cultural independence for Ireland, and believes that it is people's foremost responsibility to serve their country. In the brief conversation between Stephen and Davin, we get a clear and useful exposition of Stephen's point of view on these issues, which is consistent with his intention to remain detached from all external responsibilities.

Stephen calls Davin a "tame little goose" for signing the petition, thus equating his nationalistic ideals with subservience. Stephen is especially prone to recognize and condemn subservience lately, as he implies that Davin's enthusiasm for Irish independence is on the same scale as the bowing and fawning servitude he saw in the dean. Davin, on the other hand, criticizes Stephen as a "sneerer," indicating his dissatisfaction with Stephen's pose of detachment. A "sneerer" would not consider the issues at stake carefully, but would criticize from a safe distance. In Davin's view, to be Irish is not merely hereditary or racial—it necessarily involves a responsibility to the cause of the Irish people, and a love for the Irish culture and language. He asks Stephen, "Are you Irish at all?" When Stephen offers to show him his family tree to prove it, Davin's response is, "Then be one of us." To *be* Irish means to demonstrate your affiliation through your actions. When he asks Stephen why he dropped out of a class on Irish language and culture, Stephen indicates that "one reason" is because Emma was flirting with the priest who teaches the class. His other remarks indicate, however, that his objections run much deeper—Stephen is not very interested in Irish culture, and especially Irish nationalism. Stephen expresses his view of the situation in the following exchange:

> —This race and this country and this life produced me, he said. I shall express myself as I am.
> —Try to be one of us, repeated Davin. In your heart you are an Irishman but your pride is too powerful.
> —My ancestors threw off their language and took another, Stephen said. They allowed a handful of foreigners to subject them. Do you fancy I am going to pay in my life and person debts they made? What for?

Stephen perceives the Irish as "subjects" to another power—a situation that he cannot abide. He feels that his ancestors made the mistake, and that it should not be for him, as an individual, to pay for it. Stephen accepts the political (and therefore linguistic) circumstances of his birth and, far from feeling any responsibility on this count, seeks rather to escape the constraints these circumstances impose upon the individual:

> When the soul of a man is born in this country there are nets flung at it to hold it back from flight. You talk to me of nationality, language, religion. I shall try to fly by those nets.

We can read Davin's response to this proclamation—"Too deep for me, Stevie"—in at least two ways: either as a "serious" expression of bafflement (which would fit into Stephen's sentimental picture of him as a simple peasant), or as a critique of Stephen's extreme pose of detachment. Perhaps Davin is saying that to be "deep," in this case, is not necessarily good, if it causes one to avoid all immediate responsibilities.

Whereas Davin challenges Stephen, and provides a serious foil to his point of view, Stephen apparently finds a much more receptive audience in Lynch, whom he speaks with extensively just after his conversation with Davin. Though Lynch seems to be a more receptive audience, he is actually only a more appealing version of the dean. He playfully resists Stephen's "lecture," claiming that he has a hangover, and never seems particularly interested in the question of aesthetic value which Stephen is so fascinated by. His sarcastic commentary is his version of the dean's polite pretensions of being interested. There is the sense that no one will argue extensively with Stephen on these points because aesthetic questions are not as important to anyone else as to him.

Stephen's conversation with Lynch is more like a lecture, or a monologue, than a dialogue in earnest. Stephen is espousing his aesthetic theory, while Lynch serves as the opportunity for Stephen to talk. His contributions to the conversation are in the form of crude jokes, mock protestations, and halfhearted objections. Their long conversations, while they walk through Dublin on the way to the library, represents Stephen's intellectual development up to this point—he gives a detailed exposition of his aesthetic theory, which is impressive in its scope and sophistication.

Stephen is seeking both to define beauty and the concept of the beautiful, and to define the proper place of the artist in relation to his or her creation. Stephen bases his definition of beauty mostly on the work of Aristotle and Aquinas. He describes it as a "static" emotion—the beautiful does not evoke the "kinetic" emotions of desire or loathing, but exists outside of this realm in a state of purity. Stephen's view emphasizes the structure, wholeness, and harmony of a piece of art, and asserts that we can in fact define the "necessary qualities of beauty" despite the fact that different people in different cultures perceive and appreciate different qualities as beautiful:

> Though the same object may not seem beautiful to all people, all people who admire a beautiful object find in it certain relations which satisfy and coincide with the stages themselves of all esthetic apprehension.

Stephen identifies three essential forms of art: the lyrical, epical, and dramatic. Stephen values the dramatic most highly, in which the author is most removed from the work of art, when the "personality of the artist...finally refines itself out of existence." Stephen's ideal image of the artist is:

> Like the God of the creation, [who] remains within or behind or beyond or above his handiwork, invisible, refined out of existence, indifferent, paring his fingernails.

This passage is often cited as Joyce's own credo of artistic creation, although, paradoxically, this would be used to warn us against identifying Joyce with his fictional self, Stephen Dedalus, too completely. Here we see how Stephen can justify his rejection of national and political concerns in favor of his pose of detachment. In his conception, the duty of the artist is first to the unity and beauty of the work of art itself—the less the personality (and therefore the political or religious agenda) of the artist comes into play, the better.

The seriousness with which Stephen's sophisticated system of aesthetics is presented to undercut significantly, however, by Lynch's persistently crude and sarcastic humor, and his only partial engagement with Stephen's monologue. Stephen seems to like Lynch, however, perhaps because he will not challenge Stephen's assertions the way Davin or Cranly will. As soon as their conversation begins, Stephen recognizes with pleasure evidence of Lynch's "culture":

> —Damn your yellow insolence, answered Lynch.
> This second proof of Lynch's culture made Stephen smile again.
> —It was a great day for European culture, he said, when you made up your mind to swear in yellow.

Apparently Lynch is more cultured than Davin, which encourages Stephen that he will be a better (less hostile) audience, although Stephen's evidence for considering him cultured amounts to nothing more than the fact that he curses in a literary way.

Earlier, Stephen had been offended by the sound of Cranly's accent, associating it with all that is ugly and unpleasant about Dublin:

> Cranly's speech, unlike that of Davin, had neither rare phrases
> of Elizabethan English nor quaintly turned versions of Irish
> idioms. Its drawl was an echo of the quays of Dublin given
> back by a bleak decaying seaport, its energy an echo of the
> sacred eloquence of Dublin given back flatly by a Wicklow
> pulpit.

Surely Davin's speech, though "quaint," is not "cultured," and
neither is Cranly's. However, from what we can tell, Lynch's "culture"
amounts to a habitual repetition of stock literary phrases, in order
to curse. Lynch's appeal is as artificial as Cranly's offense. In neither
case is Stephen interested in the substance of the person, but in
how good they sound. After Stephen remarks about how fond he is
of Lynch "cursing in yellow," almost every remark out of Lynch's
mouth involves some variation on "yellow." Stephen exercises a
certain amount of control over Lynch, and seems to have his respect. But the overall sense is that this is still something of a joke
to Lynch; he still seems like little more than Stephen's "yes man."
When Stephen finishes a long tirade, and Lynch does not reply right
away, he imagines "that his words had called up around them a
thought enchanted silence." The narrator is clear to phrase this as
Stephen's perception of the scene; we may suspect, instead, that
Lynch merely has not been paying attention.

In his conversation with Cranly, which marks the end of the
narrative proper, Stephen finds a much more challenging audience.
There is the distinct sense that Stephen values Cranly as a friend
whose opinion is important. In their dialogue, there is none of the
condescension which characterized Stephen's attitude toward
Davin, Lynch, and even the dean of studies. Cranly is not afraid to
be directly critical of Stephen's ideas and actions, and he raises
significant and considerable objections to Stephen's plan to forsake
his country and family in favor of art. Stephen recognizes a certain
connection between the two of them early in their conversation:

> Their minds, lately estranged, seemed suddenly to have been
> drawn closer together, one to the other.

Cranly is perhaps the first person in the novel who Stephen seems
to engage with on equal terms—earlier in the novel he had been
intimidated by his peers and authority figures, and later in the novel

he generally feels superior to both his peers and authority figures.

Cranly raises humanistic objections to Stephen's plan, trying to show him how his rejection of church and family will cut him off from those close to him. For Cranly, it is not a matter of rejecting "religion" or "family" or "nation" in the abstract—he reminds Stephen of the real people who will be hurt by his actions. Cranly tries to turn Stephen's attention away from the abstract principle (which Stephen expresses by quoting Lucifer, "I will not serve") and toward a more practical and human level. Stephen does not view his quarrel with his mother in terms of *her* feelings—from his point of view, she is asking him to observe a false homage, a move which his integrity of soul cannot abide. Cranly urges him to consider how much she has suffered in her life, and how Stephen, by compromising and observing his Easter duty, can reduce her suffering a little. When Cranly asks him, however, if he loves his mother, Stephen claims not to understand the question. Just as Stephen tried and failed to love God, he has not been able to feel any meaningful connection with any people in his life, family or otherwise. His one-sided obsession with Emma can hardly be called "love," and his relationship with his family is, by now, as distant and detached as can be. When Cranly asks Stephen if his mother has had "a happy life," Stephen responds honestly "How do I know?" It is clear that her feelings do not come into play in his decision not to observe Easter—it is a personal matter, that has to do in his mind with his rejection of the Catholic church. Cranly's sentimental language of human compassion provides a stark contrast to Stephen's self-centered ethic of isolation and individualism:

> —Whatever else is unsure in this stinking dunghill of a world a mother's love is not. Your mother brings you into the world, carries your first in her body. What do we know about what she feels? But whatever she feels, it, at least, must be real. It must be. What are our ideas and ambitions? Play. Ideas! Why, that bloody bleating goat Temple has ideas. MacCann has ideas too. Every Jackass going the roads thinks he has ideas.

Cranly tries to appeal to Stephen's (or the reader's) sentimentality. He attempts to deflate Stephen's emphasis on the unassailable virtue of an individual pursuing his destiny outside of all society by claiming that this is not so unique, that everyone thinks his or her ideas are most important. Stephen, however, appears unaffected, and quickly moves the discussion away from himself and to the subject of other famous intellectuals in history who have offended their mothers. Cranly, however, offers a perceptive critique of Stephen's assumed pose of detachment, one which many readers will take to heart.

Cranly also challenges Stephen on the more abstract, theological and philosophical bases for his rejection of Catholicism. When Stephen assumes his pose of detachment, relishing the role of religious rebel by saying he "neither believe(s) nor disbelieve(s)," and "do(es) not want to overcome" his doubts, Cranly points out that Stephen's mind is "supersaturated" with the tenents of Catholicism. Stephen cannot set himself fully outside the structure of the church, because his pose of detachment is compromised by his long history in the church. His disbelief then is necessarily rebellious, and not disinterested and detached, since he very recently did believe. While Stephen claims that he "was someone else then," there are many indications that he is perhaps not so changed from the days when he was a believer. His conception of himself and his "mission" as an artist uses the language of the priesthood. He admits that his intellectual interests make his mind a "cloister," and cut him off from the outside world just as much as the priesthood would have.

The hold the Catholic church still has upon his mind, despite his rejection of its tenets, is made clear as Stephen admits that he is not "sure" that the religion is "false," and this is part of the reason he refuses to take communion falsely. Stephen admits that he still has a certain fear of blasphemy, although he quickly checks himself and says, "I fear more than that the chemical action which would be set up in my soul by a false homage to a symbol behind which are massed twenty centuries of authority and veneration," asserting his devotion to a personal ethic which would be morally superior to the church.

Stephen's "supersaturation" with Catholicism, despite his apparent rejection of it, is demonstrated by his reaction to Cranly's blasphemy. When Cranly suggests that Jesus was "a conscious hypocrite," and "not what he pretended to be," Stephen admits that he was "somewhat" shocked to hear Cranly say this. When Cranly asks if this is why he will not take communion, because he feels and fears that God might indeed be real, Stephen admits that this is true. It seems that Cranly is really affecting Stephen here. He seems to puncture Stephen's pose of indifference and nonchalant rebellion, showing that Stephen is still profoundly affected by the religion he claims to reject. However, Stephen's tone is difficult to gauge here. He quickly checks himself, claiming "I fear many things: dogs, horses, firearms, the sea, thunderstorms, machinery, the country road at night." He tries to lump his lingering fear of God in with other "irrational" fears.

When Stephen announces his plans to leave Ireland, Cranly is quick to point out that the church is not driving Stephen away, but that he is leaving of his own accord. When Stephen says that he "has to" go, Cranly replies, "You need not look upon yourself as driven away if you do not wish to go or as a heretic or an outlaw." Cranly is saying that Stephen is assuming this role of exile himself, that he seems to *want* to be a heretic or outlaw. This, as we know, is largely true. Stephen's conception of the artist is that he must live free of all familial, patriotic and religious obligations, and he now sees Europe as the place where this is possible. Near the end of their conversation, Stephen repeats his credo again:

> I will not serve that in which I no longer believe whether it
> call itself my home, my fatherland or my church: and I will
> try to express myself in some mode of life or art as freely as I
> can and as wholly as I can, using for my defense the only arms
> I allow myself to use—silence, exile, and cunning.

Stephen's emphasis is all on himself—he detaches himself from any obligation by dismissing his family, religion, and country as something which might "call itself" home, fatherland, or church. Stephen sees himself not necessarily as "driven away," although it is clearly necessary, for him to fulfill his vision of art, to remove himself from the circumstance, the "nets," of his birth. Cranly has pointed out, throughout their discussion, the ways this is selfish and insensitive. When he suggests that Stephen, by doing so, will alienate himself from others permanently, that he will "have not even one friend," Stephen appears unaffected. As we know, he has been alone his whole life.

Although Cranly seems to raise some serious objections, and Stephen seems to respect his point of view profoundly, we can see from his first journal entry that he has not taken Cranly's remarks to heart. Stephen's account of the situation is superficial:

> Long talk with Cranly on the subject of my revolt. He had his grand manner on. I supple and suave. Attacked me on the score of love for one's mother.

Stephen describes it as if they both had been play-acting, rather than talking about issues of real consequence in both of their lives. He is more interested in Cranly's "grand manner," and proud of his own appearance of being "supple and sauve," than any of the issues their discussion raised. Cranly's passionate appeal in favor of Mrs. Dedalus' suffering, and her love for her son, is reduced to a depersonalized move in a formal debate: "attacked me on the score of love for one's mother." Stephen shows no evidence that this conversation, which voices many reasonable and serious objections to Stephen's plan of "revolt," has had any affect on him whatsoever. It is as if his mind has been made up throughout the chapter, and it shows no tendency to change now.

Stephen in his journals appears superficial and affected. He is not afraid to be alone, and has by now embraced the role of exile fully. His brief and unemotional account of his conversation with Cranly shows how his perception is limited, and we may indeed wonder what kind of artist he will be if he has no conception of human affection or connection. His act of creation, the centerpiece of Chapter Five, bears this out. He wakes up, and almost spontaneously composes a villanelle. We have already seen him in the role of art critic, or aesthetic theorist. This is the first evidence of Stephen as artist in the novel.

Stephen's artistic inspiration is presented in religious or spiritual terms—his mind is portrayed as "pregnancy" with inspiration that came from a mysterious, divine source:

> In the virgin womb of the imagination the word was made flesh. Gabriel the seraph had come to the virgin's chamber.

He imagines himself like the Virgin Mary, and while he continues to compose the poem in his head he imagines "smoke, incense ascending from the altar of the world." As Cranly will suggest, Stephen's mind is indeed still "supersaturated" with religion, and this language suggests that in some ways his new life may not be so radically transformed from his former life. He imagines himself "a priest of eternal imagination, transmuting the daily bread of experience into the radiant body of everlasting life"—his act of creation seems to give him the same kind of power he dreamed he would have as a priest.

The "subject" of his poem is presumably Emma, although the way he imagines her while he is composing suggests how much their "relationship" exists only in his mind. As with the poem he composed for her ten years earlier, the villanelle is highly abstract, and seems to be "about" or "for" her in only the most indirect way. In some ways, his composition is quite impressive. Stephen shows a definite sensitivity to the sounds of the words, and a villanelle is a rigid and strict form—using only two rhymes, repeating the lines in a regular pattern for five three-line stanzas and a quatrain. The villanelle requires discipline, skill, and control, and gains its effects more from the formal interplay of sound and repetition than it does from emotion or passion. Therefore, Stephen's first poem is abstract, symbolic, and clearly removed from anything in his immediate life. Just as his first attempt, ten years earlier, had failed by being too far removed from the situation which had inspired it, this poem, too, is emotionally flat and detached from life. Stephen, it appears, has little conception of human love or emotion, and his art serves the purpose of removing him from daily life into the realm of fantasy and escape, sound without sense. While his poem is a somewhat impressive technical and formal achievement, we may wonder if Stephen's rigid code of individualism will cause him to suffer as an artist.

In the journal entries at the end of the novel, we have Stephen's voice directly, without the potentially ironic narrator. Over the course of the chapter we have seen him gradually become more and more alone, and this is emphasized by the univocal final pages, where Stephen is essentially "talking to himself." His tone is somewhat dramatic, and it is clear that the defense mechanisms and affectations we recognized in his interactions with his peers tend to carry over into the journals, too. However, there is a definite eagerness in the passages where he anticipates his flight to Europe.

At the end of the novel, we see the young man, whom we have followed since early childhood, now an "artist," eager to leave his dreary homeland behind in favor of life, art and experience:

> *26 April:* Mother is putting my new secondhand clothes in order. She prays now, she says, that I may learn in my own life and away from home and friends what the heart is and what it feels. Amen. So be it. Welcome, O life! I go to encounter for the millionth time the reality of experience and to forge in the smithy of my soul the uncreated conscience of my race.
> *27 April:* Old father, old artificer, stand me now and ever in good stead.

The novel in Stephen's voice, seems to end on an optimistic and forward-looking note. Most of the novel has been about rejection—Stephen has had to reject the "nets" which Dublin and Catholicism have laid upon him at birth. But his attitude now is of expectation and anticipation. Our sense is that "experience" and "life" lies elsewhere, in Europe, and that his art will feed on these. Although the narrator has been puncturing his "epiphanies" throughout, here we just have Stephen's voice in what seems to be an unambiguous affirmation. But the narration's ironies, and in particular Cranly's objections, have not been forgotten by this point, giving us a complicated and multifaceted picture of the artist. We can see many of Stephen's shortcomings, but we can also recognize in him a definite skill and ambition. We may feel, as the novel ends, that he will go off and succeed in Europe, experiencing life and creating life. Or, we may feel that this is the common delusion of youth, that, as Cranly puts it, "everyone has ideas," and we have no reason to believe that Stephen Dedalus is special. If we are willing to look outside of the text, we will see that in Joyce's next novel, *Ulysses*, Stephen Dedalus is back in Dublin—he has returned for his mother's funeral and ended up staying in town for months. In light of this later novel, the ending of *A Portrait of the Artist as a Young Man* will perhaps seem to be "punctured" much as the climaxes of the individual chapters were. The symbolism he recognizes in his name suggests both the need for flight or escape, as well as the potential hazards—Icarus, Daedalus' son, flew too high and his wings were melted by the sun. The ending of the novel is suggestively ambiguous—we may see Stephen in either, or indeed both, of these ways.

Study Questions

1. Describe Stephen's attitude toward school at the start of Chapter Five.

2. What does Davin call Stephen?

3. What is the "useful art" the dean of studies promises to teach Stephen?

4. What are the two primary influences on Stephen's artistic theory?

5. What is Davin's objection to Stephen's "revolt" against religion, family, and nation?

6. What characteristic of Lynch's speech does Stephen identify with "culture"?

7. What, according to Stephen, are the three basic forms of art?

8. What kind of poem does Stephen compose in the middle of Chapter Five?

9. Describe the attitude which the other students take toward Temple.

10. When Lynch asks Stephen if he loves his mother, what does Stephen say?

Answers

1. Stephen has a casual, even lackadaisical attitude toward his schoolwork at the start of Chapter Five. He is late for lecture, and has to borrow a scrap of notepaper from Moynihan.

2. Davin calls Stephen "Stevie."

3. The dean of studies promises to teach Stephen the "useful art" of starting a fire in a fireplace.

4. Stephen's artistic theory is based heavily on the work of Aristotle and Aquinas.

5. Davin feels that an individual's primary responsibility is to his or her country, and feels that Stephen is betraying Ireland in favor of abstract, selfish aims—a view with which Stephen does not disagree.

6. Stephen recognizes Lynch's use of "yellow" as an expletive to be an example of his "culture."

7. Stephen recognizes the three basic forms of art as the lyrical, the epical, and the tragic. The tragic is the most important, since it is when the artist is able to remove himself or herself from the creation as completely as possible.

8. Stephen composes a villanelle, a strict form which consists of only two rhymes ("ways" and "rim"), five three-line stanzas, a final quatrain, and a pattern of repetition.

9. The other students tease Temple constantly, and don't take his ideas seriously.

10. Stephen replies that he does not understand the question.

Suggested Essay Topics

1. In Chapter Five, we are given a detailed exposition of Stephen's theory of aesthetics, as well as the text of his first poem since his artistic transformation. Discuss the villanelle, using the terms of Stephen's theory as he describes it to Lynch. What can this theory tell us about the poem? How does this relate to the thematic issues in this chapter?

2. Cranly suggests that, despite his claims of rejecting the Catholic church and its faith, Stephen's mind continues to be "supersaturated" with Catholicism. Discuss how this view might be used to illuminate his character in this chapter. Aspects you may want to examine include: how the narrator describes Stephen, how he describes himself, how his inspiration and act of artistic creation is described.

3. After the entire novel has been narrated through Stephen's consciousness by a third-person narrator, the novel ends with some excerpts from Stephen's journal, as he makes final preparations to leave for Europe. How does the recession of the narrative presence affect our understanding of the ending of the novel? What are some of the effects of Joyce ending the novel this way?

Sample Analytical Paper Topics

Topic #1

Examine Stephen's relationship to Catholicism as it develops throughout the novel. Use this as a way to comment on his attitude to authority more generally.

Outline

I. Thesis Statement: *Stephen's developing ethic of individualism requires him to reject the authority of the Catholic church. We can measure the progress of his artistic and individual development in part by an examination of the changes in his attitude to the priests in the novel.*

II. When he was a child, the Jesuit priests at Clongowes represented absolute authority for Stephen.

    A. His general attitude toward the priests.

    B. The pandying incident with Father Dolan, and the "resolution" of this conflict by Father Conmee.

III. His religious awakening at the retreat.

    A. The priest's voice speaks "directly to his soul," evidence of the authority Stephen grants him.

IV. His changing attitude toward the Jesuits as he gets older.

    A. Chapter Four: the director's offer; Stephen's attraction to and rejection of the priesthood.

V.   Stephen's attitude toward Catholicism as the novel ends.

    A.   His conversation with the dean of studies.

    B.   His conversation with Cranly.

Topic #2

Examine the novel's various "climaxes." In what ways does the narrator tend to treat Stephen's triumphs ironically, suggesting that he is perhaps deluded?

Outline

I.   Thesis Statement: *The narrative works according to a pattern whereby the climactic ending of each chapter is significantly deflated by the down-to-earth, routine and habitual tone of the next chapter's opening section.*

II.   Stephen's triumph at the end of Chapter One.

    A.   The plain tone of the first paragraphs of Chapter Two.

    B.   His father telling Father Conmee's version of the story at dinner.

III. The excitement of Stephen's transgression with the prostitute at the end of Chapter Two.

    A.   How this becomes a seemingly empty and dull routine in Chapter Three.

IV.   The fervor of Stephen's confession and religious conversion at the end of Chapter Three.

    A.   How this seems passionless and routine in Chapter Four.

V.   The "climax" of the novel—Stephen's artistic conversion at the end of Chapter Four.

    A.   The narrative at the start of Chapter Five seems to suggest routine and drudgery.

    B.   This time, Stephen recognizes this, and understands that his surroundings are to blame for stifling his artistic potential (the "climax" itself is not deflated—its "puncture" has thematic significance).

VI. The eagerness and optimism of Stephen's language in the journals at the end.

    A. Is this positive tone compromised at all by this pattern of deflation in the rest of the narrative?

Topic #3

Trace the themes of exile and detachment as they develop throughout the novel.

Outline

I. Thesis Statement: *Stephen is portrayed as lonely and aloof throughout the novel, but as the novel progresses, he begins gradually to accept and embrace the role of exile until, by the end, he decides that he must leave the country and live alone in order to be happy.*

II. Stephen's "uncomfortable" loneliness at Clongowes.

    A. He feels apart from the other students, and is intimidated and uncomfortable about this.

III. In Chapter Two, his imagination (fueled by literature) causes him to detach himself from ordinary life.

    A. How this "detachment" is somewhat necessary, since the family has moved, he is no longer at school, and has no friends.

    B. How Stephen's literary imaginings suggest that he is beginning to romanticize the role of exile.

IV. After Stephen's religious conversion, his religious zeal serves to remove him from normal life.

    A. He imagines himself as a priest, separate and aloof.

V. When he has his artistic awakening at the end of Chapter Four, he decides that his pose of detachment and exile is essential toward being an artist.

    A. This pose will characterize him throughout Chapter Five.

    B. He expresses this explicitly as a personal credo of art in his conversations with Cranly and Davin.

C. His journal characterizes this, showing Stephen's voice alone, with him looking toward Europe and his self-imposed exile.

SECTION EIGHT

Bibliography

Blades, John. *A Portrait of the Artist as a Young Man*. Penguin Critical Studies. London: Penguin Books, 1991.

Ellmann, Richard. *James Joyce*. Second Ed. New York: Oxford U.P., 1982.

Joyce, James. *A Portrait of the Artist as a Young Man: Text, Criticism, and Notes*. Ed. Chester G. Anderson. Viking Critical Library. New York: Penguin Books, 1968.

Schutte, William M. ed. *Twentieth Century Interpretations of A Portrait of the Artist as a Young Man*. Englewood Cliffs, NJ: Prentice-Hall, 1968.

Seed, David. *James Joyce's A Portrait of the Artist as a Young Man*. New York: St. Martin's Press, 1992.

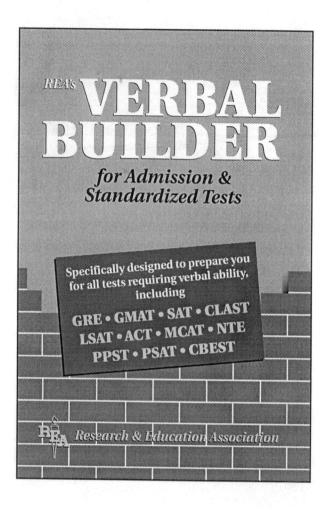

Available at your local bookstore or order directly from us by sending in coupon below.